SPECTRUM
MULTIVIEW BOOKS

The Historical Jesus

FIVE VIEWS

EDITED BY James K. Beilby
& Paul Rhodes Eddy

IVP Academic

An imprint of InterVarsity Press
Downers Grove, Illinois

InterVarsity Press
P.O. Box 1400, Downers Grove, IL 60515-1426
World Wide Web: www.ivpress.com
E-mail: email@ivpress.com

InterVarsity Press® is the book-publishing division of InterVarsity Christian Fellowship/USA®, a movement of students and faculty active on campus at hundreds of universities, colleges and schools of nursing in the United States of America, and a member movement of the International Fellowship of Evangelical Students. For information about local and regional activities, write Public Relations Dept., InterVarsity Christian Fellowship/USA, 6400 Schroeder Rd., P.O. Box 7895, Madison, WI 53707-7895, or visit the IVCF website at <www.intervarsity.org>.

Design: Cindy Kiple

Images: Profile of Christ by Burgkmair, Hans the Elder (c.1473-c.1553). Photo by Volker-H. Schneider at Kupferstichkabinett, Staatliche Museen zu Berlin, Berlin, Germany. Bildarchiv Preussischer Kulturbesitz/Art Resource, NY

ISBN 978-0-8308-3868-4

Printed in the United States of America ∞

Library of Congress Cataloging-in-Publication Data

Beilby, James K.
  The historical Jesus: five views/James K. Beilby and Paul R.
Eddy.
    p. cm.
  Includes bibliographical references and indexes.
  ISBN 978-0-8308-3868-4 (pbk.: alk. paper)
  1. Jesus Christ—Historicity—History of doctrines—21st century.
  I. Eddy, Paul R. II. Title.
  BT303.2.B365 2009
  232.9'08—dc22
                    2009026586

P	20	19	18	17	16	15	14	13	12	11	10	9	8	7
Y	26	25	24	23	22	21	20	19	18	17	16	15		

Dedicated to Michael Holmes:

department chair, colleague, friend

CONTENTS

THE QUEST FOR THE HISTORICAL JESUS
An Introduction

Paul Rhodes Eddy and James K. Beilby

Two millennia after his sojourn on earth, Jesus of Nazareth continues to capture the attention of the contemporary western world like no other figure in history. This is no less the case for popular culture than it is for the scholarly world, as his regular appearance in television specials and weekly news magazines attests. From the covers of *Time*, *Newsweek* and, yes, even *Popular Mechanics*, Jesus remains big news on into the third millennium.[1] Today, in the world of popular-level, pseudo-scholarly publications on Jesus, there is no end to the provocative and/or conspiratorial theories available. In these one can find Jesus surviving the crucifixion, getting married (most often to Mary Magdalene), having children and living to a ripe old age.[2] Some even claim that they have finally found his gravesite—and with it the very bones of Jesus.[3] Or one can find him traveling to the East, spending years learning

---

[1]Mike Fillon, "The Real Face of Jesus: Advances in Forensic Science Reveal the Most Famous Face in History," *Popular Mechanics*, December 2002, pp. 68-71.

[2]Michael Baigent, *The Jesus Papers: Exposing the Greatest Cover-up in History* (San Francisco: HarperSanFrancisco, 2006).

[3]Simcha Jacobovici and Charles Pellegrino, *The Jesus Family Tomb: The Discovery That Will Change History Forever* (London: HarperElement, 2007).

from the ancient Asian religions, and coming back to his culture as something of a Buddhist master.[4] Or, again, one can find out that the true identity of Jesus has finally been discovered: Jesus was really the apostle Paul![5]

The contemporary interest in Jesus within popular culture is, of course, fueled by a parallel interest in the academic world. At the close of the first decade of the twenty-first century, what has come to be known as the third quest for the historical Jesus has been underway for three decades and shows no sign of slowing down. This essay will begin with a relatively brief history of the modern scholarly "quest" for the historical Jesus. Next, important issues and debates within the current phase—the "third quest"—will be explored. Finally, we will conclude with an introductory word about our five contributors to this volume.

A BRIEF HISTORY OF THE QUEST FOR THE HISTORICAL JESUS

What has come to be known as the "quest for the historical Jesus" is a child of the eighteenth century and the European Enlightenment.[6] Prior to this, the notion of a "quest" for Jesus within the world of Western Christendom would have seemed a strange proposition. For, while certain tensions were apparent within and between the accounts of the four canonical Gospels, they were still seen as able to be harmonized

---

[4]Holger Kersten, *Jesus Lived in India: His Unknown Life Before and After the Crucifixion* (Rockport, Mass.: Element, 1994).

[5]Lena Einhorn, *The Jesus Mystery: Astonishing Clues to the True Identities of Jesus and Paul* (Guilford, Conn.: Lyons, 2007).

[6]Among the many helpful resources for reconstructing and interpreting the history of the quest are the following: Charlotte Allen, *The Human Christ: The Quest for the Historical Jesus* (New York: Free Press, 1998); William Baird, *History of New Testament Research: From Deism to Tübingen* (Minneapolis: Fortress, 1992); Colin Brown, *Jesus in European Protestant Thought, 1778–1860* (Durham, N.C.: Labyrinth, 1985); Gregory W. Dawes, ed., *The Historical Jesus Quest: Landmarks in the Search for the Jesus of History* (Louisville: Westminster John Knox, 1999); James M. Robinson, *A New Quest of the Historical Jesus* (London: SCM, 1959); Bernard Brandon Scott, "From Reimarus to Crossan: Stages in a Quest," *Currents in Research: Biblical Studies* 2 (1994): 253-80; W. Barnes Tatum, *In Quest of Jesus*, rev. ed. (Nashville: Abingdon, 1999); William R. Telford, "Major Trends and Interpretive Issues in the Study of Jesus," in *Studying the Historical Jesus: Evaluations of the State of Current Research*, ed. Bruce Chilton and Craig A. Evans (New York: Brill, 1994); Gerd Theissen and Annette Merz, *The Historical Jesus: A Comprehensive Guide*, trans. John Bowden (Minneapolis: Fortress, 1998 [1996]); Walter P. Weaver, *The Historical Jesus in the Twentieth Century, 1900–1950* (Harrisburg, Penn.: Trinity Press International, 1999); Ben Witherington III, *The Jesus Quest: The Third Search for the Jew of Nazareth* (Downers Grove, Ill.: InterVarsity Press, 1997).

and thus reliable.[7] From such a perspective, the Jesus of history and the Jesus of the Gospels were one and the same. There was no need to go searching for Jesus when he could be easily found in the Gospels. It took the modern age and its skepticism of both biblical and ecclesiastical authority to ignite the quest for Jesus.

Today the most commonly used schema for delineating the history of the modern scholarly quest for Jesus recognizes four distinct stages: the "old" (or "first") quest, the so-called "no quest" period, the "new" (or "second") quest, and most recently the "third quest." We will sketch each of these below, highlighting the most influential persons and ideas to emerge in each stage.

The old quest: From Reimarus to Schweitzer (1778–1906). Ever since Albert Schweitzer's 1906 landmark survey of the (old) quest (translated into English as *The Quest of the Historical Jesus*), it has become common to mark the beginning of the quest with the publication of the work of Hermann Reimarus in 1778. According to Schweitzer, Reimarus "had no predecessors."[8] This, however, is not quite accurate. Reimarus's ideas about Jesus did not spring ex nihilo from his pen. The roots of the (largely German) old quest lie in seventeenth-century British and French deism and the biblical criticism to which it eventually gave rise. Deist critiques of the notions of divine revelation and miracles fueled a growing skepticism toward the Gospels. An array of early modern thinkers such as Benedict Spinoza, Isaac La Peyrere, Richard Simon, Thomas Woolston, Peter Annet and Thomas Morgan laid the groundwork for what would eventually emerge as the mature historical-critical method.[9]

Perhaps the clearest example of a precursor to Reimarus can be found

---

[7]On premodern Christian attitudes toward the Bible and its interpretive difficulties see Baird, *History*, pp. xiii-xix; Werner Kümmel, *The New Testament: The History of the Investigation of Its Problems*, trans. S. McLean Gilmour and Howard C. Kee (Nashville: Abingdon, 1972), pp. 13-39; Craig Blomberg, *The Historical Reliability of the Gospels*, 2nd ed. (Downers Grove, Ill.: InterVarsity Press, 2007 [1987]), pp. 24-30.

[8]Albert Schweitzer, *The Quest of the Historical Jesus: A Critical Study of Its Progress from Reimarus to Wrede*, trans. W. Montgomery (New York: Collier/Macmillan, 1968), p. 26.

[9]On the rise of the historical-critical method see Baird, *History*, part 1; Brown, *Jesus*, pp. 29-55; Roy A. Harrisville and Walter Sundberg, *The Bible in Modern Culture: Baruch Spinoza to Brevard Childs*, 2nd ed. (Grand Rapids: Eerdmans, 2002).

in the work of the British deist Thomas Chubb (1679–1746).[10] In 1738 Chubb published a book about Jesus, presenting him as "a sort of first-century Palestinian Deist, garbed in the seamless robe of reason and natural religion."[11] Unfortunately, according to Chubb, much of the later Christian dogma was later foisted on the deist-like Jesus of history by the apostle Paul.

Hermann Samuel Reimarus: The "Father" of the quest. Regardless of his precursors, however, Reimarus (1694–1768), a German professor of Semitic languages, took an original and significant step in the modern study of Jesus, and with it became the "Father" of the quest. Reimarus moves beyond his deist predecessors in that he proposes a fleshed-out alternative account of Christian origins, one that situates Jewish apocalyptic thought at its center.[12] Reimarus begins by arguing for a clear distinction between the actual Jesus of history and the Gospels' presentation of him.[13] From Reimarus's perspective just who was this historian's Jesus? Simply put, "he was born a Jew and intended to remain one."[14] More specifically, Jesus was a Jew who proclaimed the "kingdom of God," by which, according to Reimarus, he must have intended "the usual meaning of this phrase among the Jews of his time"—i.e., a political kingdom centered in Jerusalem that would be established by the Messiah through the use of military force.[15] And with this interpretive move, Reimarus arrived at his famous conclusion: the real Jesus of history was a would-be Messiah figure who hoped to establish an earthly kingdom through revolutionary force—but these hopes were dashed when he was arrested and crucified. How then did the Christian faith arise? Reimarus's answer is daring: Hoping to finally attain the riches

---

[10]In fact, Charlotte Allen (*Human Christ*, p. 76) dignifies him with the title of "probably the originator of the quest for the historical Jesus." On Chubb's view of Jesus and/or his role as a precursor to the quest see Allen, *Human Christ*, pp. 76-80, 108-9; Baird, *History*, pp. 54-56; Brown, *Jesus*, p. 46.

[11]Baird, *History*, p. 55.

[12]On the deistic influence on Reimarus see Henk J. De Jonge, "The Loss of Faith in the Historicity of the Gospels: Hermann S. Reimarus on John and the Synoptics," in *John and the Synoptics*, ed., Adelbert Denaux (Leuven: Leuven University Press, 1992), pp. 409-21.

[13]Hermann S. Reimarus, *Reimarus: Fragments*, reprint ed., ed. Charles H. Talbert, trans. Ralph S. Fraser (Chico, Calif.: Scholars Press, 1985), p. 64.

[14]Ibid., p. 71.

[15]Ibid., p. 124.

and glory they had planned on receiving when Jesus became king, his disciples stole his body, fabricated a resurrection story and eventually concocted "the doctrine of a spiritual suffering savior of all mankind."[16]

Reimarus wrote all of this and more, put the manuscript in his desk drawer, and there it remained until he died. Concern for the consequences that might follow kept him from publishing it. Upon his death, his daughter gave the manuscript to a friend, the German literary critic Gotthold Lessing, and gave him permission to publish it anonymously. This he did, claiming he had found the text in the Wolfenbüttel Library in Hamburg, and presenting it to the public in small sections ("fragments") between 1774 and 1778. It was only many years later that the truth was revealed and Reimarus's true identity discovered.

Over the last few centuries only a few have concluded, similar to Reimarus, that Jesus was in fact a politically minded revolutionary.[17] Nor have many agreed with him that Jesus' disciples consciously intended to perpetrate a religious fraud for selfish gain. Rather, it is certain elements of his method that have continued to find relevance in later stages of the quest. First, the firm line drawn by Reimarus between the Jesus of history and the Christ figure of the Gospels has remained an unquestioned presupposition for many scholars throughout the quest. Second, Reimarus raised a question that continues to be hotly debated to this day: namely, what role, if any, does historical investigation of Jesus have to play within the context of the Christian faith? Here Reimarus's own answer is clear:

> Now, where the doctrine is not controlled by the history but vice versa, both history and doctrine are to this extent unfounded; the history because it is not taken from events themselves . . . ; and the doctrine because it refers to facts that originated in the writers' thinking only after the doctrine was altered and which were simply fabricated and false.[18]

---

[16]Ibid., p.129.

[17]Those who have adopted this model in one form or another over the last century include Robert Eisler, *The Messiah Jesus and John the Baptist* (London: Methuen, 1931); S. G. F. Brandon, *Jesus and the Zealots* (New York: Scribner, 1967); George Wesley Buchanan, *Jesus: The King and His Kingdom* (Macon, Ga.: Mercer University Press, 1984); Robert H. Eisenman, *James the Brother of Jesus: the Key to Unlocking the Secrets of Early Christianity and the Dead Sea Scrolls* (New York: Penguin, 1998).

[18]Reimarus, *Fragments*, p. 134.

Finally, in setting Jesus firmly within the world of Jewish eschatology, Reimarus ignited a debate that continues raging to this day—the question of to what extent, if any, Jesus embraced views associated with first-century apocalyptic eschatology. Schweitzer, who likewise believed that Jewish eschatology held the key to understanding Jesus (though in a manner different from that argued by Reimarus), praised Reimarus at this very point.[19]

Between Reimarus and Strauss: Early "lives" of the old quest. Following his survey of Reimarus's thought, Schweitzer turns in *Quest of the Historical Jesus* to consider what he dubs "the lives of Jesus of the earlier rationalism."[20] Names such as J. J. Hess, F. V. Reinhard, E. A. Opitz, J. A. Jakobi and J. G. Herder dominate this period. A characteristic feature of these studies was an embrace, to one degree or another, of "rationalist" explanations of the Gospel materials.[21] These early pioneers of the quest tended to place their emphasis on Jesus' moral teachings and did their best to render him palatable to the more rational, "enlightened" thought of the times.

The work of two scholars in particular is worth noting. In his four-volume *A Non-supernatural History of the Great Prophet of Nazareth* (1800–1802), K. H. Venturini offers various "rational" explanations for the reported miracles of Jesus. For example, Jesus' miracles of healing are explained by the fact that Jesus was a proficient herbalist, always accompanied by his "portable medicine chest."[22] Adding a twist of conspiracy to things, Venturini also argues that Jesus, along with his cousin John the Baptist, was nurtured and groomed by a covert faction of the Essenes. Although undergoing crucifixion, Jesus only appeared to die and was later revived in the tomb with the help of an Essene collaborator, Joseph of Arimathea.[23] While few could take Venturini's theory seriously at the time, since the 1947 discovery of the Dead Sea Scrolls at Qumran and the attendant burst of interest in the ancient Jewish sect

---

[19]Schweitzer, *Quest*, p. 23.
[20]Schweitzer, *Quest*, pp. 27-37.
[21]Ibid., p. 161.
[22]Ibid., p. 44.
[23]The idea that Jesus merely appeared to die on the cross—later dubbed the "swoon" theory—had already been proposed in 1744 by Peter Annet in his *The Resurrection of Jesus Considered*.

of the Essenes, Venturini-like theories have come to life again. They remain, however, generally the fruit of either eccentric scholars or non-academic conspiracy theorists.[24]

In the 1828 work of H. E. G. Paulus, *The Life of Jesus as the Basis of a Purely Historical Account of Early Christianity*, we find the epitome of the eighteenth-century "rationalist" approach to Jesus. Here Paulus famously does his best to explain the miraculous elements in the Gospels as nothing more than the disciples' mistaken interpretations of what were, in fact, purely natural events in the life of Jesus. And so, for example, the account of Jesus walking on the water is explained as something of an optical illusion—Jesus had been walking in the shallow water off the shores of the Sea of Galilee, but from a distance it had appeared to the disciples that he was farther out, and thus walking upon the very waves themselves. From Paulus's view, and in good liberal fashion, this approach should not in any way detract from the achievement of Jesus, since it is not his miracles but rather his admirable character that truly matters.

D. F. Strauss: Jesus and "myth." One of the most influential figures of the "old" quest is David Friedrich Strauss (1808–1874). His book *The Life of Jesus Critically Examined*, originally published in 1835, became one of the most controversial studies of Jesus ever written.[25] Like his more robust rationalist predecessors, he was a thoroughgoing methodological naturalist. But to Strauss's mind, the rationalist attempts to explain the Gospels as mistaken interpretations of historically occurring natural phenomena entirely missed one of the most important elements of the

---

[24]With respect to the former see John M. Allegro, *The Dead Sea Scrolls and the Christian Myth* (Buffalo: Prometheus, 1984); Barbara Thiering, *Jesus and the Riddle of the Dead Sea Scrolls: Unlocking the Secrets of His Life Story* (San Francisco: HarperSanFrancisco, 1992). With respect to the latter see, e.g., Michael Baigent and Richard Leigh, *The Dead Sea Scrolls Deception* (New York: Summit, 1991). For a survey and critique of various twentieth century claims that Jesus survived the crucifixion see Gerald O'Collins and Daniel Kendall, "On Reissuing Venturini," *Gregorianum* 75 (1994): 241-65.

[25]*The Life of Jesus Critically Examined*, ed. Peter C. Hodgson, trans. George Eliot (Philadelphia: Fortress, 1972). Strauss would go on to produce *A New Life of Jesus*, 2 vols. (London: Williams and Norgate, 1865), which was intended for a wider, more popular readership. Then, within a year, he would publish a critique of Schleiermacher's (Strauss's former teacher) book on Jesus: *The Christ of Faith and the Jesus of History: A Critique of Schleiermacher's The Life of Jesus*, ed. and trans. Leander E. Keck (Philadelphia: Fortress, 1977 [1866]).

Gospels—namely the robust religious imagination of the early followers of Jesus and the expression of this imagination in the category of myth. In comparison to the theories of his predecessors, Strauss explains, the advantage of the "mythical view" is that it "leaves the substance of the narrative unassailed; and instead of venturing to explain the details, accepts the whole, not indeed as true history, but as a sacred legend."[26] As Schweitzer notes, while Strauss was not the first to use the notion of myth to understand the Gospels, he applied this interpretive lens in a more ruthlessly consistent fashion than anyone before him.[27]

Armed with this critical perspective, Strauss's study of Jesus largely consists of analyzing the various contents of the Gospels with an eye to unmasking and explaining the many instances of myth contained therein. Over and over again, Strauss concludes, early Christian imagination served to fabricate material about Jesus out of various Old Testament stories and concepts. In the end, all that was left for Strauss, historically speaking, was a small core of bare facts about Jesus.

While the response to Strauss was swift and overwhelmingly negative—with some more conservative voices going so far as to claim that he was the "antiChrist"—the impact of Strauss's work on the quest is felt to this day, and he continues to function as something of a patron saint for those who aspire to hard-nosed criticism of the Gospels.[28] In several ways he anticipated important future developments in critical study of the Gospels. His consideration of the myth-making process at work within the early oral Jesus tradition would eventually develop and mature, almost a century later, into the discipline of form criticism. His privileging of the category of myth would be followed by the single most influential New Testament scholar of the twentieth century—Rudolf Bultmann. And his use of comparative non-Christian religious material foreshadowed the full flowering

---

[26]Strauss, *Life*, p. 56.

[27]Schweitzer, *Quest*, p. 79.

[28]For example, Robert Funk and the Jesus Seminar dedicated their first major volume (*The Five Gospels: The Search for the Authentic Words of Jesus* [San Francisco: HarperSanFrancisco, 1993]) to Strauss (along with Galileo and Thomas Jefferson). Funk's Westar Institute has also created the "D. F. Strauss Medal" to honor scholars who have made significant contributions to the study of Jesus, recipients of which include former Anglican Bishop John Shelby Spong and John Dominic Crossan.

of this method at the end of the nineteenth century in the *Religions-geschichtliche Schule* (i.e., the old "history of religions school") made famous by Wilhelm Bousset and others.

Finally, we can recognize in Strauss a quality that is both admirable and all-too-rare within the history of the quest: an explicitly stated self-consciousness concerning the religio-philosophical presuppositions that guide (both motivationally and methodologically) his critical study of Jesus. He was always quite forthright about the influence of Hegel on his study of Jesus: "My criticism of the life of Jesus was from its origin intimately related to Hegelian philosophy." Equally self-revealing is his comment: "I am no historian; with me everything has proceeded from a dogmatic (or rather anti-dogmatic) concern."[29] Strauss has often been criticized for allowing his Hegelianism to infect his historical study of Jesus. And while this is a point well taken, no scholar has ever come to the quest free of philosophical presuppositions and religious (or antireligious, as the case may be) biases. What can be learned from Strauss here is that metacritical values and assumptions always already influence one's historiographical philosophy and method, and that every Jesus scholar owes it to oneself and one's fellow scholars both to be self-aware about these influences and, where appropriate, to explicitly state and defend them. We will pick up this issue again below.

Between Strauss and Schweitzer: Later "lives" of the old quest. The negative historical results and resultant skepticism of the Gospels displayed in Strauss's *Life of Jesus* spurred a variety of reactions. At one extreme, Bruno Bauer, taking his cue from Strauss's critical methodology and concept of myth, pushed the thesis to its furthest possible point and concluded that *all* was myth and *nothing* was history—Jesus never was an actual person in history.[30] With this move Bauer became a leading early proponent of the "Christ-Myth" theory, with others like Paul-Louis Couchoud, Arthur Drews and John M. Robertson eventually following in his wake.[31] While Bauer's Christ-Myth the-

---

[29]Cited in Brown, *Jesus*, p. 204.
[30]On Bruno Bauer see Schweitzer, *Quest*, 137-60; Brown, *Jesus*, pp. 227-31.
[31]Paul-Louis Couchoud, "The Historicity of Jesus: A Reply to Alfred Loisy," *Hibbert Journal* 37

ory has had minimal impact on the scholarly quest, it captured the attention of Karl Marx and became a common feature of Soviet Marxist thought.[32]

In the face of such skepticism, others sought to shore up some basis for the historical credibility of the Gospels. One effect of this effort was the rise of modern source criticism of the Gospels. During this time, the "two-source" theory of Gospel relations came to prominence—the view that Mark was written first and that, along with an early written collection of Jesus' sayings labeled "Q" (from the German word *Quelle*, meaning "source"), was used by both Matthew and Luke in the composition of their Gospels.[33] One of the attractive features of the two-source theory is that it allows Mark (with no embarrassing infancy narrative) and Q (sayings of Jesus without any narrative and thus without miracles) to provide a generally reliable basis from which to reconstruct the life of Jesus. Though the two-source theory has always faced its challengers, it remains to this day the most widely held solution to the infamous "Synoptic Problem."[34]

While Schweitzer's famous account of the old quest is largely focused on the German scene, other things were happening elsewhere. In France, Ernest Renan, an erstwhile Roman Catholic, produced his famous *Life of Jesus* in 1863, which went on to become a best-selling work with multiple editions. Renan's book presents a Jesus who began as a wise teacher of ethical principles who reveals the loving character of the heavenly Father, but who, inspired by apocalyptic hopes, eventually became a would-be messiah who was crucified for his efforts. Like his

---

(1938): 193-214; Arthur Drews, *The Christ Myth*, 3rd ed., trans. C. D. Burns (Amherst, N.Y.: Prometheus, 1998 [1910]); John M. Robertson, *Christianity and Mythology* (London: Watts, 1900).

[32]See Zvi Rosen, *Bruno Bauer and Karl Marx: The Influence of Bruno Bauer on Marx's Thought* (The Hague: Nijhoff, 1977).

[33]On the rise to prominence of the two-source theory see Baird, *History*, pp. 295-311.

[34]For a defense of the theory, see Robert Stein, *The Synoptic Problem: An Introduction* (Grand Rapids: Baker, 1987). For recent critiques of the two-source theory from different perspectives see Mark Goodacre and Nicholas Perrin, *Questioning Q: A Multidimensional Critique* (Downers Grove, Ill.: InterVarsity Press, 2005); A. J. McNicol, D. B. Peabody and L. Cope eds., *One Gospel from Two: Mark's Use of Matthew and Luke* (Harrisburg, Penn.: Trinity Press International, 2002); Armin D. Baum, *Der mündliche Faktor und seine Bedeutung für die synoptische Frage* (Tübingen: Francke, 2008).

rationalist German counterparts, Renan denied any room for the supernatural in his reconstruction.

One might raise the question here of why there are not more conservative voices in the choir of first questers? Part of the answer lies in the fact that more conservative renderings of Jesus are short on new and daring proposals, following a course instead that is heavily dependent on the Gospel accounts themselves. In the history of the quest, old news (i.e., traditional conclusions about Jesus) is often regarded as no news. Beyond this, many of the more conservative studies of this time were written as responses to the more radical proposals rather than as independent lives of Jesus. Be that as it may, from Frederic Farrar and Alfred Edersheim in Britain to August Neander and August Tholuck in Germany, more conservative voices played a significant role in the ongoing European deliberations concerning the true identity of Jesus of Nazareth.[35]

Culminating the old quest: Wrede and Schweitzer. As the nineteenth century drew to a close, the critical quest had left in its wake a wonderfully "liberal" Jesus—a Jesus stripped of the more unenlightened entanglements associated with the Gospels and Christian orthodoxy such as miracles and divine status. This Jesus was a moral reformer to be sure, a teacher who revealed the fatherhood of God, the brotherhood of humankind, and the simple tenets of a reasonable, love-based religion. This Jesus, elaborated by such theological giants as Albrecht Ritschl and Adolf von Harnack, could still appeal to an enlightened European culture.

As the new century dawned, however, two new voices served to cut the ground from beneath this reasonable, manageable Jesus of the old quest. In 1901 William Wrede produced his famous essay on the "messianic secret" theme in the Gospel of Mark. Among the implications of his study was the disturbing conclusion that, contrary to the current liberal consensus, the Gospel of Mark did not supply the generally reliable chronological framework for the life of Jesus that so many of the

---

[35]Frederic Farrar, *The Life of Christ* (Portland, Ore.: Fountain, 1972 [1874]); Alfred Edersheim, *The Life and Times of Jesus the Messiah*, 2 vols., 8th ed. (New York: Longmans, Green, 1896). On Neander and Tholuck see Baird, *History*, pp. 235-42, 283-86.

nineteenth-century questers had relied on. Rather, in a move that fore-shadowed future redaction-critical studies, Wrede argued that both Mark's framework and much of its detail derives not from reliable traditions about Jesus, but from fabrications fed by post-Easter theological reflection of the early church.[36]

In 1906 Albert Schweitzer published his renowned *The Quest of the Historical Jesus*—a book so far-reaching in its impact that its publication date now marks the end of the old quest (though not an outcome that Schweitzer necessarily desired or anticipated). Following the prior work of Johannes Weiss, Schweitzer argued strongly that the proper context for understanding Jesus was Jewish apocalyptic eschatology. In this context, Jesus appears not merely as a (liberal) social reformer and teacher of love, but as an end-times enthusiast who fervently believed that his own sufferings would play a vital role in the apocalyptic culmination of this world. In Schweitzer's memorable words:

> There is silence all around. The Baptist appears, and cries: "Repent, for the Kingdom of Heaven is at hand." Soon after that comes Jesus, and in the knowledge that he is the coming Son of Man lays hold of the wheel of the world to set it moving on that last revolution which is to bring all ordinary history to a close. It refuses to turn, and He throws Himself upon it. Then it does turn; and crushes Him. Instead of bringing in the eschatological conditions, He has destroyed them. The wheel rolls onward, and the mangled body of the one immeasurably great Man, who was strong enough to think of Himself as the spiritual ruler of mankind and to bend history to His purpose, is hanging upon it still. That is his victory and His reign.[37]

For Schweitzer, Jesus was ultimately a failed apocalyptic prophet—he predicted the end of the world and it never came. What then is salvageable from Jesus for the contemporary Christian faith? Once the eschatological beliefs of Jesus are dispensed with as an outdated Jewish worldview, one can still embrace the message of love that characterized Jesus' teachings.[38]

---

[36]William Wrede, *The Messianic Secret*, trans. J. C. G. Greig (Greenwood, S.C.: Attic, 1971 [1901]).
[37]Schweitzer, *Quest*, pp. 370-71.
[38]Ibid., p. 207.

The (so-called) "no quest" period: From Schweitzer to Käsemann (1906–1953). It is common to designate the next period of time as that of "no quest," which suggests that the quest came to a halt for nearly a half-century. As many have pointed out, this is simply not true. During this time, a good number of studies on Jesus were produced.[39] Nonetheless, it is true that within certain German circles (which no doubt created some ripple effects beyond themselves) the quest for the historical Jesus was severely hampered by some new developments in the field. Two of these developments can be tied to Schweitzer's book.

First, a common criticism of Schweitzer's regarding those questers who had come before him was that they inevitably "found" in their sources a Jesus created in their own image—or at least a Jesus who was very palatable to them. As George Tyrrell's memorable analogy put it, whenever the scholar gazes into the deep well of history in search of Jesus, there is always the real hazard of seeing merely one's own reflection gazing back, and mistaking that for Jesus.[40] This insight about inevitable scholarly subjectivity fostered skepticism of ever arriving at an objective portrait of Jesus.

Second, Schweitzer's own conclusions about Jesus—that, ultimately, he was something like a wild-eyed and ultimately mistaken prophet of doom—left little for modern Europeans to embrace. Schweitzer put it delicately:

> The study of the Life of Jesus has had a curious history. It set out in quest of the historical Jesus, believing that when it found him it could bring Him straight into our time as a Teacher and Savior. . . . But he does not stay; he passes by our time and returns to his own.[41]

Beyond these two effects of Schweitzer's work, at least two other factors served to call into question the viability of the quest. The first involves the rise of a new method of Gospel analysis: form criticism. Between 1919 and 1921, three important German works, au-

---

[39]See Weaver, *Historical Jesus;* Dale C. Allison, "The Secularizing of the Historical Jesus," *Perspectives in Religious Studies* 27 (2000): 149-50.
[40]George Tyrrell, *Christianity at the Cross-Roads* (London: Longmans, Green & Co., 1913), p. 44.
[41]Schweitzer, *Quest*, p. 399.

thored by K. L. Schmidt, Martin Dibelius and Rudolf Bultmann, launched New Testament form-critical studies. Of these, Bultmann's *The History of the Synoptic Tradition* quickly became the classic statement of this approach for years to come.[42] While form criticism focuses on the question of the pre-Gospel oral Jesus tradition, it brought with it (particularly in Bultmann's influential version) several methodological assumptions that served to further amplify skeptical attitudes toward the Gospels as historical sources. Among these was the conviction that the Gospels were a mixture of historically rooted tradition and early Christian mythology reflecting the post-Easter faith. And so, in the eyes of many, form criticism served to reveal that a largely impenetrable veil of myth separated the modern scholar from the Jesus of history.[43] This conviction led Rudolf Bultmann to conclude:

> I do indeed think that we can know almost nothing concerning the life and personality of Jesus, since the early Christian sources show no interest in either, are moreover fragmentary and often legendary; and other sources do not exist.[44]

Through Bultmann's influence (particularly in Germany), this skeptical perspective did much to douse hopes that the Jesus of history could ever be recovered in any detail.

If the first three factors presented historical obstacles to the quest, the fourth added to this a *theological* objection. An early articulation of this theological assault on the quest came in the form of Martin Kähler's famous little book, *The So-called Historical Jesus and the Historic Biblical Christ*

---

[42]Rudolf Bultmann, *The History of the Synoptic Tradition*, rev. ed. (Oxford: Blackwell, 1963 [1921]). On the rise and nature of form criticism see Edgar V. McKnight, *What Is Form Criticism?* (Philadelphia: Fortress, 1969); Stephen Neill and N. T. Wright, "The Gospel Behind the Gospels," in *The Interpretation of the New Testament, 1861–1986*, 2nd ed. (New York: Oxford University Press, 1988), pp. 252-312.

[43]It is worth noting that form-critical analysis can be used without adopting these skeptical presuppositions. See, e.g., Vincent Taylor, *The Formation of the Gospel Tradition* (London: Macmillan, 1953); Stein, *Synoptic Problem*, pp. 217-28.

[44]Rudolf Bultmann, *Jesus and the Word*, trans. L. P. Smith and E. H. Lantero (New York: Scribner's Sons, 1958), p. 8. Although John Painter argues that Bultmann had more optimism and a greater interest in the historical Jesus than is often portrayed; see "Bultmann, Archaeology and the Historical Jesus," in *Jesus and Archaeology*, ed.James H. Charlesworth (Grand Rapids: Eerdmans, 2006), pp. 619-38.

(1892). In essence Kähler argued that the quest was theologically unnecessary—even illegitimate. It was little more than a journey down "a blind alley" since "*the historical Jesus of modern authors conceals from us the living Christ.*"[45] For Kähler, what is at stake is the very nature of Christian faith: the certitude of mountain-moving faith cannot be dependent on the always tentative and changing conclusions coming out of the quest. Thus for Kähler, "Christian faith and a history of Jesus repel each other like oil and water."[46] Kähler's convictions were picked up and deepened in the influential theological movement of post–World War I neo-orthodoxy. Here leading (mostly German) theological voices of the twentieth century such as Karl Barth, Emil Brünner, Paul Tillich and even Bultmann himself expressed their theological reserve regarding quest-like activity. The apostle Paul himself provided the biblical proof text: "Though we have known Christ after the flesh, yet now henceforth we know him no more" (2 Cor 5:16 KJV). Furthermore, from the neo-orthodox perspective, any attempt to render the Christian faith dependent on an objective, historical foundation was seen as a violation of the defining Reformation principle of "justification by faith alone."[47] In sum one could describe the neo-orthodox assessment of the quest as not unlike that of many contemporary people's perspective on human cloning: "It can't be done; and if it can, it shouldn't."

As noted earlier, despite these challenges, the conviction that the Jesus of history *could* (historically) be pursued and *should* (theologically) be pursued continued right on through this period. It was during these very decades that notable works on Jesus by the British scholars T. W. Manson and C. H. Dodd were produced.[48] D. M. Baillie captured well the sentiment of many during this time:

> I cannot believe that there is any good reason for the defeatism of those

---

[45]Martin Kähler, *The So-called Historical Jesus and the Historic Biblical Christ*, ed. and trans. Carl E. Braaten (Philadelphia: Fortress, 1988), pp. 46, 43 (emphasis in text).

[46]Ibid., p. 74. For a more detailed discussion of Kähler see Carl E. Braaten "Revelation, History, and Faith in Martin Kähler," in introduction to *The So-called Historical Jesus*, pp. 1-38.

[47]See William Baird, *The Quest of the Christ of Faith: Reflections on the Bultmannian Era* (Waco, Tex.: Word, 1977); James M. Robinson, *A New Quest for the Historical Jesus* (London: SCM Press, 1959), pp. 9-47.

[48]See T. W. Manson, *The Servant-Messiah* (Cambridge: Cambridge University Press, 1966); C. H. Dodd, *Historical Tradition in the Fourth Gospel* (Cambridge: Cambridge University Press, 1963); idem, *The Founder of Christianity* (London: Macmillan, 1970).

who give up all hope of penetrating the tradition and reaching assured knowledge of the historical personality of Jesus. Surely such defeatism is a transient nightmare of Gospel criticism, from which we are now awakening to a more sober confidence in our quest of the Jesus of history.[49]

The new quest (1953–1970s). Several ironies are tied to what has come to be known as the "new" (second) quest for the historical Jesus. The first involves the fact that it was launched in Bultmann's very presence by one of his own former students who, along with most of the significant scholars in this quest, largely shared Bultmann's generally skeptical views regarding the Gospels as historical sources. This forces the question: What could ever motivate a group of Bultmannian scholars to renew the very quest that had been largely abandoned by their own professor—Rudolf Bultmann himself—due to seemingly insurmountable historical and theological roadblocks? The answer to this question is tied to an occurrence at the University of Marburg, Germany (where Bultmann taught), in 1953.

Ernest Käsemann and the beginning of the new quest. It is customary to trace the beginning of the new quest to a very specific date: October 20, 1953. On this date, Ernest Käsemann presented a lecture titled "The Problem of the Historical Jesus" at an annual meeting of Bultmann and his former students.[50] He began by noting the factors, both historical and theological, that had contributed to the demise of the first quest in Germany. But he went on to suggest that these obstacles could not be the end of the story—and his reason for saying so was, interestingly enough, decidedly *theological* in nature:

we also cannot do away with the identity between the exalted and the

---

[49]D. M. Baillie, *God Was in Christ: An Essay on Incarnation and Atonement* (New York: Scribner's Sons, 1948), p. 58.

[50]Ernst Käsemann, "The Problem of the Historical Jesus," in his *Essays on New Testament Themes*, trans. W. J. Montague (London: SCM Press, 1964), pp. 15-47. For a variety of perspectives on the new quest see Carl E. Braaten and Roy A. Harrisville, eds., *The Historical Jesus and the Kerygmatic Christ: Essays on the New Quest of the Historical Jesus* (Nashville: Abingdon, 1964); P. Joseph Cahill, "Rudolf Bultmann and Post-Bultmannian Tendencies," *Catholic Biblical Quarterly* 26 (1964): 153-78; Ralph P. Martin, "The New Quest of the Historical Jesus," in *Jesus of Nazareth: Savior and Lord*, ed. Carl F. H. Henry (Grand Rapids: Eerdmans, 1966), pp. 23-45; John Reumann, "Jesus and Christology," in *The New Testament and Its Modern Interpreters*, ed. Eldon Jay Epp and George W. MacRae (Philadelphia: Fortress; Atlanta: Scholars Press, 1989), pp. 501-64; Robinson, *New Quest*.

earthly Lord without falling into docetism. . . . Conversely, neither our sources nor the insights we have gained from what has gone before permit us to substitute the historical Jesus for the exalted Lord. . . . The clash over the historical Jesus has as its object a genuine theological problem.[51]

And so, motivated (among other things) by the desire to avoid recapitulating something like the ancient heresy of docetism—the denial of Jesus' true humanity—Käsemann called for a renewal of the quest on the grounds of theological necessity. Ironically, whereas the old quest began with Reimarus's attempt to reveal an unbridgeable gulf between the Jesus of history and the Christ of faith presented in the Gospels, the new quest was inspired by the necessity of demonstrating *continuity* between them.

Fruits of the new quest. Within three years of Käsemann's call for a renewal of the quest, another of Bultmann's former students, Günther Bornkamm, answered that challenge with a slim volume entitled *Jesus of Nazareth*.[52] From the very first sentence, it is clear that the pessimism surrounding the no quest period has not been entirely dispelled within the new quest: "No one is any longer in the position to write a life of Jesus."[53] But, while Bornkamm does explicitly deny that we can any longer pursue an historical understanding of Jesus "along biographical, psychological lines," he nonetheless clearly affirms that not all is lost; we can still talk about "occurrence and event" in the life of Jesus.[54] Bornkamm goes on to reconstruct something of the characteristic teachings and conduct of Jesus. When it comes to the question of whether Jesus thought he was the Messiah, he agrees with Bultmann's view that Jesus never proclaimed himself to be the Messiah as such. However, he manages to retain some continuity here between history and faith when he states that "the Messianic character of his being is contained *in* his words and deeds and *in* the unmediatedness of his historical appearance."[55]

---

[51]Käsemann, "Problem," p. 34.

[52]Günther Bornkamm, *Jesus of Nazareth*, trans. Irene and Fraser McLuskey and James Robinson (New York: Harper & Row, 1960).

[53]Ibid., p. 13.

[54]Ibid., pp. 24-25.

[55]Ibid., p. 178 (emphasis in text). For appreciative, while critical, reflections on Bornkamm's study, see Leander E. Keck, "Bornkamm's *Jesus of Nazareth* Revisited," *Journal of Religion* 49 (1969): 1-17.

Other studies followed, though not all were hampered by vestigial Bultmannian pessimism. Beyond Bornkamm, significant figures in the new quest period (in terms of methodology and/or practice) include Herbert Braun, C. H. Dodd, Ernst Fuchs, Ferdinand Hahn, Leander Keck, Norman Perrin, Edward Schillebeeckx and Ethelbert Stauffer.[56] In 1959, the formal name for this stage of the quest was secured when James Robinson published his survey and assessment, titled *A New Quest of the Historical Jesus*.[57]

During this phase of the quest, a number of new developments took place in Gospels research. First was the rise of redaction criticism in the 1950s.[58] The thrust of the redaction-critical enterprise is driven by the conviction that the authors of the Gospels did not function as mere collectors of earlier tradition, but rather allowed their own literary and theological tendencies to shape the gospel texts. One of the effects of this perspective was to add a new layer of editorial fabrication that separates the reader of the Gospels and the historical Jesus, this one a factor of the literary creativity of the Gospel authors themselves. Second, the Q document took on a new importance in this era as many within the Bultmannian wing of scholarship came to see it not merely as a supplementary sayings list, but rather as a full-blown "Gospel" in its own right.[59] In time, these first two developments would coalesce, and redactional analysis of perceived editorial layers of Q itself got underway.[60] Today a number of scholars have pressed on to attempt to identify

---

[56]Herbert Braun, *Jesus of Nazareth: the Man and His Time*, trans. E. R. Kalin (Philadelphia: Fortress, 1979 [1969]); Dodd, *The Founder of Christianity*; Ernst Fuchs, *Studies of the Historical Jesus*, trans. A. Scobie (London: SCM, 1964 [1960]); Ferdinand Hahn, *Historical Investigation and the New Testament: Two Essays*, ed. Edgar Krentz, trans. Robert Maddox (Philadelphia: Fortress, 1983 [1974]); Leander Keck, *A Future for the Historical Jesus: The Place of Jesus in Preaching and Theology* (Nashville: Abingdon, 1971); Norman Perrin, *Rediscovering the Teaching of Jesus* (New York: Harper & Row, 1976); Edward Schillebeeckx, *Jesus: An Experiment in Christology*, trans. Hubert Hoskins (New York: Seabury, 1979 [1974]); Ethelbert Stauffer, *Jesus and His Story*, trans. Dorothea M. Barton (London: SCM, 1960 [1957]).

[57]James M. Robinson, *A New Quest of the Historical Jesus* (London: SCM, 1959).

[58]See Norman Perrin, *What Is Redaction Criticism?* (Philadelphia: Fortress, 1969).

[59]The first move in this direction was the 1956 dissertation of Heinz Tödt, later published as *The Son of Man in the Synoptic Tradition*, trans. D. M. Barton (Philadelphia: Westminster Press, 1965 [1959]).

[60]The most influential study here has been John Kloppenborg, *The Formation of Q: Trajectories in Ancient Wisdom Collections* (Philadelphia: Fortress, 1987).

the early Christian communities and sociological forces behind each hypothesized layer of Q.[61]

Finally, it was during the new quest that criteria designed to determine the potential historical authenticity of the Gospel material were more formally assessed and utilized.[62] Most notorious among these authenticity criteria is the "(double) dissimilarity" criterion, which states that

> the earliest form of a saying we can reach may be regarded as authentic if it can be shown to be dissimilar to characteristic emphases both of ancient Judaism and of the early Church.[63]

The end of the new quest. Unlike the terminus points of the old and no quest periods, there is no universally agreed upon date that marks the demise of the new quest and the beginning of the third quest. The most common assessment is that the new quest period slowly ground to a halt over the course of the 1970s.[64] There were a variety of reasons for this, and most have to do with reactions—for or against—the Bultmannian tendencies within the new quest. Some, like Schubert Ogden, moved back toward a more pessimistic perspective reminiscent of Bultmann himself.[65] Others, seeing the new quest as little more than an exercise in "puttering around in Bultmann's garden,"[66] challenged its methodology, its meager results or both.[67] Even the

---

[61]E.g., Burton Mack, *The Lost Gospel: The Book of Q and Christian Origins* (San Francisco: HarperSanFrancisco, 1993).

[62]Dennis Polkow surveys over twenty different criteria used by scholars up through the 1980s; see "Method and Criteria for Historical Jesus Research," *Society of Biblical Literature Seminar Papers* 26 (1987): 336-56.

[63]Perrin, *Rediscovering*, p. 39. For a history and critique of this criterion see Gerd Theissen and Dagmar Winter, *The Quest for the Plausible Jesus: The Question of Criteria*, trans. M. Eugene Boring (Louisville: Westminster John Knox, 2002), pp. 1-171.

[64]By 1974 some were talking about the "post-New Quest period"; e.g., see John Reumann "'Lives of Jesus' During the Great Quest for the Historical Jesus," *Indian Journal of Theology* 23 (1974): 53.

[65]Schubert M. Ogden, *The Point of Christology* (Dallas: SMU Press, 1982).

[66]Walter P. Weaver, "Forward: Reflections on the Continuing Quest for Jesus," in *Images of Jesus Today*, ed. James H. Charlesworth and Walter P. Weaver (Valley Forge, Penn.: Trinity Press International, 1994), p. xiii.

[67]E.g., Raymond E. Brown, "After Bultmann, What?—An Introduction to the Post-Bultmannians," *Catholic Biblical Quarterly* 26 (1964): 1-30; John G. Gager, "The Gospels and Jesus: Some Doubts about Method," *Journal of Religion* 54 (1974): 244-72; James MacDonald, "New Quest—Dead End? So What about the Historical Jesus," in *Studia Biblica 1978*, vol. 2: *Papers on the Gos-*

question of whether the new quest was really "new" at all was raised.[68] In any case, by the early 1980s it was becoming increasingly clear that something "newer" than the new quest itself was underway—and the "third quest" was born.

The third quest (1980s–present). The term "third quest" was first coined by N. T. Wright in a 1982 article.[69] While it is widely used today, there remains debate as to what exactly it refers to and whether in fact it even exists as such. Some dismiss the term as unhelpful, arguing either that the hard distinctions of "old," "no," "new," and "third" quests serve erroneously to ignore the very real *continuity* throughout the history of the quest[70] or, at the very least, that what we call the "third" quest is simply a revitalization of the "new" quest.[71] Even among those who embrace the label "third quest," a significant disagreement about its definition remains. Wright originally used the term in a synchronic fashion—to demarcate not a distinct chronological period, but rather a new methodological orientation. Thus for Wright and some others the new (or "new 'new,'" or "renewed") quest and the "third" quest are both operative today, running as parallel tracks with distinct methodological approaches (the former continuing in the broad skeptical wake left by Bultmann and, before him, Wrede; the latter departing from that influence, being more Schweitzerian in nature).[72] Others, however, have

---

pels, ed. E. A. Livingstone (Sheffield: JSOT Press, 1980), pp. 151-70.

[68]E.g., Van A. Harvey and Schubert M. Ogden, "How New is the 'New Quest of the Historical Jesus,'" in *The Historical Jesus and the Kerygmatic Christ*, ed. Carl E. Braaten and Roy A. Harrisville (Nashville: Abingdon, 1964), pp. 197-242.

[69]N. T. Wright, "Towards a Third 'Quest'? Jesus Then and Now," *ARC* (Montreal, Quebec) 10 (1982): 20-27. While others have proposed alternate rubrics for this current stage of Jesus studies—e.g., "post-Quest" (Tatum, *In Quest*, p. 102); "Jesus research" (J. H. Charlesworth, *Jesus Within Judaism* [New York: Doubleday, 1988], p. 26)—it appears that Wright's "Third Quest" has won the day.

[70]E.g., Allison, "Secularizing," pp. 141-45; Stanley E. Porter, *The Criteria for Authenticity in Historical-Jesus Research: Previous Discussion and New Proposals* (Sheffield: Sheffield Academic Press, 2000), pp. 56, 239-42; Tom Holmén, "A Theologically Disinterested Quest? On the Origins of the 'Third Quest' for the Historical Jesus," *Studia Theologica* 55 (2001): 189. Weaver (*Historical Jesus*, pp. xi-xii) questions the appropriateness of the common four-stage typology given its indebtedness to an overly narrow, parochially German perspective.

[71]E.g., Telford, "Major Trends," pp. 60-61.

[72]N. T. Wright, "Quest for the Historical Jesus," in *Anchor Bible Dictionary*, 6 vols.; ed. David N. Freedman (New York: Doubleday, 1992), 3:799-800; idem, *Jesus and the Victory of God* (Minneapolis: Fortress, 1996), chaps. 2-3. Those who appear to follow Wright's synchronic approach include Pieter Craffert, "Historical-Anthropological Jesus Research: The Status of Authentic

rejected Wright's original definition and instead use the term "third quest" in a diachronic sense—to designate the all-inclusive current (since the late 1970s / early 1980s) chronological stage of the quest.[73] It appears that the majority of scholars today use the term "third quest" in this chronological fashion, and we will do the same in this essay.

Unlike the other stages of the quest, the beginning of the third quest is not easily marked by a specific year. For convenience's sake, some have proposed 1985 as the inauguration of the third quest, since this year saw both the publication of E. P. Sander's groundbreaking volume *Jesus and Judaism* and the launch of the Jesus Seminar.[74] Things are not that neat and simple, however. Others trace the origins of the third quest back into the late 1970s with works such as Ben Meyer's *The Aims of Jesus.*[75] In any case, disagreement on the precise launch date of the third quest notwithstanding, there is widespread agreement that a new stage of the quest was incrementally inaugurated through the 1970s and early 1980s with works by scholars such as Meyer, Sanders, Anthony Harvey, John Riches, Geza Vermes, Marcus Borg, John Dominic Crossan and Robert Funk (with his launching of the Jesus Seminar).[76] Since then the last three decades have seen a flood of scholarly works

---

Pictures beyond Authentic Material," *Hervormde Teologiese Studies* 58 (2002): 440-71; Craig Evans, "Assessing Progress in the Third Quest of the Historical Jesus," *Journal for the Study of the Historical Jesus* 4 (2006): 54; and Robert Funk, *Honest to Jesus: Jesus for a New Millennium* (San Francisco: HarperSanFrancisco, 1996): 62-76 (although Funk relabels Wright's "third questers" the "pretend questers" [p. 64]).

[73]E.g., Colin Brown, "Quest of Historical Jesus," in *Dictionary of Jesus and the Gospels,* eds. Joel B. Green, Scot McKnight and I. Howard Marshall (Downers Grove, Ill.: InterVarsity Press, 1992), p. 337; John Dominic Crossan, "What Victory? What God? A Review Debate with N. T. Wright on *Jesus and the Victory of God,*" *Scottish Journal of Theology* 50 (1997): 346-47; Donald L. Denton, *Historiography and Hermeneutics in Jesus Studies: An Examination of the Work of John Dominic Crossan and Ben F. Meyer* (New York: T & T Clark, 2004), pp.4-8; Theissen and Merz, *Historical Jesus,* pp. 7-12; Witherington, *Jesus Quest,* pp. 11-12.

[74]E.g., David Gowler, *What are They Saying about the Historical Jesus?* (Mahwah, N.J.: Paulist, 2007), p. 27.

[75]Ben F. Meyer, *The Aims of Jesus* (London: SCM Press, 1979).

[76]Meyer, *Aims*; E. P. Sanders, *Jesus and Judaism* (Philadelphia: Fortress, 1985); Marcus Borg, *Conflict, Holiness, and Politics in the Teachings of Jesus* (New York: Mellen, 1984); John Dominic Crossan, *In Fragments: The Aphorisms of Jesus* (San Francisco: Harper & Row, 1983); Robert Funk, "The Issue of Jesus," *Forum* 1 (1985): 7-12; Anthony Harvey, *Jesus and the Constraints of History* (Philadelphia: Westminster Press, 1982); John Riches, *Jesus and the Transformation of Judaism* (London: Darton, Longman, & Todd, 1980); Geza Vermes, *Jesus the Jew: A Historian's Reading of the Gospels* (New York: Macmillan, 1973); idem, *Jesus and the World of Judaism* (Philadelphia: Fortress, 1984).

on Jesus. Among these studies are multivolume projects like those by John Meier and N. T. Wright;[77] landmark works like Crossan's *The Historical Jesus* and James Dunn's *Jesus Remembered* (with both of these scholars being contributors to this present volume);[78] insightful survey's such as Mark Allan Powell's *Jesus as a Figure in History*, Theissen and Merz's *The Historical Jesus*, and Ben Witherington III's *The Jesus Quest;*[79] and a number of useful reference works, status reports and resource guides, such as those produced by Darrell Bock (also a contributor to this volume).[80]

THE CURRENT STATE OF THE THIRD QUEST
CONTOURS AND QUESTIONS

The bulk of the remainder of this essay is devoted to canvassing the broad contours and some of the important questions that characterize the present state of the third quest. First, a range of methodological issues will be touched on. We will begin with the question of the viability of the quest itself, and move from there to terminological issues, issues related to philosophy of historiography and historical method,

---

[77]John Meier, *A Marginal Jew: Rethinking the Historical Jesus*, vol. 1, *The Roots of the Problem and the Person* (New York: Doubleday, 1991); vol. 2, *Mentor, Message and Miracles* (New York: Doubleday, 1994); vol. 3, *Companions and Competitors* (New York: Doubleday, 2001); vol. 4, *Law and Love* (New York: Doubleday, 2009). N. T. Wright, *Christian Origins and the Question of God*, vol. 1: *The New Testament and the People of God* (Minneapolis: Fortress, 1992); vol. 2: *Jesus and the Victory of God* (Minneapolis: Fortress, 1996); vol. 3: *The Resurrection of the Son of God* (Minneapolis: Fortress, 2003).

[78]John Dominic Crossan, *The Historical Jesus: The Life of a Mediterranean Jewish Peasant* (San Francisco: HarperSanFrancisco, 1991); James D. G. Dunn, *Jesus Remembered* (Grand Rapids: Eerdmans, 2003); see as well Martin Hengel and Anna Maria Schwemer, *Geschichte des frühen Christentums*, vol. 1, *Jesus und das Judentum* (Tübingen: Mohr Siebeck, 2007).

[79]Mark Allan Powell, *Jesus as a Figure in History* (Louisville, Ky.: Westminster John Knox, 1998); Theissen and Merz, *Historical Jesus* (1998); Witherington, *Jesus Quest* (1995).

[80]Darrell L. Bock, *Studying the Historical Jesus: A Guide to Sources and Methods* (Grand Rapids: Baker Academic, 2002); Darrell Bock and Gregory J. Herrick, eds., *Jesus in Context: Background Readings for Gospel Study* (Grand Rapids: Baker Academic, 2005). See also Chilton and Evans, eds., *Studying the Historical Jesus*; James D. G. Dunn and Scot McKnight, eds., *The Historical Jesus in Recent Research* (Winona Lake, Ind.: Eisenbrauns, 2005); Craig A. Evans, ed., *Encyclopedia of the Historical Jesus* (New York: Routledge, 2008); Joel B. Green, Scot McKnight and I. Howard Marshall, eds., *Dictionary of Jesus and the Gospels* (Downers Grove, Ill.: InterVarsity Press, 1992); Amy-Jill Levine, Dale C. Allison and John Dominic Crossan, eds., *The Historical Jesus in Context* (Princeton, N.J.: Princeton University Press, 2006); and especially Tom Holmén and Stanley E. Porter, eds., *The Handbook of the Study of the Historical Jesus*, 4 vols. (Boston: Brill, forthcoming).

the interdisciplinary nature of the contemporary quest, and the question of ancient literary sources for Jesus. Finally, the "results" of the contemporary quest will be considered. Here, the Jewishness of Jesus and the question of Jesus and apocalyptic eschatology will be touched on, as will a number of the portraits of the historical Jesus that have been proposed for consideration.

Methodology and related issues. One of the distinctive features of the contemporary quest is a widely represented self-awareness on the part of scholars of the importance of historical methodology. In the words of Crossan: "Method, method, and once again, method."[81] Reminiscent of the "no quest" posture, this conscious awareness of the complexities surrounding the issue of methodology has led some to question the very possibility of the quest itself.

Questioning the quest. There are several ways, and even senses, in which the legitimacy of the quest itself is being questioned today. Some, following the basic sentiments of Bultmann, question whether it is possible to convincingly trace enough of the Gospel tradition back to Jesus himself to warrant the efforts of the quest.[82] For example, William Hamilton, with a nod to Bultmann and Paul Tillich, determined that "Jesus is inaccessible by historical means," and thus he proposes a "Quest for the Post-Historical Jesus."[83] Others—starting from a poststructuralist inspired rejection of historiography in general, and/or following from the observation that current scholars continue to discover a plethora of discordant, often mutually exclusive historical Jesuses—have concluded that the quest itself is a "failing enterprise."[84] Yet still others see the quest as a nonstarter not

---

[81]Crossan, "Historical Jesus as Risen Lord," in John Dominic Crossan, Luke Timothy Johnson and Werner Kelber, *The Jesus Controversy: Perspectives in Conflict* (Harrisburg, Penn.: Trinity Press International, 1999), p. 5.

[82]Practically speaking, this appears to be the view of Helmut Koester, "The Historical Jesus and the Historical Situation of the Quest: An Epilogue," in *Studying the Historical Jesus: Evaluations of the State of Current Research*, ed. Bruce Chilton and Craig A. Evans (New York: Brill, 1994), pp. 535-45.

[83]William Hamilton, *A Quest for the Post-Historical Jesus* (New York: Continuum, 1994), p. 19. Along similar lines see Thomas J. J. Altizer, *The Contemporary Jesus* (Albany: SUNY Press, 1997); Dieter Georgi, "The Interest in Life of Jesus Theology as a Paradigm for the Social History of Biblical Criticism," *Harvard Theological Review* 85 (1992): 51-83.

[84]Jacob Neusner, "Who Needs the 'Historical Jesus'? A Review Essay," *Bulletin for Biblical Re-*

so much because of the historical difficulties but rather because of its sheer lack of historical interest or relevance. William Arnal, suggesting that a new no quest period is the best scholarly route to take, captures this sentiment:

> And so perhaps the quest for the historical Jesus should be abandoned once again. . . . Not because scholars cannot agree on their reconstructions. . . . Not even because reasonable conclusions are impossible in light of our defective sources. . . . But because, ultimately, the historical Jesus does not matter, either for our understanding of the past, or our understanding of the present . . . The Jesus who is important to our day is not the Jesus of history, but the symbolic Jesus of contemporary discourse.[85]

Finally, for some scholars today, the third quest is put in jeopardy not from the beginning, but in hindsight. Similar to Bruno Bauer of the old quest, they have embarked on the historical search for Jesus only to conclude that a person named Jesus of Nazareth never did exist.[86] And so, Robert Price, one of the most provocative Christ-Myth theorists writing today (and a contributor to this volume), concludes that at the end of a truly critical study, we find that the "historical Jesus" has in fact "shrunk to the vanishing point."[87]

If it is historical matters that lead to a rejection of the quest for some, for others their critique is tied to things theological. From Reimarus and the beginnings of the quest, the question of the proper role, if any, of the historical study of Jesus within the Christian faith has been at play. Today, some follow the same general path as Martin Kähler and conclude that the historical quest for Jesus has no real bearing on the faith life of the Christian believer. No one has stated this more strongly

---

search 4 (1994): 119. See also Hal Childs, *The Myth of the Historical Jesus and the Evolution of Consciousness* (Atlanta: Scholars Press, 2000).

[85]William E. Arnal, *The Symbolic Jesus: Historical Scholarship, Judaism and the Construction of Contemporary Identity* (Oakville, Conn.: Equinox, 2005), p. 77. This sentiment seems to characterize that group of scholars who, following Jonathan Z. Smith and Burton Mack, are most interested in the early Christian enterprise as little more than an instance of myth-making in the service of social formation and experiment. See Mack, "The Historical Jesus Hoopla," in *The Christian Myth: Origins, Logic and Legacy* (New York: Continuum, 2003), pp. 25-40.

[86]Robert M. Price, *Deconstructing Jesus* (Amherst, N.Y.: Prometheus, 2000); idem, *The Incredible Shrinking Son of Man* (Amherst, N.Y.: Prometheus, 2003); Earl Doherty, *The Jesus Puzzle: Did Christianity Begin with a Mythical Christ?* (Ottawa: Canadian Humanist, 1999).

[87]Price, *Incredible Shrinking*, p. 354.

in recent years than the Roman Catholic New Testament scholar Luke Timothy Johnson (another contributor to this volume). For Johnson the attempt to render the Christian faith in any way dependent on the historically reconstructed Jesus is "impossible" since historical proposals are always contingent and open to later revision—hardly the type of thing the Christian community could base its very identity on over time.[88] For Johnson, none of this should bother the believer, since it is also the case that "historical research is *irrelevant* to Christian faith."[89] This is because Christian faith is focused not on historical reconstructions of the pre-Easter Jesus of the past, but rather on the living and active presence of the risen Jesus in the present. Thus, for Johnson,

> Christians direct their faith not to the historical figure of Jesus but to the living Lord Jesus. Yes, they assert continuity between that Jesus and this. But their faith is confirmed, not by the establishment of facts about the past, but by the reality of Christ's power in the present.[90]

To those who remind Johnson that it was a theological motivation that got the new quest itself up and running—namely the conviction that contemporary Christianity must not devolve into a new form of docetism—he responds by pointing out that there are resources within the tradition itself that safeguard against this error.[91]

Johnson is not alone in this perspective. Some contemporary evangelical Protestant scholars have come to similar conclusions. Frank Thielman, for example, taking a cue from Johnson himself, hopes to convince fellow evangelicals to consider whether the quest "may not be merely theologically unnecessary" but, in fact, "theologically ill-

---

[88]Luke Timothy Johnson, "The Real Jesus: The Challenge of Current Scholarship and the Truth of the Gospels," in *The Historical Jesus through Catholic and Jewish Eyes*, ed. Bryan F. LeBeau et al. (Harrisburg, Penn: Trinity Press International, 2000), p. 57. For his sustained case see idem, *The Real Jesus: The Misguided Quest for the Historical Jesus and the Truth of the Traditional Gospels* (San Francisco: HarperSanFrancisco, 1996).

[89]Johnson, "Real Jesus," p. 59 (emphasis added).

[90]*Real Jesus*, pp. 142-43. For a similar, if more moderate, take on things see Robert Morgan, "Christian Faith and Historical Jesus Research: a Reply to James Dunn," *Expository Times* 116 (2005): 217-23.

[91]Johnson, "The Humanity of Jesus: What's at Stake in the Quest for the Historical Jesus?" in John Dominic Crossan, Luke Timothy Johnson and Werner Kelber, *The Jesus Controversy: Perspectives in Conflict* (Harrisburg, Penn.: Trinity Press International, 1999), pp. 61-66.

advised."[92] Even Jacob Neusner, a Jewish scholar, has tried to warn Christians about the dangers of too closely associating the products of the quest with the historic Christian faith: "And since when do matters of fact have any bearing on the truths of faith?"[93]

In defense of the quest. Not surprisingly, most scholars involved in discussions about the merits of the quest conclude quite differently from the more skeptical perspectives surveyed above. For most questers, despite the challenges and inherent limitations of contemporary historiography, the quest remains a viable historical enterprise. And while most questers acknowledge the dangers of allowing personal theological biases to a priori determine and/or distort historical conclusions, statistically speaking most (though certainly not all) also self-identify with the label "Christian" and remain convinced that the historical study of Jesus is not only an *allowable* activity for a believer, but is, in fact, an *important* one.[94] This is an important observation since, while some argue that one distinctive of the third quest is a general theological disinterestedness, others have seriously questioned this claim.[95]

In his 1971 book, *A Future for the Historical Jesus*, Leander Keck defends the theological legitimacy of the quest against the counter-

---

[92]Frank Thielman, "Evangelicals and the Jesus Quest: Some Problems of Historical and Theological Method," *Churchman* 115 (2001): 70-71. Even broader concerns are expressed about any use by evangelicals of the historical-critical method itself in Eta Linnemann, *Historical Criticism of the Bible: Methodology or Ideology?* (Grand Rapids: Baker, 1990); Robert Thomas and David Farnell, *The Jesus Crisis: The Inroads of Historical Criticism into Evangelical Scholarship* (Grand Rapids: Kregel, 1998).

[93]Neusner, "Who Needs," p. 121.

[94]E.g., John Dominic Crossan, "Why Is Historical Jesus Research Necessary?" in *Jesus Two Thousand Years Later*, ed. James H. Charlesworth and Walter P. Weaver (Harrisburg, Penn.: Trinity Press International, 2000), pp. 7-37; Dunn, *Jesus Remembered*, pp. 99-136; Craig Evans, "The Historical Jesus and Christian Faith: A Critical Assessment of a Scholarly Problem," *Christian Scholar's Review* 18 (1988): 48-63; Werner H. Kelber, "The Quest for the Historical Jesus from the Perspectives of Medieval, Modern and Post-Enlightenment Readings, and in View of Ancient, Oral Aesthetics," in John Dominic Crossan, Luke Timothy Johnson and Werner Kelber, *The Jesus Controversy: Perspectives in Conflict* (Harrisburg, Penn.: Trinity, 1999), pp. 75-155; Meier, *Marginal Jew*, 1:4; Powell, *Jesus*, pp. 182-84; Wright, *Jesus*, pp. 13-16, 25-26, 660-62.

[95]E.g., see respectively Theissen and Winter, *Quest for the Plausible*, pp. 142-43; Holmén, "Theologically Disinterested Quest?" Theological "interest" in the quest can, of course, be antitheologically motivated. E.g., see Paul Hollenbach's claim that the value of the quest is tied to the need to "overthrow . . . the 'mistake called Christianity'"; "The Historical Jesus Question in North America Today," *Biblical Theology Bulletin* 19 (1989): 19.

arguments that characterized the "no quest" period. His concerns are shared by many Christian scholars of various stripes within the quest today, and so his case is worth summarizing here. Among his contentions are the following: (1) The integrity of Christian preaching—and thus of preachers themselves—is at stake if "claims for Jesus are not really supportable but only useful for persuasion"; (2) historical study of Jesus can serve as "a major bulwark" against contemporary "ideological distortion" of Jesus and his message; (3) responsible historical study of Jesus assists the church in retaining a robust and fully orbed Christology, one that safeguards itself from a new form of "docetism" on one hand, or a well-meaning but inappropriately "self-validating" fideism on the other; and finally (4) given the "demise of Christendom" in the Western world and the "pluralistic marketplace of ideas" (itself quite similar to the setting of the early church) in which the contemporary believer now finds herself, a faith divorced from serious historical considerations invites its intellectual marginalization within the surrounding culture, leaving it to appear to others as little more than a curious but ultimately irrelevant vestige of a belief system from the premodern past.[96]

Keck goes on to suggest that once a correct view of Christian "faith" is in view—faith as relational "trust," and thus not in diametrical opposition to, but rather in potentially complementary relationship with, human reason and historical evidence—then much of the theological resistance to the quest dissipates.[97] Moreover, Keck points out that while not "every believer must be a critical historian in order to believe," nonetheless every believer "has central things at stake in the historical study of Jesus, just as citizens of all sorts have their lives at stake in the work of scientists, economists, and politicians whose work they may not comprehend or even know about."[98]

It is worth noting that among those who take historical study of the earthly life of Jesus as central to their Christological endeavors are a number of Third World theologians for whom Jesus' life functions as

---

[96]Keck, *Future*, pp. 36-39.
[97]Ibid., chap. 2.
[98]Ibid., p. 39.

the concrete, historically rooted model for, and biblical legitimization of, the call for contemporary Christians to imitate his commitment to human liberation.[99] In sum, most questers associated with the Christian faith—including many self-professed evangelical Christians— would take issue with the Kähler-Johnson tradition's claim that the quest is largely "irrelevant" to the Christian faith.[100] Instead, it appears that many would resonate with the words of Ronald Preston: "A religion which believes in an Incarnation is compelled to lay itself open to the hazards of critical and historical enquiry."[101]

The terminology problem. Terminological equivocation and confusion in any field of study creates problems, and historical Jesus research has had its share over the years. With Kähler came a distinction between the "Jesus of history" and the "Christ of faith" or, from his famous book title, the "historical Jesus" and the "historic [i.e., historically influential], biblical Christ." Others have tried to get at this same distinction with other labels: "pre-Easter Jesus" and "post-Easter Jesus"; "historical Jesus" and "Jesus of piety"; "Jesus of history" and "Jesus of story"; "historical Jesus" and "real Jesus."[102] This last set of terms—"historical Jesus" and "real Jesus"—has been proposed by John Meier as a replacement to any others. Here, the "historical Jesus," or the "Jesus of history," refers to "the Jesus we can 'recover' and examine by using the scientific tools of modern historical research."[103] By the "real Jesus" he means to signify something

---

[99]E.g., see Jon Sobrino, *Jesus the Liberator: A Historical-Theological Reading of Jesus of Nazareth*, trans. Paul Burns and Francis McDonagh (Maryknoll, N.Y.: Orbis, 1993); Leonardo Boff, *Jesus Christ Liberator: A Critical Christology of Our Time*, trans. Patrick Hughes (Maryknoll, N.Y.: Orbis, 1978).

[100]For two representative evangelical statements in defense of participation in the quest see Colin Brown, "Christology and the Quest of the Historical Jesus," in *Doing Theology for the People of God: Studies in Honour of J. I. Packer*, ed. Donald Lewis and Alister McGrath (Downers Grove, Ill.: InterVarsity Press, 1996), pp. 67-83; Michael Bird, "Shouldn't Evangelicals Participate in the 'Third Quest for the Historical Jesus?'" *Themelios* 29, no. 2 (2004): 5-14.

[101]Ronald Preston, "The Presuppositions of Christian Theology," in *Vindications: Essays on the Historical Basis of Christianity*, ed. Anthony Hanson (New York: Morehouse-Barlow, 1966), p. 15.

[102]See respectively Marcus Borg, *Jesus in Contemporary Scholarship* (Valley Forge, Penn.: Trinity Press International, 1994), p. 195; Elisabeth Schüssler Fiorenza, "The Jesus of Piety and the Historical Jesus," *Catholic Theological Society of America Proceedings* 49 (1994): 90-99; Powell, *Jesus*, pp. 8-9; Meier, *Marginal Jew*, 1:21-26.

[103]Meier, *Marginal Jew*, 1:25. Meier also sets out his proposal in "The Historical Jesus: Rethinking Some Concepts," *Theological Studies* 51 (1990): 3-24.

like the sum total of the actual Jesus, most of the data about whom is lost forever to the sands of time. Thus Meier warns:

> The reader who wants to know the real Jesus should close this book right now, because the historical Jesus is neither the real Jesus nor the easy way to him. The real Jesus is not available and never will be. This is true not because Jesus did not exist—he certainly did—but rather because the sources that have survived do not and never intended to record all or even most of the words and deeds of his public ministry— to say nothing of the rest of his life.[104]

While some scholars have embraced Meier's terminological proposal, others have expressed their reservations.[105] Nonetheless, whatever terms they use, most scholars in the field today find a way to express their conviction that the reconstructed product that arises from the contemporary historical study of Jesus is not to be confused with the total reality of the man Jesus of Nazareth who lived for roughly thirty-three years in first-century Palestine.

Philosophy of historiography and historical method. An interesting irony of the contemporary quest is the remarkable attention given to questions of historical method (compared to the prior stages of the quest) on one hand, and, on the other, the frequent claim that far too little attention has been paid to these very issues thus far.[106] From Ben Meyer's 1979 *The Aims of Jesus* onward, many of the notable works of the third quest have included significant, self-reflective statements on the proper historical method by which the historical Jesus is to be pursued.[107] Less often does one find evidence of a Jesus scholar pushing back beyond the

---

[104]Meier, *Marginal Jew*, 1:22.

[105]Among those who take issue with Meier's terms for one reason or another are C. Stephen Evans, *The Historical Christ and the Jesus of Faith: The Incarnational Narrative as History* (Oxford: Clarendon, 1996), pp. 8-11; Witherington, *Jesus Quest*, p. 199.

[106]See Denton, *Historiography*; Evans, *Historical Christ*; Robert J. Miller, "Historical Method and the Historical Jesus," in his *The Jesus Seminar and Its Critics* (Santa Rosa, Calif.: Polebridge, 1999), pp. 27-46.

[107]Perhaps most remarkable is Wright's first volume, *The New Testament and the People of God*, which is largely devoted to methodological issues beginning with epistemology itself. See also Crossan, *Historical Jesus*, pp. xxvii-xxxiv; Dunn, *Jesus Remembered*, chaps. 6-10; idem, *A New Perspective on Jesus: What the Quest for the Historical Jesus Missed* (Grand Rapids: Baker Academic, 2005); Meier, *Marginal Jew*, vol. 1, part 1; Meyer, *Aims of Jesus*, part 1; Sanders, *Jesus and Judaism*, pp. 1-58.

practical elements of historical method to the theoretical groundings of
these methods in a self-conscious philosophy of historiography and its
religio-philosophical moorings (e.g., epistemology, metaphysics).[108] As
Wright has noted, much of the discord in Jesus studies today is the result of "the projection of an undiscussed metaphysic."[109] More and
more, however, scholars are challenging each other and themselves to
"come clean" on the often hidden worldview presuppositions that inevitably influence their historiographical decisions about Jesus.[110] As
William Lyons observes:

> Only with a clear acknowledgment of one's wider presuppositions can
> such decisions be made coherently and only with the attainment of some
> degree of resolution on the wider issues can such decisions be made
> consensually.[111]

One place where the issue of worldview presuppositions has direct
bearing on Jesus studies involves historical decisions on Jesus' miracles.
Contrary to previous times, virtually everyone in the field today acknowledges that Jesus was considered by his contemporaries to be an
exorcist and a worker of miracles.[112] However, when it comes to historical assessment of the miracles tradition itself, the consensus quickly

---

[108]Wright is one of the notable exceptions; see *New Testament*, part 2. It appears that many
in the post-Bultmannian tradition continue to rely on Van Harvey's work in this respect;
see *The Historian and the Believer: The Morality of Historical Knowledge and Christian Belief*
(Philadelphia: Westminster Press, 1966). Harvey's work has been subjected to critique from
alternative perspectives; see, e.g., Evans, *Historical Christ*, pp. 184-202; Paul Rhodes Eddy
and Gregory A. Boyd, *The Jesus Legend: A Case for the Historical Reliability of the Synoptic
Jesus Tradition* (Grand Rapids: Baker Academic, 2007), chap. 1. For a brilliant statement on
contemporary philosophy of historiography see Aviezer Tucker, *Our Knowledge of the Past:
A Philosophy of Historiography* (Cambridge: Cambridge University Press, 2004).

[109]Wright, *New Testament*, p. 31.

[110]Mark Allan Powell, "Authorial Intent and Historical Reporting: Putting Spong's Literaliza-
tion Thesis to the Test," *Journal for the Study of the Historical Jesus* 1 (2003): 248.

[111]William John Lyons, "The Hermeneutics of Fictional Black and Factual Red: The Markan
Simon of Cyrene and the Quest for the Historical Jesus," *Journal for the Study of the Historical
Jesus* 4 (2006): 154. See also Eddy and Boyd, *Jesus Legend*, pp. 21-24.

[112]Scholars ranging from evangelical quarters to the Jesus Seminar agree here; e.g., see respectively Graham H. Twelftree, *Jesus the Miracle Worker: A Historical and Theological Study*
(Downers Grove, Ill.: InterVarsity Press, 1999); Robert W. Funk and the Jesus Seminar, *The
Acts of Jesus: The Search for the Authentic Deeds of Jesus* (San Francisco: HarperSanFrancisco,
1998), p. 566. Meier finds this consensus on Jesus as a miracle worker to be one of the "seven
notable gains" (p. 461) of the third quest; see John P. Meier, "The Present State of the 'Third
Quest' for the Historical Jesus: Loss and Gain," *Biblica* 80 (1999): 477-83.

shatters. Some, following in the footsteps of Bultmann, embrace an explicit methodological naturalism such that the very idea of a miracle is ruled out a priori.[113] Others defend the logical possibility of miracle at the theoretical level, but, in practice, retain a functional methodological naturalism, maintaining that we could never be in possession of the type and/or amount of evidence that would justify a historical judgment in favor of the occurrence of a miracle.[114] Still others, suspicious that an uncompromising methodological naturalism most likely reflects an unwarranted metaphysical naturalism, find such a priori skepticism unwarranted and either remain open to, or even explicitly defend, the historicity of miracles within the Jesus tradition.[115]

Another methodological issue that emerges in Jesus studies today can be termed the "atomism" vs. "holism" debate. Here the question at hand is whether (following the Bultmannian tradition) it is better to begin by isolating historically authentic bits of Jesus material and then working outward to flesh out the historical Jesus (i.e., "atomism"), or whether, conversely, it is best to begin with a large-scale, fleshed out hypothesis about Jesus that is then subsequently tested and either verified or falsified by the data ("holism"). The methodological approaches of the Jesus Seminar (i.e., voting on small bits of the Jesus tradition), Crossan and Meier typify the atomistic approach, while the alternative approaches of Sanders, Wright and Dunn exemplify the more "holistic" method.[116] Tied to this discussion is the debated question of whether,

---

[113]For Bultmann's famous statements rejecting miracles see Rudolf Bultmann "Is Exegesis Without Presuppositions Possible?" in *Existence and Faith*, trans. S. M. Ogden (Cleveland: Meridian / New York: World, 1966), pp. 291-92; idem, "The Problem of Miracle," *Religion in Life* 27 (1958): 63-75. Robert Funk, for example, maintains the Bultmannian a priori moratorium on miracles; see "Twenty-one Theses," *Fourth R*, July-August (1998): 8.

[114]E.g., Miller, *Jesus Seminar*, p. 39; Price, *Incredible Shrinking*, pp. 19-20.

[115]E.g., Barry L. Blackburn, "The Miracles of Jesus," in *Studying the Hisotrical Jesus: Evaluations of the State of Current Research*, ed. Bruce Chilton and Craig A. Evans (New York: Brill, 1994), pp. 353-94; Eddy and Boyd, "Miracles and Method," in *Jesus Legend*, pp. 39-90; Meier, *Marginal Jew*, 2:509-32; Twelftree, *Jesus the Miracle Worker*, pp. 241-77; Wright, *New Testament*, pp. 92-98.

[116]See Funk and Jesus Seminar, *Five Gospels;* Crossan, *Historical Jesus*, pp. xxvii-xxxiv; Meier, *Marginal Jew*, 1:167-95; Sanders, *Jesus and Judaism*, pp. 3-22; Wright, *New Testament*, pp. 98-118; Dunn, *New Perspective on Jesus*, pp. 57-78. For a helpful discussion of atomism and holism—using Crossan and Ben Meyer respectively as exemplars—see Denton, *Historiography*.

in reconstructing the historical Jesus, one should privilege a focus on his *words* or his *deeds/activities*.[117]

A final issue of historical methodology under constant discussion in the quest today is the question of historical criteria by which to assess the Jesus tradition—traditionally known as "authenticity criteria."[118] Here the most controversial of the criteria is the so-called double dissimilarity criterion. As noted above, this criterion played an important role for many in the new quest. Today some still see it as a vital tool for discriminating between fabrications of the early church and material that actually originated with Jesus.[119] Most, however, appear to have decisively rejected this criterion, and that for several reasons. Chief among them is the fact that the double dissimilarity criterion tends to have the effect of distancing Jesus from his Jewish context. With the virtually unanimous consensus today that Jesus must be understood squarely within his first-century Jewish context, at least the "dissimilar from Judaism" side of this criterion has been widely abandoned.[120] Other scholars have challenged the flip side of this double-edged criterion as well—"dissimilar from early Christianity"—including those who have recently launched the "Jesus in Continuum" project which "seeks to uncover a Jesus who is both fitting within his Jewish context and in a comprehensible relation to early Christian attitudes."[121]

Other historical/authenticity criteria continue to be discussed, evalu-

---

[117]See respectively Lane C. McGaughy, "Words before Deeds: Why Start with the Sayings," *Forum* (n.s.) 1 (1998): 387-98; Sanders, *Jesus and Judaism*, pp. 3-18.

[118]Important statements on criteria include Bruce Chilton and Craig A. Evans, eds., *Authenticating the Activities of Jesus* (Boston: Brill, 1999); Bruce Chilton and Craig A. Evans, eds., *Authenticating the Words of Jesus* (Boston: Brill, 2002); Porter, *Criteria for Authenticity;* Theissen and Winter, *Quest for the Plausible;* Wright, *New Testament*, pp. 99-109.

[119]E.g., Price, *Incredible Shrinking*, pp. 16-19. Robert Funk and the Jesus Seminar (*Five Gospels*, pp. 30-32) seem to embrace a form of this criterion when they advocate the importance of isolating Jesus' "distinctive discourse."

[120]E.g., Dunn, *Jesus Remembered*, pp. 82-83; Tom Holmén, "Doubts about Double Dissimilarity: Restructuring the Main Criterion of Jesus-of-History Research," in *Authenticating the Words of Jesus*, ed. Bruce Chilton and Craig A. Evans (Boston: Brill, 2002), pp. 47-80; Sanders, *Jesus and Judaism*, pp. 16-17; Wright, *Jesus*, pp. 131-32; and especially Theissen and Winter, *Quest for the Plausible*, parts 1–2.

[121]Tom Holmén, "An Introduction to the Continuum Approach," in *Jesus from Judaism to Christianity: "Continuum" Approaches to the Historical Jesus*, ed. Tom Holmén (New York: T & T Clark, 2007), pp. 1-2.

ated and proposed. Among the more commonly appealed to are the "multiple independent attestation" (i.e., any element of the Jesus tradition that is found in multiple, unrelated early sources has a strong likelihood of originating with Jesus) criterion[122] and the "embarrassment" (i.e., any element of the Jesus tradition that would have posed embarrassment to the early church was probably not fabricated by it and thus most likely goes back to Jesus) criterion.[123] More recently proposed (and sometimes rather idiosyncratic) criteria include: Wright's "double criterion of similarity and dissimilarity,"[124] Theissen and Winter's "historical plausibility" criterion[125] and the "characteristic Jesus" criterion of Dunn.[126]

The interdisciplinary quest. In the words of Bernard Brandon Scott, "The historical quest for the historical Jesus has ended; the interdisciplinary quest for the historical Jesus has just begun."[127] And many see this fact as one of the most distinctive and fruitful features of the third quest. It is no longer merely New Testament scholars and historians who are wading into the rushing waters of the quest, but an entire cadre of interdisciplinary explorers, each bringing their own distinctive disciplinary methods, tools and insights to the historical study of Jesus and the Gospels. And so, for example, in recent times one can find a variety of philosophers and philosophical theologians weighing in on relevant matters.[128] Even more widespread today is the interaction between New Testament scholars and archaeologists on the question of Jesus and his first-century Palestinian context.[129] With the help of archaeol-

---

[122]E.g., this is such a dominant criterion for Crossan that he advocates "the complete avoidance of any unit [of the Jesus tradition] found only in single attestation even within the first stratum [i.e., a very early text]"; *Historical Jesus*, p. xxxii.

[123]E.g., for Meier (*Marginal Jew*, 1:168-71), this is the first of the "primary criteria." See also Funk, *Honest to Jesus*, p. 138.

[124]Wright, *Jesus*, pp. 131-33, 613-14.

[125]Theissen and Winter, *Quest for the Plausible*, part 3.

[126]Dunn, *Jesus Remembered*, pp. 332-33; idem, *New Perspective on Jesus*, pp. 57-78. Dunn was preceded here by Keck, *Future*, p. 33.

[127]Cited in Marcus Borg, "A Renaissance in Jesus Studies," *Theology Today* 45 (1988): 284.

[128]E.g., see the relevant essays in Craig Bartholomew et al., eds., *"Behind" the Text: History and Biblical Interpretation* (Grand Rapids: Zondervan, 2003); Gregory A. Boyd, *Cynic, Sage or Son of God?* (Wheaton: Bridgepoint, 1995); Evans, *Historical Christ*; Raymond Martin, *The Elusive Messiah: A Philosophical Overview of the Quest for the Historical Jesus* (Boulder, Colo.: Westview, 1999); and the essays by Gary Habermas and William Lane Craig in *Jesus Under Fire*, ed. Michael J. Wilkins and J. P. Moreland (Grand Rapids: Zondervan, 1995).

[129]E.g., see Mark Alan Chancey, *Greco-Roman Culture and the Galilee of Jesus* (Cambridge: Cam-

ogy and related disciplines, we now have a much better handle on everything from the religious nature of first-century Galilee to the
socioeconomic conditions that characterized both city and countryside
in the Palestine of Jesus' day.[130] A continuing area of debate is that of
the degree to which first-century Palestine was "hellenized" and, more
controversially, just what effects that Mediterranean-wide cultural force
had on ancient Jews and their religion.[131]

A third important interdisciplinary conversation has been occurring at
the intersection of Jesus studies and the social sciences (e.g., cultural anthropology, sociology, socioeconomics).[132] Two broad trends can be discerned in this area. There is, on one hand, a widespread—and relatively

---

bridge University Press, 2005); J. H. Charlesworth, ed., *Jesus and Archaeology*; John Dominic
Crossan and Johnathan L. Reed, *Excavating Jesus: Beneath the Stones, Behind the Texts* (San
Francisco: HarperSanFrancisco, 2001); Douglas R. Edwards and C. T. McCollough, eds.,
Archaeology and the Galilee: Texts and Contexts in the Graeco-Roman and Byzantine Periods
(Atlanta: Scholars Press, 1997); Sean Freyne, *Galilee and Gospel: Collected Essays* (Tübingen:
Mohr Siebeck, 2000); Lee I. Levine, ed., *The Galilee in Late Antiquity* (New York: Jewish
Theological Seminary of America, 1992).

[130]It should be noted that tensions can and do exist between the study of "text" and "artifact"
within historical Jesus studies. See Dunn, "On the Relation of Text and Artifact: Some Cau-
tionary Tales," in *Text and Artifact in the Religions of Mediterranean Antiquity: Essays in Honour
of Peter Richardson*, ed. S. G. Wilson and M. Desjardins (Waterloo, Ont.: Wilfrid Laurier
University Press, 2000), pp. 192-206; D. E. Groh, "The Clash between Literary and Archaeological Models of Provincial Palestine," in *Archaeology and the Galilee: Texts and Contexts
in the Graeco-Roman and Byzantine Periods*, ed. Douglas R. Edwards and C. T. McCollough
(Atlanta: Scholars Press, 1997), pp. 29-37.

[131]Since the groundbreaking work of Martin Hengel on the widespread hellenization of Jews
in the ancient world, few argue for anything like a hermetically sealed Judaism. See Hengel,
Judaism and Hellenism: Studies in their Encounter in Palestine during the Early Hellenistic Period,
2 vols., trans. John Bowden (Philadelphia: Fortress, 1974 [1973]); idem, *The 'Hellenization'
of Judea in the First Century after Christ*, trans. John Bowden (Philadelphia: Trinity Press
International, 1989). However, even Hengel agrees that when it came to their religious worldview, Palestinian Jews of Jesus' day generally refused to countenance "paganism" within their
spheres of influence, and remained Torah-true in orientation. See Hengel, *'Hellenization' of
Judea*, p. 54; idem, "Judaism and Hellenisim Revisited," in *Hellenism in the Land of Israel*, ed.
John J. Collins and Gregory E. Sterling (Notre Dame, Ind.: University of Notre Dame Press,
2001), pp. 6-37.

[132]Helpful orientations include John H. Elliot, *What is Social-Scientific Criticism?* (Minneapolis:
Fortress, 1993); K. C. Hanson and Douglas E. Oakman, *Palestine in the Time of Jesus: Social
Structures and Social Conflict* (Minneapolis: Fortress, 1998); Richard Horsley, *Sociology and
the Jesus Movement* (New York: Crossroad, 1989); Howard C. Kee, *Christian Origins in So-
ciological Perspective: Methods and Resources* (Philadelphia: Westminster Press, 1980); Gerd
Theissen, *The Sociology of Early Palestinian Christianity*, trans. John Bowden (Philadelphia:
Fortress, 1978 [1977]); idem, *Social Reality and the Early Christians*, trans. M. Kohl (Minneapolis: Fortress, 1992 [1977]).

uncontroversial—use of *social history and description* within the quest today. On the other hand, there is an influential, if less widespread and often contested, application of *sociological models and methods* to the interpretation of the early Jesus tradition. With regard to this latter trend, John Dominic Crossan has become one of the most influential voices today. For example, his envisioning of a pan-Mediterranean context—with the help of such sociological resources as Gerhard Lenski's theory of social stratification—within which to situate Jesus has invited both accolades and critique.[133] Pieter Craffert has gone as far as to argue that an "anthropological-historical" approach to Jesus should, in significant ways, supplant the dominant "historical-critical" method that has driven the quest thus far.[134] Others, while appreciating certain aspects that the social sciences (e.g., social description) can bring to the quest, fear that sociological models imposed on the data of the Jesus tradition bring with them ideologically deterministic and/or reductionistic conclusions.[135]

A final major area of interdisciplinary ferment in the quest today involves the crossfertilization between contemporary oral tradition/orality studies and Jesus/Gospels research. Important voices in this conversation include Kenneth Bailey, Richard Bauckham, John Dominic Crossan, Jonathan Draper, James Dunn, Richard Horsley and Werner Kelber.[136] Here at least two separate issues come to the fore. First, there is the issue of the nature of the early oral Jesus tradition and

---

[133]See Crossan, *Historical Jesus*. For a contrasting perspective see Sean Freyne, "Galilean Questions to Crossan's Mediterranean Jesus," in *Galilee and Gospels*, pp. 208-29.

[134]Craffert, "Historical-Anthropological"; idem, *The Life of a Galilean Shaman: Jesus of Nazareth in Anthropological-Historical Perspective* (Eugene, Ore.: Cascade, 2008), part 1.

[135]For a range of expressed concerns see Dunn, "Testing the Foundations: Current Trends in New Testament Study," Inaugural lecture, February 9, 1984 (Durham, U.K.: University of Durham, 1984), 8-10; Johnson, "Humanity of Jesus," p. 57 n. 33, pp. 65-66; Ben Meyer, "Master Builder and Copestone of the Portal: Images of the Mission of Jesus," *Toronto Journal of Theology* 9 (1993): 187-209; Jens Schröter, "New Horizons," pp. 77-83.

[136]Kenneth Bailey, "Informal, Controlled Oral Tradition and the Synoptic Gospels," *Asia Journal of Theology* 5 (1991): 34-54; Richard Bauckham, *Jesus and the Eyewitnesses: The Gospels as Eyewitness Testimony* (Grand Rapids: Eerdmans, 2006); John Dominic Crossan, *The Birth of Christianity* (San Francisco: HaperSanFrancisco, 1998), part 2; Dunn, *Jesus Remembered*, chap. 8; Richard Horsley with Jonathan Draper, *Whoever Hears You Hears Me: Prophets, Performance, and Tradition in Q* (Harrisburg, Penn.: Trinity Press International, 1999); Werner Kelber, *The Oral and the Written Gospel: The Hermeneutics of Speaking and Writing in the Synoptic Tradition, Mark, Paul, and Q* (Philadephia: Fortress, 1983).

the resultant implications for the historical recovery of Jesus.[137] The second involves exploration of the ramifications—both for interpretation and historical reconstruction—of the fact that the Gospels themselves (along with virtually all ancient texts) were written with what can be called an "oral sensibility" (i.e., written with features characteristic of the oral/aural style itself).[138] This—along with social/collective memory studies—appears to be one of the most fertile areas of Jesus/ Gospels research currently under investigation.[139]

The question of literary sources. The last methodological issue to be touched on here, and one of obviously great importance, is the issue of *sources*—important both for understating Jesus' context, first-century Palestine and the wider Mediterranean world, and for the historical recovery of Jesus himself.[140] Throughout the history of the quest, the primary sources consulted by most Jesus scholars in their historical reconstruction efforts have been the four canonical Gospels.[141] When, in the nineteenth century, the Gospel of John came to be seen by many as a less-

---

[137]There is currently no consensus on the implications of oral tradtion/orality studies for the question of the historical reliability of the early Jesus tradition. For two contrasting views see Crossan, *Birth of Christianity*, part 2; Eddy and Boyd, *Jesus Legend*, chaps. 6-10

[138]Important interdisciplinary studies touching on the "oral" sensibilities of texts written within an orally dominant environment include Mark Amodio, *Writing the Oral Tradition: Oral Poetics and Literate Culture in Medieval England* (Notre Dame, Ind.: University of Notre Dame Press, 2004); E. J. Bakker, "How Oral is Oral Composition?," in *Signs of Orality: The Oral Tradition and Its Influence in the Greek and Roman World*, ed. E. A. MacKay (Boston: Brill, 1999), pp. 29-37; John Miles Foley, "Oral Tradition into Textuality," in *Texts and Textuality: Textual Instability, Theory and Interpretation*, ed. P. Cohen (New York: Garland, 1997), pp. 1-24; idem, "What's in a Sign?," in *Signs of Orality: The Oral Tradiion and Its Influence in the Greek and Roman World*, ed. E. A. MacKay (Boston: Brill, 1999), pp. 1-27; Amin Sweeney, *A Full Hearing: Orality and Literacy in the Malay World* (Berkeley: University of California Press, 1987); Rosalind Thomas, *Literacy and Orality in Ancient Greece* (New York: Cambridge University Press, 1992).

[139]See, e.g., Stephen C. Barton, Loren T. Stuchenbruck and Benjamin G. Wold, eds., *Memory in the Bible and Antiquity* (Tübingen: Mohr Siebeck, 2007); Richard Horsley, Jonathan Draper and John Miles Foley, eds., *Performing the Gospel: Orality, Memory and Mark, Essays Dedicated to Werner Kelber* (Minneapolis: Fortress, 2006); Alan Kirk and Tom Thatcher, eds., *Memory, Tradition, and Text: Uses of the Past in Early Christianity* (Atlanta: SBL Press, 2005).

[140]The question of ancient literary sources inevitably includes text-critical issues. For a helpful reflection on the implications for Jesus research see Michael F. Bird, "Textual Criticism and the Historical Jesus," *Journal for the study of the Historical Jesus* 6 (2008): 133-56.

[141]This remains the case for the vast majorty of questers today. See James H. Charlesworth, "The Historical Jesus: Sources and a Sketch," in *Jesus Two Thousand Years Later*, ed. James H. Charlesworth and Walter P. Weaver (Harrisburg, Penn.: Trinity Press International, 2000), pp. 87-88.

than-reliable historical source, the three "Synoptic" Gospels (i.e., Matthew, Mark and Luke) became the focus of inquiry. And so to this day the "synoptic" Jesus remains for most scholars the obvious starting point for their own historical investigations. However, while many continue to sideline the Fourth Gospel, others, protesting this methodological annexation, argue that John, in significant ways, is an independent and historically important witness to Jesus.[142] In the words of Paul Anderson, it is well past time that we call for a reassessment of the all-too-common "de-historicization of John" and the "de-Johannification of Jesus." The resulting rapprochement between the Johannine and synoptic sources, he muses, just may "lead to a *fourth* quest for Jesus."[143] Whatever particular decisions one makes about the use of the canonical Gospels as sources, one question that must be faced is the nature of the "Gospel" *genre*. Currently, proposals include Greco-Roman biography (a widely held view), ancient historiography, romance novel, Homeric-inspired fiction, Jewish midrash/pesher and a distinct, sui generis genre.[144] Obviously, one's decision on the genre question will have a significant impact upon any subsequent assessment of the historical value of the Gospels for reconstructing Jesus. Comparatively speaking, the other twenty-three New Testament documents are less valuable sources for reconstructing the life of Jesus. While most scholars conclude that there are elements of the Jesus tradition to be found there, particularly in Paul's epistles, what there is does not add much beyond what is already found in the Gospels.[145]

---

[142]Earlier calls to take John seriously in this regard came from C. H. Dodd (*Historical Tradition in the Fourth Gospel* [Cambridge: Cambridge University Press, 1963]) and John A. T. Robinson (*The Priority of John* [London: SCM Press, 1985]). For a range of more recent positive assessments of John's historical possibilities see Paul N. Anderson, *The Fourth Gospel and the Quest for Jesus: Modern Foundations Reconsidered* (New York: T & T Clark, 2006); Craig Blomberg, *The Historical Reliability of John's Gospel: Issues and Commentary* (Downers Grove, Ill.: InterVarsity Press, 2001); Peter W. Ensor, *Jesus and His "Works": The Johannine Sayings in Historical Perspective* (Tübingen: Mohr Siebeck, 1996); Francis J. Moloney, "The Fourth Gospel and the Jesus of History," *New Testament Studies* 46 (2000): 42-58; Marianne Meye Thompson, "The Historical Jesus and the Johannine Christ," in *Exploring the Gospel of John: In Honor of D. Moody Smith*, eds. R. Alan Culpepper and C. Clifton Black (Louisville, Ky.: Westminster John Knox, 1996), pp. 21-42.

[143]Anderson, *Fourth Gospel*, pp. 191, 192 (emphasis in text).

[144]For a recent survey and assessment (including implications for the historicity question) of the more common proposals see Eddy and Boyd, *Jesus Legend*, chap. 8.

[145]On the Jesus tradition in Paul see James D. G. Dunn, "Jesus-tradition in Paul," in *Studying the Historical Jesus: Evaluations of the State of Current Research*, ed. Bruce Chilton and Craig A.

For many scholars throughout the history of the quest, significant primary sources for recovery of the historical Jesus effectively end with the canonical Gospels.[146] For others today, however, these Gospels are merely the beginning. It has been noted that one of the distinctive developments in the third quest is the widespread use of new sources for reconstructing Jesus and his context.[147] One of the reasons for this is that scholars within the third quest have made significant use of the two amazing textual discoveries of the 1940s—the Nag Hammadi library (1945) and the Dead Sea Scrolls (1947). Particularly among those within the post-Bultmannian stream of the third quest, certain extracanonical Gospels play a crucial role in liberating historical Jesus studies from the "tyranny of the synoptic Jesus."[148] Among the most important of these are the so-called Q Gospel[149] and the *Gospel of Thomas* (found within the Nag Hammadi collection).[150] Other Gospels that have come to play a role in some scholars' work today are the *Secret Gospel of Mark* (made famous by Morton Smith) and the *Gospel of Peter.*[151]

Among non-Christian sources, the works of Flavius Josephus (A.D. 37–c. 100), particularly his *Jewish Antiquities* and *The Jewish War*, stand head and shoulders above all others in terms of importance for reconstructing the first-century Palestinian context within which Jesus

---

Evans (New York: Brill, 1994), pp. 155-78; Michael Thompson, *Clothed with Christ: The Examples and Teaching of Jesus in Romans 12:1-15:13* (Sheffield: Sheffield Academic Press, 1991).

[146]Among the more influential contemporary questers who have come to this conclusion are Meier, *Marginal Jew*, 1:139-41; idem, "Present State," pp. 464-66; Wright, *Jesus.*

[147]Theissen and Merz, *Historical Jesus*, p. 11; Weaver, "Forward: Reflections," pp. xiii-xiv.

[148]Charles W. Hedrick, "Introduction: The Tyranny of the Synoptic Jesus," *Semeia* 44 (1988): 1-8. For a selection of extracanonical Gospels in English translation see Robert J. Miller, ed., *The Complete Gospels*, rev. ed. (San Francisco: HarperSanFrancisco, 1994 [1992]).

[149]See Arland Jacobson, *The First Gospel: An Introduction to Q* (Sonoma, Calif.: Polebridge, 1992); Mack, *Lost Gospel;* John S. Kloppenborg Verbin, *Excavating Q: The History and Setting of the Sayings Gospel* (Minneapolis: Fortress, 2000).

[150]For an English translation of the *Gospel of Thomas* see Miller, ed., *Complete Gospels*, pp. 301-29. Robert Funk and the Jesus Seminar famously elevated the *Gospel of Thomas* to the level of the four canonical Gospels in the title of their first major volume, *The Five Gospels*. See also Stephen J. Patterson, *The Gospel of Thomas and Jesus* (Sonoma, Calif.: Polebridge, 1993); Marvin Meyer, *The Gospel of Thomas: The Hidden Sayings of Jesus* (San Francisco: HarperSanFrancisco, 1992). Others argue, from various vantage points, that the *Gospel of Thomas* is a later document that is largely dependent on the canonical gospels, and so is not of much help to the quest. See, e.g., Meier, *Marginal Jew*, 1:123-41; Nicholas Perrin, *Thomas and Tatian: The Relationship between the Gospel of Thomas and the Diatessaron* (Boston: Brill, 2002); Wright, *New Testament*, pp. 442-43.

[151]Each can be found in English translation in Miller, ed., *Complete Gospels*, part 4.

lived.[152] Beyond this, our current texts of Josephus' *Jewish Antiquities* contain two controversial passages that directly mention Jesus. While virtually all scholars concede that the longest and most famous of these two passages—known as the *Testimonium Flavianum* (*Jewish Antiquities*, 18.3.3)—includes elements added in by a Christian copyist at some point, most nonetheless conclude that Josephus's original text did mention Jesus by name.[153] A number of other ancient non-Christian authors appear to mention Jesus (e.g., Tacitus, Suetonius, Lucian of Samosata, Thallus). While advocates of the Christ-Myth theory consistently challenge the reliability and/or authenticity of these reports, others deem a number of them to be authentic and even independent of Christian hearsay.[154]

Results: Images of the historical Jesus in the third quest. With characteristic candor, John Dominic Crossan begins his major study by stating that "historical Jesus research is becoming something of a scholarly bad joke." The primary reason for this, he notes, is "the number of competent and even eminent scholars producing pictures of Jesus at wide variance with one another."[155] For some this radically divergent assortment of historical Jesuses at the end of the day suggests the quest has hit a dead end.[156] For many, however, this plurality of Jesus-portraits seems to represent an exciting opportunity for more rigorous methodological reflection, more careful historical study and more engagement in interdisciplinary dialogue.

But while consensus in Jesus studies today is elusive, it is not entirely absent. For example, there is widespread (if not always total) consensus that Jesus was baptized by John, that he taught and preached in Galilee, that he drew followers to himself, that he was known as an effective miracle worker and exorcist, and that he made a final journey to Jeru-

---

[152]For an English translation see William Whiston, trans., *The Works of Josephus, Complete and Unabridged* (Peabody, Mass.: Hendrickson, 1987).

[153]For a likely reconstruction of Josephus's original text at this point see Meier, *Marginal Jew*, 1:61. For a recent defense of the authenticity of such a reconstruction see Eddy and Boyd, *Jesus Legend*, pp. 190-99. Jesus is also mentioned in the famous "James passage" later in *Jewish Antiquities* 20.9.1.

[154]For discussion see Eddy and Boyd, *Jesus Legend*, chap. 4.

[155]Crossan, *Historical Jesus*, p. xxvii.

[156]Neusner, "Who Needs," p. 119.

salem for Passover where, in conjunction with an incident in the temple, he was arrested, convicted by Pilate and crucified. And if even some of these general points of consensus are disputed by some, there seems to be one point at which everyone is in firm agreement today.

A rare consensus: The Jewishness of Jesus. There appears to be one overwhelmingly common feature within the third quest today—a commitment to taking seriously the Jewishness of Jesus.[157] In John Meier's estimation:

> Even if the third quest has no other impact on contemporary Christology, the emphatic reaffirmation of the Jewishness of Jesus will make the whole enterprise worthwhile. Something lasting will have been gained.[158]

This emphasis has been spurred by several factors, including: (1) awareness of the pressing need to address the tragedy of the German "Aryanizing" of Jesus during the Nazi era, (2) the growing awareness of the ways in which "Jesus" and "Judaism" have been played off against each other over the last two millennia—with the latter being painted as the hypocritical, legalistic religion of dead works from which Jesus and the Christian tradition were liberated by the alien (i.e., anti-Jewish) message of grace, faith and love—and (3) a now widespread recognition of the simple historical fact that a Jesus divorced from first-century Palestinian Judaism cannot be the Jesus of history.[159] And so, from the very beginnings of the third quest and landmark works like Vermes' *Jesus the Jew* and Sander's *Jesus and Judaism*, a recovery of the Jewishness of Jesus

---

[157]See, e.g., James H. Charlesworth, "Jesus Research Expands with Chaotic Creativity," in *Images of Jesus Today*, ed. James H. Charlesworth and Walter P. Weaver (Valley Forge, Penn.: Trinity, 1994), pp. 5, 9; Meier, "The Present State," pp. 483-86; Theissen and Merz, *Historical Jesus*, pp. 10-11.

[158]Meier, "Present State," p. 486.

[159]On the Aryanization of Jesus in Nazi Germany see Peter M. Head, "The Nazi Quest for the Aryan Jesus," *Journal for the Study of the Historical Jesus* 2 (2004): 55-89. On the caricature and misuse of Judaism as a negative comparison to Jesus and/or early Christianity throughout the centuries see Paula Fredriksen, "What You See is What You Get: Context and Content in Current Research on the Historical Jesus," *Theology Today* 52 (1995): 75-97; Paula Fredriksen and Adele Reinhartz, eds., *Jesus, Judaism, and Christian Anti-Judaism: Reading the New Testament after the Holocaust* (Louisville: Westminster John Knox, 2002). For several recent representative statements emphasizing the need to take seriously the Jewishness both of Jesus and his context, see James H. Charlesworth, ed., *Jesus' Jewishness: Exploring the Place of Jesus within Early Judaism* (New York: Crossroad, 1996); Tom Holmén, "The Jewishness of Jesus in the 'Third Quest,'" in *Jesus, Mark and Q: The Teaching of Jesus and Its Earliest Records*, ed. Michael Labahn and Andreas Schmidt (Sheffield: Sheffield Academic Press, 2001), pp. 143-62; Sanders, *Jesus and Judaism*.

has been a chief hallmark of the enterprise.[160] One of the most scathing critiques that a contemporary scholar can receive today is that he has ignored or even underappreciated the Jewishness of Jesus.[161] A common response to such scrutiny includes an appeal to the wide diversity within first-century Judaism. And here we hit a practical point where the theoretical consensus on Jesus' Jewishness begins to fracture—the debate on whether there was anything like a "common Judaism" that served to bind together the variety of Jewish sects and expressions of the ancient world.[162] William Arnal, for example, rejects the "common Judaism" thesis, and so proclaims much of the "Jewish Jesus" discussion to be little more than a "red herring," since, within a radically diverse Judaism, Jesus could turn out to be just about anything and still potentially qualify as "Jewish."[163]

A consensusless "consensus": The apocalyptic Jesus. Again, claims of "consensus" within the third quest are rare. But just such a claim has been made repeated times with regard to the question of Jesus' relationship to Jewish apocalyptic eschatology. The irony is that "consensus" has been claimed by both sides on this matter! James Charlesworth, for example, writes:

> One of the strongest consensuses in New Testament research is that Jesus' mission was to proclaim the dawning of God's Rule, the Kingdom of God. Research on Mark 9:1 has convinced virtually every specialist that Jesus' teaching was emphatically apocalyptic and eschatological.[164]

Yet Marcus Borg—and with him Robert Funk and the Jesus Seminar—can be found explicitly denying this very state of affairs. Borg writes:

---

[160]For a brief historical survey of this recovery effort see Dunn, *Jesus Remembered*, pp. 86-92.

[161]See Freyne, "Galilean Questions to Crossan's," p. 91; E. P. Sanders, "Jesus, Ancient Judaism, and Modern Christianity: The Quest Continues," in *Jesus, Judaism, and Christian Anti-Judaism: Reading the New Testament After the Holocaust*, ed. Paula Fredriksen and Adele Reinhartz (Louisville: Westminster John Knox, 2002), pp. 31-55; Wright, *New Testament*, p. 437.

[162]Those who identify something of a "common Judaism" with normative elements include Dunn, *Jesus Remembered*, pp. 280-81; Meier, "Present State," p. 468; E. P. Sanders, *Judaism: Practice and Belief, 63 BCE–66 CE* (Philadelphia: Trinity Press International, 1992); Wright, *New Testament*, part 3. For perspectives resisting this claim see Arnal, *Symbolic Jesus*; Jacob Neusner, William Scott Green and Ernest S. Frerichs, eds., *Judaisms and Their Messiahs at the Turn of the Christian Era* (Cambridge: Cambridge University Press, 1987).

[163]Arnal, *Symbolic Jesus*, p. 20.

[164]Charlesworth, "Jesus Research Expands," p. 10.

The old consensus [i.e., pre–third quest] that Jesus was an eschatological prophet who proclaimed the imminent end of the world has disappeared . . . [and] is no longer held by the majority of North American
scholars actively engaged in Jesus research.[165]

From the time of the old quest itself, the question of Jesus' relation to
apocalyptic Judaism—and the nature of its conviction regarding the imminent in-breaking of God into the natural world—has been a central
point of contention. And it remains so to this day. Despite claims and
counterclaims of "consensus," the fact is that scholars currently remain
deeply divided on this issue.[166] This issue is complicated by the fact that
even the very nature of the end-time expectations of apocalyptic Judaism
is under debate. And so, some hold that, while John the Baptist before
him and the early church after him embraced an apocalyptic worldview,
Jesus himself rejected this orientation.[167] Others hold that Jesus did embrace an apocalyptic worldview, but that, despite highly metaphorical,
cosmically oriented ways of expressing this conviction, Jewish expectations of the "end" did not involve the literal undoing of the space-time
universe itself.[168] Finally, others hold that Jewish apocalyptic thought in
Jesus' day did in fact await the very literal transformation of the cosmic
order, most likely involving both cosmic conflagration and re-creation.[169]
Since the days of Schweitzer himself, lurking behind this debate is the
troubling question: Was Jesus mistaken about the timing of the "end"
and thus a failed prophet? Some, with Schweitzer, have simply concluded:

---

[165]Borg, "Renaissance," p. 285. Similarly Funk and the Jesus Seminar (*Five Gospels*, p. 4) have
claimed that one of the "seven pillars of scholarly wisdom" with regard to contemporary Jesus
studies is the "liberation of the non-eschatological Jesus" from the previous, and mistaken,
"apocalyptic Jesus" paradigm.

[166]For a recent (if unbalanced) entree into the debate, see Robert J. Miller, ed., *The Apocalyptic
Jesus: A Debate* (Sonoma, Calif.: Polebridge, 2001).

[167]John Dominic Crossan is a well-known exponent of this view. See his essay in this present
volume, "Jesus and the Challenge of Collaborative Eschatology."

[168]The most well-known representative here is N. T. Wright; see *New Testament*, pp. 280-99.

[169]E.g., Dale C. Allison, *Jesus of Nazareth: Millenarian Prophet* (Minneapolis: Fortress, 1998);
Bart Ehrman, *Jesus: Apocalyptic Prophet of the New Millennium* (New York: Oxford University
Press, 2001). Edward Adams has recently argued that first-century Judaism (as well as the
New Testament) contained "two distinct cosmic-eschatological schemes . . . destruction and
creation anew and non-destructive transformation." *The Stars Will Fall from Heaven: Cosmic
Catastrophe in the New Testament and its World* (New York: T & T Clark, 2007), p. 257.

Yes.[170] Some, like Wright, avoid this conclusion by arguing that Jesus' eschatological predictions were actually fulfilled in the fall of Jerusalem.[171] Others avoid it in recognizing an "already–not yet" dynamic at the heart of Jesus' eschatology that still allows for future fulfillment.[172] And others still, as noted above, simply avoid the whole question in denying an eschatological Jesus altogether.

The quest for the aims and intentions of Jesus. Standing in the shadows of the failures of the old quest and the pessimism of Bultmann, many twentieth-century questers explicitly gave up any hopes of ever retrieving anything like the inner thought world of Jesus. Schweitzer himself criticized the apparently futile attempts within the old quest to produce psychological portraits of Jesus.[173] Henry Cadbury expanded on this concern with a warning about the inevitable anachronistic "modernizing" of Jesus that takes place whenever we try to recover anything like his unified aims and intentions.[174] With the coming of the new quest, talk of Jesus' "intentions" was reinvigorated, but was also quickly identified with twentieth-century existentialist categories that fueled the post-Bultmannian project—categories that no longer hold attraction for most contemporary Jesus scholars. And so, for many questers still today, the subquest for the inner aims or "self-consciousness" of Jesus remains a nonstarter. Theissen and Winter, for example, suggest that the question of Jesus' "aims" cannot be a part of the scholar's quest for "historical factuality."[175]

In the eyes of a growing number, however, while old quest naiveté must certainly be avoided, exploring questions about Jesus' "aims," "intentions" and, for some, even "self-consciousness" remains a legiti-

---

[170]E.g., Allison, *Jesus.*

[171]Wright, *Jesus,* chap. 8. See Allison's challenge to Wright on this question in "Jesus and the Victory of Apocalyptic," in *Jesus and the Restoration of Israel: A Critical Assessment of N. T. Wright's* Jesus and the Victory of God, ed. Carey C. Newman (Downers Grove, Ill.: Inter-Varsity Press, 1999), pp. 126-41; and Wright's rejoinder (in the same volume) in "In Grateful Dialogue: A Response," pp. 262-63.

[172]E.g., Witherington, *Jesus Quest,* pp. 209-10.

[173]Albert Schweitzer, *The Psychiatric Study of Jesus: Exposition and Criticism,* trans. C. R. Joy (Boston: Beacon, 1958 [1911]).

[174]Henry Cadbury, *The Peril of Modernizing Jesus* (New York: Macmillan, 1937), pp. 148, 152.

[175]*Quest for the Plausible,* p. 150. Similar skepticism about retrieving Jesus' "self-consciousness" is expressed by Stephen Fowl, "Reconstructing and Deconstructing the Quest of the Historical Jesus," *Scottish Journal of Theology* 42 (1989): 331.

mate aspect of historiography.[176] Within the third quest no one has defended and explored the idea of Jesus' "aims" more thoroughly than Wright.[177] Intrinsic to the very historiographical enterprise, argues Wright, is "the study of aims, intentions, and motivations."[178] Charlesworth agrees: "I am convinced that an exegete interested in Jesus Research is obligated to reflect on Jesus' self-understanding."[179] Within this context, a number have argued for a messianic self-understanding on the part of Jesus.[180] One might imagine that a natural tension exists between the use of large-scale social science models for understanding Jesus, on one hand, and the search for Jesus' own individual, and thus possibly unique, aims and intentions. But as Donald Denton has rightly argued, this potential tension need not materialize in actual practice:

> The danger of reducing the particularity of intentional actions to larger categories, such as social science models, is real. But I would also note the danger of "reduction" in the opposite direction. . . . Some such interconnection of both would seem to be most appropriate, without conceiving either in exclusivistic terms.[181]

Models of Jesus within the third quest. The culminating goal for any quester, of course, is to present an historically responsible reconstruction of Jesus of Nazareth, one that others find "plausible"—hopefully even "probable" (which is, of course, as good as it gets in the realm of

---

[176]At the very headwaters of the third quest, Ben Meyer forced this issue front and center with the title of his 1979 book: *The Aims of Jesus.* For two more recent positive statements on such an endeavor see Denton, *Historiography*, pp. 107-13; Evans, "Assessing Progress," pp. 43-49. Some have even dared to reopen the "psychological" investigation of Jesus in explicit terms. See, e.g., John W. Miller, *Jesus at Thirty: A Psychological and Historical Portrait* (Minneapolis: Fortress, 1997).

[177]For his methodological defense of such an endeavor see *New Testament*, pp. 109-12, 125-26; *Jesus*, pp. 99-105.

[178]Wright, *New Testament*, p. 111.

[179]Charlesworth, *Jesus within Judaism*, p. 131. For his exploration of this issue see ibid., chap. 6.

[180]Markus Bockmuehl, *This Jesus: Martyr, Lord, Messiah* (Edinburgh: T & T Clark, 1994); Ragnar Leivestad, *Jesus in His Own Perspective: An Examination of His Sayings, Actions and Eschatological Titles*, trans. David E. Aune (Minneapolis: Fortress, 1987 [1982]); Martin Hengel and Anna Maria Schwemer, *Jesus und das Judentum* (Tübingen: Mohr Siebeck, 2007); Martin Hengel, "Jesus, the Messiah of Israel," in *Studies in Early Christology* (Edinburgh: T & T Clark, 1995), pp. 1-72; Wright, *Jesus*, chap. 11.

[181]Denton, *Historiography*, p. 113.

historiography). Over the last several decades that compose the third quest, an impressive (some, with Crossan, would say "embarrassing") number of such scholarly reconstructions have been proposed for consideration. Among them (in no particular order) are: an eschatological prophet, a Galilean holy man, an occultic magician, an innovative rabbi, a trance-inducing psychotherapist, a Jewish sage, a political revolutionary, an Essene conspirator, an itinerant exorcist, an historicized myth, a protoliberation theologian, a peasant artisan, a Torah-observant Pharisee, a Cynic-like philosopher, a self-conscious eschatological agent, a socioeconomic reformer, a paradoxical Messianic claimant and, finally, as one who saw himself as, in some sense, the very embodiment of Yahweh-God. For many in the third quest, a single, monochromatic model cannot capture the Jesus of history, and so often two or more images are combined to form a richly textured, multidimensional portrait. Of these many images, none are embraced by all; some are embraced by many; and all are put forward by someone as the most historically plausible reconstruction of the historical Jesus.

The historical Jesus: Five views. In this present volume, five noted scholars of the third quest—Robert M. Price, John Dominic Crossan, Luke Timothy Johnson, James D. G. Dunn and Darrel L. Bock—come together for the purpose of dialogue about the historical Jesus. Each contributor has produced a number of volumes on the topic.[182] Several have had entire volumes and/or journal issues dedicated to interaction with their own work.[183] Each brings to the dialogue table a different set of methodological lenses—and thus arrives at a different reconstruction of the historical Jesus—than the others.

In each of the five major essays, issues related to historical method as

---

[182]E.g., Price, *Deconstructing Jesus;* idem, *Incredible Shrinking;* Crossan, *Historical Jesus;* idem, *Jesus: A Revolutionary Biography* (San Francisco: HarperSanFrancisco, 1994); Johnson, *Real Jesus;* idem, *Living Jesus: Learning the Heart of the Gospel* (San Francisco: HarperSanFrancisco, 1999); Dunn, *Jesus Remembered;* idem, *New Perspective on Jesus;* Bock, *Studying the Historical Jesus;* idem, *Blasphemy and Exaltation in Judaism: The Charge against Jesus in Mark 14:53-65* (Grand Rapids: Baker Academic, 2000).

[183]E.g., Jeffrey Carlson and Robert A. Ludwig, eds., *Jesus and Faith: A Conversation on the Work of John Dominic Crossan* (Maryknoll, N.Y.: Orbis, 1994); Craig A. Evans, Adela Yarbro Collins, Walter Wink and Luke Timothy Johnson, "The 'Real Jesus' in Debate," *Bulletin for Biblical Research* 7 (1997): 225-54; Robert B. Stewart, ed., *Memories of Jesus: A Critical Assessment of James D. G. Dunn's Quest of the Historical Jesus* (Nashville: B&H Academic, forthcoming).

well as their own reconstruction (or, in the case of one, deconstruction) of the historical Jesus are covered. Each major essay is followed by a set of responses from the other four contributors. We trust that the reader will find the resulting dialogue as enlightening as it is lively.

We would like to thank each of our five contributors for their valuable role in this project and for their unwavering collegiality throughout the process. Working with each of them has been for us an honor. We also thank our InterVarsity Press editor, Dan Reid, for his ongoing support of this project from start to finish. To our wives, Kelly Eddy and Michelle Beilby, we offer our unending gratefulness for their tireless support of our academic ventures. Finally, we want to express our thankfulness to our Bethel University department chairperson, Michael Holmes. Mike has been to us not only a faithful supporter of our vocational callings, but also an example of what a Christian scholar should be. It is to him that we dedicate this book.

1

JESUS AT THE
VANISHING POINT

Robert M. Price

At the outset of a controversial essay, let me try for a moment to make it easier for readers to resist the temptation to dismiss what I say based on tired stereotypes. I will argue that it is quite likely there never was any historical Jesus. Some will automatically assume I am doing apologetics on behalf of "village atheism," as some do. For what it may be worth, let me note that I began the study of the historical Jesus question as an enthusiastic would-be apologist. Eventually quite surprised to find myself dis-illusioned with "our" arguments, I shifted toward a more mainstream critical position more or less like Bultmann's. I was even more surprised, as the years went on, to find that I was having a greater and greater difficulty poking holes in what I had regarded as extreme, even crackpot, theories. Finally and ironically, I wound up espousing them for reasons I will shortly be recounting. In all this time, while I gladly admit I wrote with some indignation against what Albert Schweitzer called "the twisted and fragile thinking of apologetics,"[1]

---

[1]Albert Schweitzer, *Out of My Life and Thought: An Autobiography*, trans. C. T. Campion (New York: Mentor; New American Library, 1953), pp. 185-86: "Because I am devoted to Christianity in deep affection, I am trying to serve it with loyalty and sincerity. In no wise do I undertake to enter the lists on its behalf with the crooked and fragile thinking of Christian apologetics, but I call on it to set itself right in the spirit of sincerity with its past and with thought in order that it may thereby become conscious of its true nature."

I have never come to disdain Christianity. Indeed, I was for half a dozen years pastor of a Baptist church and am now a happy Episcopalian. I rejoice to take the Eucharist every week and to sing the great hymns of the faith. For me the Christ of faith has all the more importance since I think it most probable that there was never any other.

METHODOLOGICAL PRESUPPOSITIONS

Which is the greatest commandment for historians? The first and greatest is the *principle of analogy*. It is for seeming failure to understand this important axiom that many hurl charges of "antisupernaturalist bias" and "naturalistic presuppositions" in the study of the Gospels. Historians do not have access to H. G. Wells's time machine. We cannot know what occurred in the past and thus do not dogmatize about it. We deal only in probabilities. How do we decide what probably did or probably did not happen in the past? When we are looking at an ancient account, we must judge it according to the analogy of our experience and that of our trustworthy contemporaries (people with observational skills, honest reporters, etc., regardless of their philosophical or religious beliefs). There is no available alternative. Again, we weren't there and thus do not know that natural law always operated as it does now (the "uniformitarianism" decried by "scientific creationists"), but there is no particular reason not to think so, and unless we do, we have no criterion at all. We will be at the mercy of old stories of people turning lead into gold, turning into werewolves, using magic to win battles. If in our experience it takes a whole army to defeat an army, we will judge improbable any ancient tale that has a single man defeating an army. What else can we do? So we will judge an account improbable if it finds no analogy to current experience. Regarding the Gospels, for instance, this means that we will not reject out of hand stories in which Jesus heals the sick and casts out demons. We cannot do clinical follow-ups in these cases, but we do know such scenes may be found in our world today, and so they do not present a stumbling block to historical Jesus research. Even Bultmann admitted Jesus must have done what he and his contemporaries considered miracles.[2] (There may be other reasons for doubting it, of course, but not that it violates the principle of analogy.)

On the other hand, the historian must ask if an old account that does not fit the analogy of present-day experience does happen to match the analogy of legend or myth.

If it looks more like a legend than like any verifiable modern experience, what are we to conclude? If the story of Jesus walking on the water bears a strong resemblance to old stories in which Hermes, Pythagoras, the Buddha and others walk on water, mustn't we conclude we are probably dealing with a legend in the case of Jesus too? We don't know. We weren't there. But we could say the same thing about the Hercules myths. Must we gravely admit it is entirely likely that the Son of Zeus killed the Hydra just because someone once said so?

The principle of analogy is simply a "surprise-free method,"[3] like that of the sociologist, the futurologist, the meteorologist. These three specialists predict what probably will happen based on current trends, and they can be wrong since there are sometimes factors in play that are invisible to them. But what can they do? We do not reproach them because they are not oracles, infallibly predicting what will happen. Likewise, the historian does not claim clairvoyant knowledge of the past as Rudolf Steiner did. The historian, so to speak, "postdicts" based on traceable factors and analogy. But it is all a matter of probabilities. This is why Gospel critics who reject the spectacular nature miracles of Jesus feel they must. They are judging those Gospel reports "improbable." One may not be satisfied with this and decide to believe in them anyway, but that will be a matter of faith, the will to believe, not of historical judgment, and the two must not be confused.

---

[2]Rudolf Bultmann, *Jesus and the Word*, 2nd ed., trans. Louise Pettibone Smith and Erminie Huntress Lantero (New York: Scribner's, 1958), p. 173: "there can be no doubt that Jesus did the kind of deeds which were miracles to his mind and to the minds of his contemporaries . . . undoubtedly he healed the sick and cast out demons."

[3]Herman Kahn and Anthony J. Wiener, *The Year 2000—A Framework for Speculation on the Next Thirty-Three Years* (New York: Macmillan, 1967), cited in Peter L. Berger, *A Rumor of Angels: Modern Society and the Rediscovery of the Sacred* (Garden City, N.J.: Doubleday Anchor, 1970), pp. 16-19. B. B. Warfield adopted this "methodological atheism" as a matter of course in his scrutiny of Popish, Pentecostal and pagan miracle stories in his *Counterfeit Miracles* (1918; reprint, London: Banner of Truth Trust, 1972).

I will momentarily explain why I believe the principle of analogy compels us to go much further than this in our judgment of the historical Jesus question. But first, one more observation. The principle of analogy is important even in our choice of criteria for evaluating the sayings tradition. It underlies the criterion of dissimilarity (concerning which, more just below), but it also enters into the question of how we view the transmission of the sayings material. As is well known, Harald Riesenfeld and Birger Gerhardsson[4] urged critics to view the oral transmission of Jesus-sayings as analogous to the oral tradition of the Tannaim, the early Torah sages (if the term "rabbi" be deemed slightly anachronistic) who strove to be like "a plastered cistern that loses not a drop" (*Avot* 2.11), that is, not a word of one's master's teaching. That is a possible analogy, available in a closely related historical-cultural milieu, to be sure. But there is another, only slightly later, and that is the transmission of the hadith of Muhammad, which Muslims themselves were the first to realize had grown like a cancer to the point where only a century after Muhammad there were thousands of spurious sayings and precedents ascribed to him. Al-Bukhari, Muslim, and others began the process of weeding them out, but they retained a huge number, and today's Western, critical study of the hadith suggests virtually the whole corpus is inauthentic, that is, for the purpose of reconstructing Muhammad's teaching.[5] What all this means is that the early Muslim savants simply had no problem with fabricating hadith if they thought the content was valid.[6] It must have been no different for the creators of

---

[4]Harald Riesenfeld, *The Gospel Tradition and Its Beginnings: A Study in the Limits of "Form-geschichte"* (London: Mowbray, 1957). Birger Gerhardsson, *Memory and Manuscript: Oral Transmission in Rabbinic Judaism and Early Christianity*, trans. Eric J. Sharpe (Uppsala, Sweden: Almqvist & Wiksells, 1961). I believe that, in light of the more recent work of Jacob Neusner, the rabbinic model tends in exactly the opposite direction to that indicated by Reisenfeld and Gerhardsson. See Robert M. Price, "Messiah as Mishnah: The Problem of the Jesus-Attributed Saying," in Jacob Neusner, *Approaches to Ancient Judaism*, New Series 13, University of South Florida Studies in the History of Judaism 164 (Atlanta: Scholars Press, 1998), pp. 1-19.
[5]Henri Lammens, "The Koran and Tradition: How the Life of Muhammad Was Composed," trans. Ibn Warraq, in *The Quest for the Historical Muhammad*, ed. Ibn Warraq (Amherst, N.Y.: Prometheus, 2000), pp. 169-87.
[6]Ignaz Goldziher, *Etudes sur la Tradition Islamique*, trans. L. Bercher (Paris: Adrien-Maisonneuve, 1952), pp. 58-59, 195, cited in Robert D. Smith, *Comparative Miracles* (New York: B. Herder, 1965), pp. 128-32. Ignaz Goldziher, *Introduction to Islamic Theology and Law*, trans. Andras and Ruth Hamori, Modern Classics in Near Eastern Studies (Princeton, N.J.: Prince-

the *Pistis Sophia* and many Nag Hammadi Gospels to coin huge amounts of teaching and ascribe it to Jesus.[7] So were the Gospel tradents more like the rabbis and their disciples, or more like the Muslim hadith-masters, or even the Nag Hammadi writers? Only a close scrutiny of the various sayings can tell us, if anything can. No a priori decision can short-circuit the critical process. One certainly cannot go into the study of the Gospels armed with the assurance that the material *must* be authentic or inauthentic.

If the principle of analogy is the first historiographical commandment, the second, the *criterion of dissimilarity*, is like unto it. Norman Perrin formulated this axiom most clearly, though as he himself pointed out, it was nothing new. The idea is that no saying ascribed to Jesus may be counted as probably authentic if it has parallels in Jewish or early Christian sayings. Perrin was no fool. He understood well enough that if Jesus taught among Jewish colleagues, his opinions would frequently overlap theirs, and that if he founded a movement (even inadvertently!), the members of it would repeat his ideas.[8] But he was right: even in rabbinic sources it becomes clear that the same saying, not just the same sentiment, might be attributed to various rabbis (Jacob Neusner has made this even clearer),[9] and so the same was likely to be true with Jesus. Someone might naturally like a Jewish saying he heard without attribution and ascribe it to Jesus. This is all the more true in light of a discernible Judaizing tendency in early Christianity. And as for the early church, the contradictions between Gospel sayings on eschatology, divorce, fasting, and preaching to Gentiles and Samaritans are most easily explained as church factions ascribing their diverse views to Jesus because they thought them valid inferences (or revelations from the risen Lord).

---

ton University Press, 1981), pp. 43-44. See also Alfred Guillaume, *The Traditions of Islam: An Introduction to the Study of the Hadith Literature* (New York: Oxford University Press, 1924), pp. 52-53, 78-79.

[7]Christopher Tuckett, *Nag Hammadi and the Gospel Tradition: Synoptic Tradition in the Nag Hammadi Library*, Studies of the New Testament and Its World (Edinburgh: T & T Clark, 1986). Majella Franzmann, *Jesus in the Nag Hammadi Writings* (Edinburgh: T & T Clark, 1996).

[8]Norman Perrin, *Rediscovering the Teaching of Jesus* (New York: Harper & Row, 1976), p. 39.

[9]Jacob Neusner, *In Search of Talmudic Biography: The Problem of the Attributed Saying*, Brown Judaic Studies 70 (Chico, Calif.: Scholars Press, 1984).

No, I believe the opposition aroused by Perrin's proposal was that it made the game too difficult to play: too little data would be left; so why not change the rules of the game? Indeed, I think Perrin's own application of the criterion of dissimilarity was selective and inconsistent. Worse yet, he failed to see that the criterion of dissimilarity must be all devouring because of the central tenet of form criticism, which is that in order to be transmitted, every Gospel pericope must have had some pragmatic use. On that assumption, an entirely natural one as it appears to me, form critics sought with great ingenuity to reconstruct the *Sitz im Leben* of each and every Gospel pericope, and with great success. (Again, remember that it is all a matter of probability; of course, it is speculative, but who has anything better to offer?) But Perrin did not seem to see that this meant that *every single* Gospel bit and piece must have had a home in the early church, belonged to the early church (no big surprise! The Gospels, after all, weren't written by Buddhists!), and thus *all* must be denied to Jesus by the criterion of dissimilarity. A saying may have been preserved because of its relevance, but it may as easily have been created, as many appear to have been, and so one must assume the latter. As F. C. Baur said, anything is possible, but what is probable? And if the criterion of dissimilarity is valid, then we must follow unafraid wherever it leads. I know many will protest at this point, saying I have reduced the criterion to its ultimate absurdity, demonstrated despite myself how wrong-headed it always was. But no: this is just to cut and run when the going gets tough. When one objects that the criterion is too strict because it doesn't leave us enough pieces of the puzzle, agnosticism is transforming into fideism. The objection presupposes the conclusion that there was a historical Jesus and that we ought to be able to find out about him.

The third commandment is to remember what an *ideal type* means. Conveniently forgetting it, many have ignored the importance of the mystery religions,[10] the *theios anēr* (divine man),[11] the dying-and-rising

---

[10]Helmut Koester, *Introduction to the New Testament: History and Culture and Religion of the Hellenistic Age* (Berlin: Walter de Gruyter, 1987).

[11]Jack Dean Kingsbury, *The Christology of Mark's Gospel* (Minneapolis: Fortress, 1989), pp. 33-37.

gods,[12] and, most recently, Gnosticism,[13] for the historical Jesus question. An *ideal type* is a textbook definition made up of the regularly recurring features common to the phenomena in question. The ideal type most certainly does not ignore points of distinctiveness of the member phenomena, nor does it presuppose or require absolute likeness between all members of the envisioned category. Rather, the idea is that if discreet phenomena possess enough common features that a yardstick may be abstracted from them, then each member may be profitably measured and better understood against the yardstick. If the ideal type of "religion" includes the feature "belief in superhuman entities," then we do not conclude that Buddhism is not a religion after all. Rather, we turn around and use the yardstick of what is generally true of religions to better understand this particular exception.

Nor do we conclude that, since all members of the proposed category do not match up in every respect, that there is no such category after all. There is a natural range of variations on the theme, and it is only the broad theme that the ideal type sets forth. Neither do we expect that all typical features will be present in all specific cases. We do not deny there is such a thing as a form of miracle stories just because not every one of them contains, say, the feature of the skepticism of the onlookers, though most do.

Fourth, we must keep in mind that *consensus is no criterion*. The truth may not rest in the middle. The truth may not rest with the majority. Every theory and individual argument must be evaluated on its own. If we appeal instead to "received opinion" or "the consensus of scholars," we are merely abdicating our own responsibility, as well as committing the fallacy of *appeal to the majority*. I dare say that, had we really been content to accede to received opinion, none of us would ever have entered the field of New Testament scholarship. I accept the dictum of

---

[12]Jonathan Z. Smith, "Dying and Rising Gods," in *The Encyclopedia of Religion*, ed. Mircea Eliade (New York: Macmillan, 1987), 4:521-27. See my refutation of Smith in Robert Price, *Deconstructing Jesus* (Amherst: Prometheus, 2000), pp. 88-91.

[13]Michael Allen Williams, *Rethinking "Gnosticism": An Argument for Dismantling a Dubious Category* (Princeton, N.J.: Princeton University Press, 1996). Karen L. King, *What Is Gnosticism?* (Cambridge, Mass.: Belknap Press, 2003). If there's no such thing as Gnosticism, then there's no Buddhism or Presbyterianism either.

Paul Feyerabend at this point. The only axiom that does not inhibit research is "anything goes."[14] Let's just see *how far.* It matters not whether a particular hypothesis comports easily with the majority paradigm or with one's own other hypotheses. Since all must be but tentatively and provisionally held anyway, we must follow the evidence wherever it seems to be taking us in this or that particular case. We may wind up overturning and replacing the regnant paradigm, though in the meantime we will expect defenders of "normative science" to do their best defending the ramparts of their cherished paradigm—as they should, since a new one must show its worth by bearing the scrutiny of one's peers.[15]

In the same vein, the fifth commandment is to remember that *scholarly "conclusions" must be tentative and provisional, always open to revision.* Our goal is to try out this and that paradigm/hypothesis to see which makes the most natural sense of the evidence without "epicycling." We must seek the minimum of special pleading for fitting an item of recalcitrant evidence into the framework.

THE TRADITIONAL CHRIST-MYTH THEORY

Virtually everyone who espoused the Christ-Myth theory has laid great emphasis on one question: *Why no mention of a miracle-working Jesus in secular sources?* Let me leapfrog the tiresome debate over whether the *Testimonium Flavianum* is authentic. For the record, my guess is that Eusebius fabricated it[16] and that the tenth-century Arabic version[17] represents an abridgement of the Eusebian original, not a more primitive, modest version. My opinion is that John Meier and others are rewriting a bad text to make it a good one, to rehabilitate it for use as a

---

[14]Paul Feyerabend, *Against Method,* rev. ed (New York: Verso, 1988), p. 14; see also chap. 3 on "counterinduction," pp. 24-32.

[15]Thomas S. Kuhn, *The Structure of Scientific Revolutions* (Chicago: University of Chicago Press, 1962), p. 65.

[16]Solomon Zeitlin, *Josephus on Jesus: With Particular Reference to the Slavonic Josephus and the Hebrew Josippon* (Philadelphia: Dropsie College for Hebrew and Cognate Learning, 1931), chap. 7, "The Christ Passage in Josephus," pp. 61-70.

[17]Shlomo Pines, *An Arabic Version of the Testimonium Flavianum and its Implications* (Jerusalem: Israel Academy of Sciences and Humanities, 1971).

piece of evidence.[18] But who cares? It is all moot. The silence-of-the-sources argument at most implies a Bultmannian version of a historical Jesus whose relatively modest activity as an exorcist and faith healer would not have attracted much attention, any more than the secular media cover Peter Popov today. It does not go all the way to imply there was no historical Jesus. (Indeed, it may even be circular in assuming there was either a real superman or a mythic superman, without a middle option of a mortal messiah.)

The second of the three pillars of the traditional Christ-Myth case is that *the Epistles, earlier than the Gospels, do not evidence a recent historical Jesus.* Setting aside the very late 1 Timothy, which presupposes the Gospel of John (the only Gospel in which Jesus "made a good confession before Pontius Pilate"),[19] we should never guess from the Epistles that Jesus died in any particular historical or political context, only that the fallen angels (Col 2:15), the archons of this age, did him in, little realizing they were sealing their own doom (1 Cor 2:6-8). It is hard to imagine that the authors of Romans 13:3 and 1 Peter 2:13-14 (where we read that Roman governors punish only the wicked, not the righteous) believed that Jesus died at the order of Pontius Pilate. We should never even suspect he performed a single miracle, since none are mentioned. Did Paul think his Jesus had been a teacher? We just don't know, since his cherished "commands of the Lord" (1 Cor 7:10, cf. 25; 9:14), while they might represent quotations from something like the Q source, may as well be midrashically derived inferences from Old Testament commands of Adonai in the Torah, or even prophetic mandates from the Risen One.

Paul seems to know of a Last Supper of Jesus with his disciples, at which he instituted the Eucharist (1 Cor 11:23-26), but this is a weak reed. On the one hand, for reasons having nothing to do with Christ-Myth theory, some have pegged this piece of text as an interpolation.[20]

---

[18]Robert E. Van Voorst, *Jesus Outside the New Testament: An Introduction to the Ancient Evidence* (Grand Rapides: Eerdmans, 2000), pp. 88-104.

[19]Robert M. Price, "Schleiermacher's Dormant Discovery," *Journal of Higher Criticism* 9, no. 2 (2002): 203-16.

[20]Jean Magne, "Les paroles sur la coupe," in *Logia: Les paroles de Jesus—The Sayings of Jesus: Memorial Joseph Coppens*, ed. Joel Delobel, Bibliotheca ephemeridum theologicarum lovaniensum 59

On the other, suppose Paul did write it; Hyam Maccoby argued that in 1 Corinthians 11:23 we see Paul comparing himself with Moses, the one who receives material (in this case, cult law) directly from Adonai and passes it on to his fellow mortals. In other words, Paul does not mean he has received this tradition from other mortals who were present on the occasion, or even from their successors, but that, in human terms, the Last Supper pericope *originated with him*. He would have first apprehended it in a vision,[21] much as the nineteenth-century mystic Anna Katherina Emmerich[22] beheld in a series of visions the "dolorous passion of our Lord Jesus Christ," including "lost episodes" that made it into Mel Gibson's *The Passion of the Christ*. On Maccoby's entirely plausible reading, we would actually be seeing the beginnings of the historicization of the Christ figure here.

Finally, though the Epistles name the Christian savior Jesus, it is quite possible, as Paul Couchoud suggested long ago,[23] that they attest to an even earlier stage of belief in which the savior received the honorific name Jesus only as of his postmortem exaltation. For Philippians 2:9-11, read without theological embarrassment, seems to intend that it was that name, exalted above all other names, that the savior received, not the title *kyrios*. Every voice acclaiming him Lord is paralleled with every knee bowing to him, both to occur at the mention of this new name, Jesus, now bestowed on him.

(Leuven: Peeters/Leuven University Press, 1982), pp. 485-90; idem, *From Christianity to Gnosis and From Gnosis to Christianity: An Itinerary through the Texts To and From the Tree of Paradise*, trans. A. F. W. Armstrong, Brown Judaic Studies 286 (Atlanta: Scholars Press, 1993), p. 33, cited in William O. Walker Jr., *Interpolations in the Pauline Letters*, Journal for the Study of the New Testament Supplement Series 213 (London: Sheffield Academic Press, 2001), p. 19. Cf. G. A. Wells, *The Jesus of the Early Christians: A Study in Christian Origins* (London: Pemberton Books, 1971), p. 270: "In verses 22 and 33 Paul is urging the faithful to share the food in a decent and civilized way; while from verses 23 to 32 he is talking not of this ethical problem, but of the mystical properties of the Lord's body. Some have therefore regarded verses 23-32 as an interpolation." (Wells himself, however, is not convinced the passage is an interpolation.)

[21]Hyam Maccoby, *Paul and Hellenism* (Philadelphia: Trinity Press International, 1991), pp. 92-93.

[22]See the discussion of Emmerich and her novel in Albert Schweitzer, *The Quest of the Historical Jesus: A Critical Study of its Progress from Reimarus to Wrede*, trans, W. Montgomery (New York: Macmillan, 1961), pp. 108-10.

[23]Paul L. Couchoud, "The Historicity of Jesus: A Reply to Alfred Loisy," *Hibbert Journal* 37, no. 2 (1938): 193-214; idem, *The Creation of Christ: An Outline of the Beginnings of Christianity*, trans. C. Bradlaugh Bonner (London: Watts & Co., 1939), p. 438.

All the Epistles seem to know is a Jesus Christ, Son of God, who came into the world to die as a sacrifice for human sin and was raised by God and enthroned in heaven. Some mythicists (the early G. A. Wells[24] and Alvar Ellegard[25]) thought that the first Christians had in mind a Jesus who had lived as a historical figure, just not of the recent past, much as the average Greek believed Hercules and Achilles really lived somewhere back there in the past.[26] Others, like Earl Doherty,[27] believe the original Christology envisioned a Jesus who had never even appeared on earth (except in visions to his believers) and whose sacrificial death amid the angels had occurred in one of the lower heavens, where these beings were located in ancient belief. Again, as the Son of Man, his death would be of a piece with the primordial death of the primal man Purusha in the *Rig Veda* (10:90), whose self-sacrifice in the heavens gave rise to the creation.[28]

But what about the one whom Paul calls "James the brother of the Lord" (Gal 1:19)? Paul says he met him, so mustn't he have understood Jesus to be a figure of recent history? That is indeed a natural reading, but it is not the only one. Wells cautions that "brethren of the Lord" (1 Cor 9:5) may refer to a missionary brotherhood[29] such as the Johannine Epistles presuppose, and need not refer to literal siblings of the Lord any more than 1 Corinthians 3:9's "the Lord's colaborers" means Paul and Apollos had offices down the hall from God as "the Lord's colleagues." After all, Paul does not say "James the brother of *Jesus*," and he might simply have meant to identify James as one of these itinerant evangelists. Wells's theory makes all the more sense in light of Walter

---

[24]Wells, *Jesus of the Early Christians;* idem, *Who Was Jesus?* (London: Elek/Pemberton, 1975); idem, *The Historical Evidence for Jesus* (Amherst, N.Y.: Prometheus, 1988); idem, *Who Was Jesus? A Critique of the New Testament Record* (LaSalle, Ill.: Open Court, 1989).

[25]Alvar Ellegard, *Jesus One Hundred Years Before Christ: A Study in Creative Mythology* (London: Century, 1999).

[26]Paul Veyne, *Did the Greeks Believe in Their Myths? An Essay on the Constitutive Imagination,* trans. Paula Wissing (Chicago: University of Chicago Press, 1988), pp. 17-18, 88.

[27]Earl Doherty, *The Jesus Puzzle: Did Christianity Begin with a Mythical Christ?* (Ottawa: Canadian Humanist Publications, 1999), pp. 120-22.

[28]Wendy Doniger O'Flaherty, ed. and trans., *The Rig Veda: An Anthology* (Baltimore: Penguin Books, 1981), pp. 29-32.

[29]Wells, *Jesus of the Early Christians,* pp. 141-42.

Schmithals's argument[30] that in Galatians 1:19 Paul means by "apostles" (among whom he there counts James) simply itinerant preachers whose hub was Jerusalem; most of them were naturally out on the road at the time of Paul's visit, which is why he met only two who happened to be there: Cephas and James.

In any case, there is the Taiping Messiah Hong Xiuquan,[31] a nineteenth-century revolutionary leader: he proclaimed himself "the Little Brother of Jesus." Obviously he didn't mean he was a blood relative of the ancient Jesus of Nazareth. No doubt Hong Xiuquan believed in a historical Jesus, but what he had in mind was that he was the incarnation of a second heavenly Son-hypostasis of God. James's title may have implied something like that, especially since that is pretty much the same thing Gnostics meant when they called Thomas the twin of Jesus, though they didn't think Jesus had been a flesh-and-blood mortal.

JESUS: SENDER OR RECIPIENT?

Wells and others have insisted that it is just inexplicable, on the usual understanding of a historical Jesus, why the Epistles never quote him. To be sure, the Epistles do contain many gems that sound like variants on sayings that are ascribed to Jesus in the Gospels. But none of these are attributed to Jesus by the epistolarians. James D. G. Dunn asks us to believe that Paul and James did mean the reader to detect dominical logia at such points but thought it best to leave them as allusions for those who had ears to hear ("wink, wink, nudge, nudge").[32] With great respect to a great scholar, I must confess that this seems to me very strained. It is one of those arguments no one would take seriously except as a tool to extricate oneself from a tight spot. Surely if one wants to settle a question by appealing to the words of Jesus, one will make sure the reader understands that they are in fact words of Jesus—by saying so.

---

[30]Walter Schmithals, *The Office of Apostle in the Early Church,* trans. John E. Steely (Nashville: Abingdon, 1969), pp. 82-87.

[31]Jonathan D. Spence, *God's Chinese Son: The Taiping Heavenly Kingdom of Hong Xiuquan* (New York: W. W. Norton, 1996), pp. 46-49, 64-65.

[32]James D. G. Dunn, "Jesus Tradition in Paul," in *Studying the Historical Jesus,* ed. Bruce Chilton and Craig A. Evans (Leiden: Brill, 1994), pp. 177-78.

Along the same lines, Wells reasons that, if the writers of the New Testament epistles had access to anything like the sayings tradition of the Synoptics, they must surely have cited them when the same subjects came up in the situations they addressed. Is celibacy at issue (1 Cor 7:7, 25-35)? Why not quote Matthew 19:11-12? Tax evasion (Rom 13:6)? Mark 12:17 would surely come in handy. Dietary laws (Rom 14:1-4; 1 Cor 8; Col 2:20-21) in contention? Mark 7:15 would made short work of that. Controversy over circumcision (Rom 3:1; Gal 5:1-12)? *Gospel of Thomas* 53 ought to settle that one fast. On the other hand, if there were originally no dominical sayings to settle the question, it is not hard to imagine that soon people would be coining them (as they still do today in illiterate congregations where debaters try to gain points by pulling a Jesus saying or a Bible verse out of their imaginations. No one can check to prove them wrong!)[33]—or attaching Jesus' name to a saying they already liked, to make it authoritative. It makes eminent sense to suggest, in the Epistles, that we see early Christian sayings just before their attribution to Jesus.

SON OF SCRIPTURE

We can observe the same tendency in the events predicated of Jesus. Scholars have always seen Gospel echoes of the ancient Scriptures in secondary coloring or redactional juxtaposition, but the more recent scrutiny of John Dominic Crossan,[34] Randel Helms,[35] Dale and Patricia Miller,[36] and Thomas L. Brodie[37] has made it appear likely that virtually the whole Gospel narrative is the product of haggadic midrash on the Old Testament. Earl Doherty has clarified the resultant understanding of the Gospel writers' methodology. It has been customary to

---

[33]Nathan L. Gerrard, "The Holiness Movement in Southern Appalachia," in *The Charismatic Movement*, ed. Michael P. Hamilton (Grand Rapids: Eerdmans, 1975), p. 165.

[34]John Dominic Crossan, *The Cross That Spoke: The Origins of the Passion Narrative* (San Francisco: Harper & Row, 1988).

[35]Randel Helms, *Gospel Fictions* (Amherst, N.Y.: Prometheus, 1989).

[36]Dale Miller and Patricia Miller, *The Gospel of Mark as Midrash on Earlier Jewish and New Testament Literature*, Studies in the Bible and Early Christianity 21 (Lewiston/Queenston/Lampeter: Edwin Mellen Press, 1990).

[37]Thomas L. Brodie, "Luke the Literary Interpreter: Luke-Acts as a Systematic Rewriting and Updating of the Elijah-Elisha Narrative in 1 and 2 Kings" (Ph.D. diss., Pontifical University of St. Thomas Aquinas, Rome, 1988).

suppose that early Christians began with a set of remarkable facts, then sought after the fact for scriptural predictions for them. We have supposed that Hosea 11:1 provided a pedigree for Jesus' childhood sojourn in Egypt, that it was the story of the flight into Egypt that made early Christians go searching for the Hosea text. Now it seems, by contrast, that the flight into Egypt is midrashic all the way down. The words in Hosea 11:1 "my son," catching the early Christian eye, generated the whole story, since they assumed such a prophecy about the divine Son must have had its fulfillment. And the more apparent it becomes that most Gospel narratives can be adequately accounted for by reference to scriptural prototypes, Doherty suggests,[38] the more natural it is to picture early Christians beginning with a more or less vague savior myth and seeking to lend it color and detail by anchoring it in a particular historical period and clothing it in scriptural garb. We must now envision proto-Christian exegetes "discovering" for the first time what Jesus the Son of God had done and said "according to the scriptures" by decoding the ancient texts. Today's Christian reader learns what Jesus did by reading the Gospels; his ancient counterpart learned what Jesus did by reading Joshua and 1 Kings. It was not a question of memory but of creative exegesis. Let me survey the Gospel of Mark to illustrate the extent of this midrashic borrowing.[39]

At Jesus' baptism (Mk 1:9-11) the heavenly voice conflates bits and pieces of Psalm 2:7, Isaiah 42:1 and Genesis 22:12 (LXX). In the temptation narrative (Mk 1:12-13), the forty days of Jesus in the wilderness recall both Moses' period of forty years in the desert of Midian before

[38]Doherty, *Jesus Puzzle*, pp. 79-82, 225-30.

[39]For the scriptural roots of all four Gospels and Acts (and in greater detail), see Robert M. Price, "New Testament Narrative as Old Testament Midrash," in *Encyclopedia of Midrash: Biblical Interpretation in Formative Judaism*, ed. Jacob Neusner and Alan J. Avery Peck (Leiden: Brill, 2005), 1:534-73. Besides Crossan, Helms, the Millers and Brodie, I owe a great debt to the work of John Bowman, *The Gospel of Mark: The New Christian Jewish Passover Haggadah*, Studia Post-Biblica 8 (Leiden: Brill, 1965); J. Duncan M. Derrett, *The Making of Mark: The Scriptural Bases of the Earliest Gospel*, vols. 1 and 2 (Shipston-on-Stour, U.K.: P. Drinkwater, 1985); Frank Kermode, *The Genesis of Secrecy: On the Interpretation of Narrative*, The Charles Eliot Norton Lectures 1977-1978 (Cambridge, Mass.: Harvard University Press, 1979); Wolfgang Roth, *Hebrew Gospel: Cracking the Code of Mark* (Oak Park, Ill.: Meyer-Stone Books, 1988); and Rikki E. Watts, *Isaiah's New Exodus and Mark*, Wissenschaftliche Untersuchungen zum Neuen Testament 2, Reihe 88 (Tübingen: Mohr Siebeck, 1997).

returning to Egypt and the forty-day retreat of Elijah to the wilderness after the contest with Baal's prophets (1 Kings 19:5-7), where Elijah, like Jesus, is ministered to by angels. The Q tradition shared by Matthew (Mt 4:1-11) and Luke (Lk 4:1-13) and possibly abridged by Mark plays off the Exodus tradition in yet another way. Jesus resists the devil's blandishments by citing three texts from Deuteronomy, 8:3; 6:16; 6:13, all referring to trials in the wilderness. The recruitment of the first disciples (Mk 1:16-20) comes from Elijah's recruitment of Elisha in 1 Kings 19:19-21. Likewise the calling of Levi in Mark 2:14. In the Capernaum exorcism story (Mk 1:21-28) the cry of the demoniac comes directly from the defensive alarm of the Zarephath widow in 1 Kings 17:18. The incident of Peter's mother-in-law (Mk 1:29-31) is also cut from the cloth of Elijah's mantle. In 1 Kings 17:8-16, Elijah meets the widow of Zarephath and her son, and he delivers them from imminent starvation. As a result she serves the man of God. In 2 Kings 4, Elisha raises from the dead the son of the Shunammite woman, who had served him. Mark has reshuffled these elements so that this time it is the old woman herself who is raised up from her illness, not her son, who is nonetheless important to the story (Peter), and she serves the man of God, Jesus.

The story of a paralyzed man's friends tearing off the roof and lowering him to Jesus (Mk 2:1-12) seems based on 2 Kings 1:2-17, where King Ahaziah gains his affliction by falling from his roof through the lattice and languishes in bed. Mark has borrowed the substance of the withered hand healing (Mk 3:1-6) from the miracle of the Judean prophet of 1 Kings 13:1-6.

Mark has sandwiched together two previous pericopes, the choosing of the Twelve and the embassy of relatives (Mk 3:13-35). We must imagine that previous to Mark someone had midrashically rewritten the Exodus 18 story of Moses' heeding Jethro's advice to name subordinates, resulting in a scene in which choosing the twelve disciples was the idea of the Holy Family of Jesus. Originally we would have read of Jesus' welcoming his family. And as Jethro voices his concern for the harried Moses, suggesting he share the burden with a number of helpers (Ex 18:21-22), so we would have read that James or Mary advised the choice of assistants "that they might be with him, and that he might send them out to preach" (Mk 3:14). And Jesus would only then have named the Twelve. Mark, acting in the interest of a church-political agenda, has broken the story into two and reversed its halves so as to bring dishonor on the relatives of Jesus and to take from them the credit for choosing the Twelve (which is also why he emphasizes that Jesus "summoned those that he *himself* wanted," i.e., it was all his own idea). Jesus, however, does not, like Moses, choose seventy (though Luke will restore this number, Lk 10:1), but only twelve, based on the choice of the twelve spies in Deuteronomy 1:23.

Matthew and Luke (hence the Q source) make an interesting addition to Jesus' response to the scribes. Luke 11:19-20, as usual, is probably closer to the Q original. Compressed into these verses is an unmistakable midrash on the exodus story of Moses' miracle contest with the magicians of Pharaoh. Initially able to match Moses feat for feat, they prove incapable of copying the miracle of the gnats and warn Pharaoh to give in, since "this is the finger of God" and no mere sorcery like theirs (Ex 8:19).

The stilling of the storm (Mk 4:35-41) has been rewritten from Jonah's adventure, with additions from certain of the Psalms. The basis for the story can be recognized in Jonah 1:4-6; 1:15b-16 plus Psalm 107:23-29. The Gerasene demoniac (Mk 5:1-20) mixes materials from Psalm 107:10, 4, 6, 14, and *Odyssey* 9.101-565. Jairus's daughter and the woman with the issue of blood (Mk 5:21-24, 35-43) are a complex retelling, again, of the tale of Elisha and the Shunammite woman (2 Kings 4). Jesus' rejection at home (Mk 6:1-6) goes back to the story of Saul as an improbable prophet in 1 Samuel 10:1-27.

Mark's version of the mission charge (Mk 6:7-13) may have been influenced by the practices of Cynic preachers, but they surely owe something to the Elisha stories. When Jesus forbids the missioners to "take along money nor two cloaks," he is warning them not to repeat Gehazi's fatal error; he had exacted from Naaman "a talent of silver and two cloaks" (2 Kings 5:22). The provision of a staff (Mk 6:8) may come from Gehazi's mission for Elisha to the Shunammite's son: "take my staff in your hand and go" (2 Kings 4:29). Luke must have recognized this, since he returned to the same text to add to his own mission charge to the seventy (Lk 10:4) the stipulation "and salute no one on the road," borrowed directly from Elisha's charge to Gehazi in 2 Kings 4:29.

In the story of the death of the Baptizer (Mk 6:14-29), Herod Antipas's words to his stepdaughter come from Esther 5:3. His painting himself into the corner, having to order John's execution, may come from Darius's bamboozlement in Daniel 6:6-15.

The basis for both miraculous feeding stories (Mk 6:30-44; 8:1-10) is the story of Elisha's multiplying the twenty barley loaves for a hundred men in 2 Kings 4:42-44. The walking on the sea (Mk 6:45-52) looks to come from Psalm 107:23-30 (LXX 106:23-30); 23-30; Job 9:8. In debate with the scribes over purity rules (Mk 7:1-23), Jesus is made to cite the LXX of Isaiah 29:13, the Hebrew original of which would not really make the required point. Less obviously, there is also a significant reference to Elijah in Mark 7:14, "and summoning the multitude again, he said to them, 'Listen to me, all of you, and understand.'" Here we are to discern a reflection of Elijah's gesture in 1 Kings 18:30, "Then Elijah said to all the people, 'Come near to me.'"

In Mark 7:24-30 Jesus meets a foreign woman in the district of Tyre and Sidon who requests his help for her child, and we find ourselves back with Elijah and widow of Sidonian Zarephath in 1 Kings 17:8-16. There the prophet encounters the foreigner and does a miracle for her and her son. In both cases the miracle is preceded by a tense interchange between the prophet and the woman in which the prophet raises the bar to gauge the woman's faith. The Syrophoenician parries Jesus' initial dismissal with a clever comeback; the widow of Zarephath is bidden to take her remaining meal and to cook it up for Elijah first, whereupon the meal is indefinitely multiplied. But why does Jesus call the poor woman and her daughter, by implication, dogs? Mark has taken it from 2 Kings 8:7-15. Mark 7:31-37 is a midrash on Isaiah 29:18 and Isaiah 35:5-6. We probably ought to add Mark 8:22-26 and Mark 10:46-52 as midrashic fulfillments of the same texts.

Jesus' ascent of the unnamed mountain and his transfiguration (Mk 9:1-13) is Mark's version of Moses' ascent of Mount Sinai and his shining visage in Exodus 24 and Exodus 34:29. The Markan introduction,

"And six days later" (Mk 9:2), must be understood as a pointer to the Exodus account, where the glory cloud covers the height for six days (Ex 24:16). The glowing apparition of Jesus is most obviously derived from Exodus 34:29, but we must not miss the influence of Malachi 3:2, especially since Elijah too appears.

Mark connects again with the story of Elisha and the Shunammite (2 Kings 4) in his story of the deaf-mute epileptic (Mk 9:14-29). Elisha dispatched his disciple with his own potent staff to restore the Shunammite's dead son, but he could not (2 Kings 4:31). But Elisha succeeded where Gehazi failed (2 Kings 4:32-35).

The account of the disciples jockeying for position (Mk 9:33-37) reaches back to the pentateuchal disputes between Moses and Aaron and Miriam (Num 12) and/or Dathan and Abiram (Num 16). Mark returns to the same portion of Numbers for his story of the independent exorcist (Mk 9:38-40). The man casting out demons outside of Jesus' retinue is based directly on Eldad and Medad (Num 11:24-30). John is a renamed Joshua who protested that "Eldad and Medad are prophesying in the camp," that is, "not following us" (Mk 9:38).

Mark modeled 10:13-16 on 2 Kings 4, again, the story of Elisha and the Shunammite. "And when she came to the mountain, to the man of God, she caught hold of his feet. And Gehazi came to thrust her away. But the man of God said, 'Let her alone, for she is in bitter distress, and the LORD has hidden it from me and has not told me'" (2 Kings 4:27).

Jesus has just announced his impending death and resurrection, prompting James and John to venture, "Teacher, we want you to do for us whatever we may ask of you. . . . Grant that we may sit in your glory, one at your right, one at your left" (Mk 10:35, 37). This comes from 2 Kings 2:9, "Ask what I shall do for you before I am taken from you." Hearing Elisha's answer, Elijah reflects, "You have asked a hard thing" (2 Kings 2:10), just as Jesus warns James and John, "You do not know what you are asking for."

The parallel stories of the preparation for the entry and the supper (Mk 11:1-6; 14:12-16) alike derive from 1 Samuel 9. Though Mark does not make it explicit, the scene of Jesus entering the holy city on a donkey (Mk 11:7-11) is a fleshing out of Zechariah 9:9. The actions and words of the crowd come right from Psalm 118:26-27. The cursing of the fig tree (Mk 11:12-14, 20) stems from Psalm 37:35-36. The cleansing of the Temple (Mk 11:15-18) must have in view Malachi's messenger of the covenant who will purify the sons of Levi (Mal 3:1-3, as hinted by Mk 1:2 and 9:3), as well as the oracle of Zechariah 14:21, "And there shall no longer be a trader in the house of the LORD of hosts on that day." The saying of Jesus is merely a conflation of Isaiah 56:7 and Jeremiah 7:11. The parable of the wicked tenants (Mk 12:1-12) has grown out of Isaiah 5:1-7.

The whole apocalyptic discourse of Mark is a cento of Scripture paraphrases and quotations: Mark 13:7 comes from Daniel 11:44; Mark 13:8 from Isaiah 19:2 and/or 2 Chronicles 15:6; Mark 13:12 from Micah 7:6; Mark 13:14 from Daniel 9:27 or 12:11 and Genesis 19:17; Mark 13:19 from Daniel 12:1; Mark 13:22 from Deuteronomy 13:2; Mark 13:24 from Isaiah 13:10; Mark 13:25 from Isaiah 34:4; Mark 13:26 from Daniel 7:13; and Mark 13:27 from Zechariah 2:10 and Deuteronomy 30:4.

The seed of the Last Supper story (Mk 14:17-31) is Psalm 41:9. Matthew embellishes the enigmatic figure and fate of Judas. He gets the precise amount Judas was paid, thirty silver pieces, from Zechariah 11:11. That Judas returned the money, throwing it into the temple treasury and that the priests decided to use it to buy the potter's field he drew from the Syriac version ("Cast it into the treasury"), then the Hebrew version ("Cast it to the *potter*"). How does Matthew know Judas hanged himself? That was the fate of David's traitorous counselor Ahithophel (2 Sam 17:23), whom scribal tradition took to be the subject of Psalm 41:9, which the Gospels applied to Judas.

Peter's avowal that he will not leave Jesus' side reminds us of Elisha's three avowals that he will not leave Elijah (2 Kings 2:2, 4, 6). Or Mark may have been thinking of Ittai's loyalty pledge to David (1 Sam 15:21). The basis of the Garden of Gethsemane scene (Mk 14:32-52) is 2 Samuel 15–16. Judas's betraying kiss (Mk 14:44-45) would seem to derive from 2 Samuel 20:7-10. Mark borrowed from Daniel 6:4 (LXX) the scene of the crossfire of false accusations during the Sanhedrin trial

(Mk 14:55-56). Mark 14:65, where Jesus suffers blows and mockery as a false prophet, comes from 1 Kings 22:24, "Then Zedekiah the son of Chenaanah came near and struck Micaiah on the cheek, and said, 'How did the spirit of the Lord go from me to speak to you?' And Micaiah said, '*Behold, you shall see* on that day when you go into an inner chamber to hide yourself.'" Jesus' silence at both trials before the Sanhedrin and Pilate (Mk 14:60-61; 15:4-5) comes from Isaiah 50:7; 53:7.

The substructure for the crucifixion in chapter 15 is, as all recognize, Psalm 22, from which derive all the major details, including the implicit piercing of hands and feet (Mk 15:24 // Ps 22:16b), the dividing of his garments and casting lots for them (Mk 15:24 // Ps 22:18), the "wagging heads" of the mockers (Mk 15:29 // Ps 22:7) and, of course, the cry of dereliction, "My God, my God, why have you forsaken me?" (Mk 15:34 // Ps 22:1). Matthew adds another quote, "He trusts in God. Let God deliver him now if he desires him" (Mt 27:43 // Ps 22:8), as well as a strong allusion ("for he said, 'I am the son of God,'" Mt 27:43) to Wisdom of Solomon 2:12-20. The darkness at noon comes from Amos 8:9, while the vinegar and gall come from Psalm 69:21. How odd that the first written account of the major event of the Christian story should be composed not of historical memories but of Scripture passages out of context.

Joseph of Arimathea (Mk 15:42-47) is surely a combination of King Priam, who comes to Achilles' camp to beg the body of his son Hector, and the Patriarch Joseph, who asked Pharaoh's permission to bury the body of Jacob in the cave-tomb Jacob had hewn for himself back beyond the Jordan (Gen 50:4-5). The empty tomb narrative requires no source beyond Joshua 10:18, 22, 26-27. The vigil of the mourning women reflects the women's mourning cult of the dying-and-rising god, long familiar in Israel (Ezek 8:14; Zech 12:11; Song 3:1-4).

We have not forgotten the criterion of dissimilarity; it is now evident that it must extend from sayings paralleled in Jewish sources to stories from the Jewish Scriptures. If the Gospel episode looks like a rewrite of an Old Testament story, it is multiplying explanations, contra Occam's razor, to suggest that the episodes *also* actually happened to Jesus. And the principle of analogy applies here as well: which do the Gospel stories resemble more closely, contemporary experience or ancient miracle tales? Which is more likely: that a man walked on water, glowed like the sun and rose from the dead, or that someone has rewritten a bunch of well-known miracle stories?

DYING-AND-RISING GODS

The Jesus story as attested in the Epistles shows strong parallels to Middle Eastern religions based on the myths of dying-and-rising gods. (And this similarity is the third pillar of the traditional Christ-Myth theory.) Originally celebrating the seasonal cycle and the yearly death and return of vegetation, these myths were reinterpreted later when peoples of the ancient nationalities relocated around the Roman Empire and in urban settings. The myths now came to symbolize the rebirth of the individual initiate as a personal rite of passage, namely new birth. Strong evidence from ancient stelae and tablets make clear that Baal and Osiris were believed to be dying-and-rising gods long before the Christian era. There is also pre-Christian evidence for the resurrection of Attis,[40] Adonis and Dumuzi/Tammuz. All these survived into the Hellenistic and Roman periods, when they were available to influence Christianity. Apologists, understandably, have tried to minimize the parallels. In view of the archaeological evidence, it is only wishful thinking to claim that these other religions borrowed the common themes from Christianity. In any case the priority of the pagan versions ought to be obvious from the simple fact that church fathers and apologists from the ancient world admitted it by arguing that Satan had counterfeited the facts of the gospel and planted them *in advance*, much as modern creationists have claimed Satan fabricated and planted the bones of nonexistent dinosaurs, just to throw potential believers off the track.

J. Z. Smith disdains the old Protestant propaganda accusing Catholicism of assimilating pagan myth and ritual, so he bends over back-

---

[40]Maarten J. Vermaseren, *Cybele and Attis: The Myth and the Cult*, trans. A. M. H. Lemmers (London: Thames and Hudson, 1977), pp. 119-24. For other pre-Christian dying-and-rising deities, see Tryggve N. D. Mettinger, *The Riddle of Resurrection: "Dying and Rising Gods" in the Ancient Near East*, Coniectanea Biblica Old Testament Series 50 (Stockholm: Almqvist & Wiksell International, 2001).

ward to try to make such borrowings impossible.[41] This makes him take up the case of the conservative apologists. His particular approach is to aver that there never was a common myth of the dying-and-rising god. This he does by forgetting or obscuring the nature of the ideal type, as discussed above. Pointing out secondary, even trivial, differences between specific myths, he would have us deny that they form a general type. But again, one might as well argue there is no such thing as a "religion" or a "miracle story" because the actual cases are not all exactly alike.

I must admit that when I first read of these mythic parallels in Gilbert Murray's *Five Stages of Greek Religion*,[42] it hit me like a ton of bricks. No assurances I received from any Christian scholar I read ever sounded like anything other than specious special pleading to me, and believe me I was disappointed. This was before I had ever read of the principle of analogy, but when I did learn about that axiom, I was able to give a name to what was so powerful in Murray's presentation. Yet I must admit that even this is not enough to make one discount the existence of a historical Jesus. It does not push us beyond Bultmann who reasoned that the resurrection faith, though based on Easter morning visions, was articulated in terms of these mystery-religion myths. Bultmann regarded Christ-Myth theorists as insane.[43] And yet Bultmann was inconsistent: trying to have his cake for the queen of heaven and eat it too. You mean, the first disciples *did* actually have visions of some type, persuading them that Jesus was risen, and *then* they adopted mystery-religion parallels? Too many explanations. There is no more reason to posit a core experience than in the case of Attis. *And* yet, for all this, there still *might* have been a historical Jesus, even if there was

---

[41]Jonathan Z. Smith, *Drudgery Divine: On the Comparison of Early Christianities and the Religions of Late Antiquity*, Jordan Lectures in Comparative Religion, XIV, School of Oriental and African Studies, University of London (Chicago: University of Chicago Press, 1990).

[42]Gilbert Murray, *Five Stages of Greek Religion*, 3rd ed. (Garden City, N.Y.: Doubleday Anchor Books, 1951), "Preface to the Third Edition," pp. v-ix.

[43]Bultmann, *Jesus and the Word*, p. 13: "Of course the doubt as to whether Jesus really existed is unfounded and not worth refutation. No sane person can doubt that Jesus stands as founder behind the historical movement whose first distinct stage is represented by the oldest Palestinian community." But one has to wonder whether Bultmann protests too much, knowing his critics charged that he himself had come close to such a view.

no historical Easter morning experience. This is why the rest of the Jesus story is vital.

THE MYTHIC HERO ARCHETYPE

I have already tried to give some idea of the extent to which the gospel story represents a tapestry of Scripture quotes from the Old Testament. That is already enough to vitiate the use of Gospel materials to reconstruct a life of Jesus. If you can explain it from systematic Old Testament borrowing, it is superfluous to look for anything else. But let me approach it from a slightly different angle, one equally powerful to my mind, namely that of the *mythic hero archetype* compiled and delineated by Lord Raglan, Otto Rank, Alan Dundes[44] and others from the hero myths, both Indo-European and Semitic. Here are the twenty-two recurrent features, with those appearing in the gospel story of Jesus in italics. They make it pretty clear that it is not merely the death-and-resurrection complex in which the Jesus story parallels myth more than history.

1. *mother is a royal virgin*
2. *father is a king*
3. father related to mother
4. *unusual conception*
5. *hero reputed to be son of god*
6. *attempt to kill hero*
7. *hero spirited away*
8. *reared* by foster parents *in a far country*
9. *no details of childhood*
10. *goes to future kingdom*
11. is victor over king
12. marries a princess (often daughter of predecessor)
13. *becomes king*
14. *for a time he reigns uneventfully*
15. *he prescribes laws*

---

[44]Alan Dundes, "The Hero Pattern in the Life of Jesus," in *In Quest of the Hero*, ed. Robert A. Segal (Princeton, N.J.: Princeton University Press, 1990).

16. *later loses favor with gods or his subjects*
17. *driven from throne and city*
18. *meets with mysterious death*
19. *often at the top of a hill*
20. his children, if any, do not succeed him [i.e., *does not found a dynasty*]
21. *his body is not buried*
22. *nonetheless has one or more holy sepulchers*

Jesus' mother Mary is a virgin, though not of royal blood, though later apocrypha, as if to fill the lack, do make Mary Davidic. Joseph is "of the house of David," though he does not reign, but that is just the point: his heir, the true Davidic king, is *coming*. Mary and Joseph are not related. Jesus' conception is certainly unusual, being virginal and miraculous. Jesus is the Son of God, as more and more people begin to recognize. He is immediately persecuted by the reigning king, Herod the Great. In most hero tales, the persecutor is not only the reigning king but also the hero's father who may fear his son overthrowing him. This role has been split in the Jesus story, Joseph being a royal heir but not king, while another, Herod, sits on Joseph's rightful throne. Fleeing persecution, the hero takes refuge in a distant land, Egypt. Mary is not a foster parent, though Joseph is. There are no details about Jesus' childhood or upbringing. The one apparent exception, Jesus' visit to the temple when he is bar-mitzvah age (Lk 2:41-52), is itself a frequent hero mytheme, that of the child prodigy.

Jesus goes to Jerusalem to be acclaimed as king, though he eschews worldly power. Nonetheless he comes into conflict with the rulers as if he had. He does not marry (though, again, as if to fill the gap, pious speculation has always suspected he married Mary Magdalene). Does Jesus have a peaceful reign, issuing laws? Not exactly. But while enjoying popular esteem as King of the Jews, for the moment unmolested, he does hold forth in the temple court, issuing teachings and moral commandments. Suddenly the once-ardent followers turn on him, demanding his blood. They drive Jesus out of the city to be crucified atop the hill of Golgotha. Though he is temporarily buried, his tomb turns up empty, and later various sites were nominated as his burial place. He has no children, except in modern additions to the Jesus story in which he founded the Merovingian dynasty of medieval France.

Some of the heroes from whose stories scholars abstracted this list of features, this ideal type, were historical individuals, but inevitably their lives become encumbered by the barnacles of myth and legend. Dibelius called this tendency the law of biographical analogy.[45] How do we know which ones have at least some historical basis? There will be collateral, "neutral" information about them, for example, details of upbringing, education, early plans, romances, likes and dislikes, physical appearance. In the case of Jesus there is absolutely none of this "secular" information. Every detail corresponds to the interest of mythology and epic.

Again, a basically historical figure will also be tied into the history of his times by well-documented events. Augustus Caesar and Cyrus of Persia would be good examples. Jesus Christ would not be. Consider the fact that at every point where the gospel story appears to obtrude on contemporary history, there are serious difficulties in taking the narratives as historical. The Matthean nativity story, in which Herod the Great persecutes baby Jesus, seems largely based on Josephus's nativity of Moses.[46] And besides, though Herod was a paranoid and a butcher, his many recorded atrocities do not include what one might consider a very conspicuous one: the butchery of all infants and toddlers in a particular town. And when the persecution of the infant hero is so common a theme in myth, it starts looking like a better alternative here too.

At the other end of Jesus' career, we see him connected to the Sanhedrin, even to Caiaphas, whose tomb has been identified. But the difficulties attaching to a trial being held on Passover Eve, as well as the procedure and the grounds for a blasphemy verdict, have made many reject the historical accuracy of the story who have never entertained the Christ-Myth theory. There is also the suspicion that Jewish involvement was a creation fostered by the same tendency to whitewash the Romans that eventuated in the canonical sainthood of Pontius

---

[45]Martin Dibelius, *From Tradition to Gospel* (New York: Scribner's, n.d.), pp. 104-8.
[46]Josephus *Jewish Antiquities* 2.9.2-3.

Pilate. And as for that worthy, it is by no means only Christ-Myth cranks and eccentrics who have rejected the story of Pilate trying to free Jesus as a piece of implausible fiction.[47] Who knows what happened? Maybe Herod the Great did try to kill the infant Messiah. Maybe the Sanhedrin did condemn Jesus as a blasphemer and a gutless Pilate finally gave in to their whims. But it does not seem very probable, and probability is the only coin in which the historian trades. He cannot build a story out of things that might possibly have happened. And this means that it is a chain of very weak links that binds Jesus to the circumstances of the first century.

CIRCULARITY AND HISTORICITY

Besides this, there are persistent alternative traditions as to his dates. Irenaeus thought Jesus was martyred under Claudius Caesar.[48] The Talmud makes Jesus the disciple of Rabbi Jeschua ben Perechiah and has him crucified in 83 B.C.E., when Alexander Jannaeus crucified so many Pharisees. The *Toledoth Jeschu* incorporated these long-lived traditions. Epiphanius reports them too.[49] The *Gospel of Peter* assigns Jesus' condemnation to Herod Antipas, and (as Loisy suggested[50]) so did one of Luke's passion sources. If Pilate had really turned the case over to Antipas, and the latter set Jesus free, why on earth does Jesus go back to Pilate? Only because Luke wants to use as much as he can of both an L story in which Antipas killed Jesus, and Mark, in which it was Pilate who did the deed. How is it that such radically different estimates of Jesus' dates grew up side by side if there was a real event at the heart of it? We have already seen that no historical memory was available to Mark when he composed the first crucifixion account.

I am of the opinion that the varying dates are the residue of various

---

[47]S. G. F. Brandon, *The Trial of Jesus of Nazareth* (New York: Stein and Day, 1968), chap. 4, "The Scandal of the Roman Cross: Mark's Solution," pp. 81-106. Burton L. Mack, *A Myth of Innocence: Mark and Christian Origins* (Minneapolis: Fortress, 1991), pp. 293-96.

[48]Irenaeus *Demonstration of the Apostolic Preaching* 74.

[49]G. R. S. Mead, *Did Jesus Live 100 B.C.?* (New Hyde Park: University Books, 1968), chap. 8, "The Talmud 100 Years B.C. Story of Jesus," pp. 135-51; chap. 16, "The 100 Years B.C. Date in the Toldoth," pp. 302-23; chap. 19, "The 100 Years B.C. Date in Epiphanius," pp. 388-412.

[50]Alfred F. Loisy, *The Origins of the New Testament*, trans. L. P. Jacks. (London: Allen and Unwin, 1950), p. 167.

attempts to anchor an originally mythic or legendary Jesus in more or less recent history. It would represent the ancient tendency toward euhemerism. In like manner, Herodotus had tried to calculate the dates of a hypothetically historical Hercules,[51] while Plutarch sought to pin Osiris down as an ancient king of Egypt.[52] Even the Christian Eusebius (in his *Chronological Tables or Summary of All Histories*) supposed that Medea and Jason really existed and dated them 780 years after the Patriarch Abraham. Ganymede and Perseus were historical figures too, living some six centuries after Abraham. Why did the Christians bother trying to anchor Jesus in recent history? For the same reason that, according to Elaine Pagels's keen insight,[53] the orthodox opposed the spiritual resurrection appearances of Jesus and preferred a version in which he showed up in the objective flesh to name apostles and give commands. As Arthur Drews had already posited,[54] the urgency for historicizing Jesus was the need of a consolidating institution for an authoritative figurehead who had appointed successors and set policy (exactly the advantage of orthodoxy over subjectivistic Gnosticism according to Irenaeus, a true company man). It was exactly the logic whereby competing churches fabricated legends of their founding by this or that apostle: the apostle (or Jesus) could not be much older than the organization for which he is being appropriated as founder and authority.

All this implies it is utterly pointless even to ask whether there was sufficient time for legends to grow up around Jesus. Sufficient time—from *when*? It is anybody's guess when the tiny mutation of an honorific epithet of some Near Eastern dying-and-rising god took over as his name (as the Vedic Rudra became too holy or dangerous to say, and

---

[51]Veyne, *Did the Greeks Believe in Their Myths?* p. 32.

[52]Plutarch *Isis and Osiris* 13.

[53]Elaine Pagels, *The Gnostic Gospels* (New York: Random House, 1979), chap. 1, "The Controversy over Christ's Resurrection: Historical Event or Symbol?" pp. 3-27.

[54]Arthur Drews, *The Christ Myth*, 3rd ed., trans. C. DeLisle Burns (Amherst, N.Y.: Prometheus, 1998), pp. 271-72. Cf. Burton L. Mack, *The Lost Gospel: The Book of Q and Christian Origins* (San Francisco: HarperSanFrancisco, 1993), p. 207: "the myths of origin were written and imagined as having happened at a recent time and in a specific place." Also Veyne, *Did the Greeks Believe in Their Myths?* p. 76: "Myth, this authorless 'it is said' that is confused with the truth, was reinterpreted as a historical or cultural memory which, starting with the eyewitnesses, would be handed down from generation to generation."

worshipers began to invoke him as "Siva," "Auspicious One").[55] Some god or savior was henceforth known as "Jesus," "Savior," and Christianity was off and running. The savior would eventually be supplied sayings borrowed from Christian sages, Jewish rabbis and Cynics, and clothed in a biography drawn from the Old Testament. It is futile to object that monotheistic Jews would never have held truck with pagan godlings. We know they did in the Old Testament, though Ezekiel didn't like it much. And we know that first-century Judaism was not the same as Yavneh-era Judaism. There was no normative mainstream Judaism before Yavneh. And, as Margaret Barker has argued, there is every reason to believe that ancient Israelite beliefs, including polytheism, continued to survive despite official interdiction, from before the time of Josiah and Deuteronomy.[56] Barker suggests that the first Jesus worshipers understood Jesus to be the Old Testament Yahweh, the Son of God Most High, or El Elyon, head of the Israelite pantheon from time immemorial. When he spoke of or to his Father, he meant El Elyon. And, according to Geo Widengren,[57] this ancient Yahweh was celebrated as a dying-and-rising god. When early Christians gave the Easter shout, "The Lord is risen!" they were only repeating the ancient acclamation, "Yahweh lives!" (Ps 18:46), and they meant the same thing by it.

Bultmann, despite his disdain for the Christ-Myth theory, came perilously near to it when he argued that we know the *Das* of Jesus but not the *Was*.[58] Maybe the *Was* was a myth, not a man. For if we are that short on historical content, it begins to look as if there never was any.

[55]W. J. Wilkins, *Hindu Mythology, Vedic and Puranic*, 2nd ed. (Calcutta: Thacker, Spink and Co., 1882; reprint, Calcutta: Rupa and Co., 1989), p. 266. In a hymn from the White Yajur Veda addressed to Rudra: "Thou art gracious [Siva] by name." Mahadev Chakravarti, *The Concept of Rudra Siva Through the Ages*, 2nd rev. ed. (Dehli: Motilal Banarsidass, 1994), p. 28: "The name Siva is euphemistic and is used as an attributive epithet not particularly of Rudra, but of several other Vedic deities. One of the earliest uses of Siva as a proper name of Rudra is found in the *Svetasvatara Upanisad*, in which the beginning of the cult of Rudra-Siva was traced."

[56]Margaret Barker, *The Great Angel: A Study of Israel's Second God* (Louisville, Ky.: Westminster John Knox Press, 1992).

[57]Geo Widengren, "Early Hebrew Myths and Their Interpretation," in S. H. Hooke, *Myth, Ritual, and Kingship: Essays on the Theory and Practice of Kingship in the Ancient Near East and in Israel* (New York: Oxford University Press, 1958), pp. 149-203.

[58]Rudolf Bultmann, *Theology of the New Testament*, trans. Kendrick Grobel, Scribner Studies in Contemporary Theology (New York: Scribner's, 1955), 2:66.

Might there still have been a historical Jesus who, however, has been irretrievably lost behind the stained glass curtain of his own glorification? Indeed. But I should think the burden of proof lies with the one who would affirm such a Jesus.

RESPONSE TO ROBERT M. PRICE

John Dominic Crossan

Situated on the foothills of the Drakensberg west of Durban, the city of Pietermaritzburg is the capital of the province of KwaZulu-Natal in South Africa. On Church Street a bronze statue of Mohandas Karamchand Gandhi (1869–1948) faces towards the City Hall and proclaims: "my life is my message." This "Statue of Hope" was erected, as its inscription states, to mark "the centenary of the event on the night of 7 June 1893 when M. K. Gandhi was forcibly removed from a train compartment at the Pietermaritzburg station because of discrimination based on race. 'My active non-violence began from that date' (Mahatma Gandhi)."

There is also a plaque inside the city's railroad station which cites Gandhi's reply to a question about his life's most creative experiences. He describes that incident when, despite his first-class ticket, he was forced by a white objection off the Durban-Charlestown train at nightfall as "one experience that changed the course of my life." From Pietermaritzburg "the train steamed away leaving me shivering in the cold. Now the creative experience comes there. I was afraid for my very life. I entered the dark waiting-room. There was a white man in the room. I was afraid of him. What was my duty? I asked myself. Should I go back to India, or should I go forward, with God as my helper and face whatever was in store for me? I decided to stay and suffer. My active non-violence began from that date."

Inaugural event in 1893, autobiographical comment in 1938, city-statue in 1993, rail-station plaque in 1998. And recall what happened to India and South Africa in between. But do you think there was any mention of Gandhi's detrainment in *The Natal Witness* for Wednesday, 8 June 1893? Was anyone watching, noticing, recording that constitutive moment? Does anyone ever recognize mustard seeds?

My response will not take up the multiple items mentioned in Price's essay, because I simply agree with vast swaths of them. But I still have a few very important negatives.

First of all, incident after incident in the life and death of Jesus have indeed been articulated through earlier biblical models and/or Greco-Roman types. As Price acknowledges, I argued that in great detail with regard to the execution and resurrection in *The Cross That Spoke*. But watching that very process convinced me of the opposite conclusion from his own.

Second, the hero typology Price mentions is also at work with Jesus, but that no more negates his historical existence than the similar investment for Augustus negates that emperor's historical identity. One example. The virginal or with-no-intercourse conception of Jesus exalts this child over any predestined child in either Jewish tradition, with its intercourse between aged and/or infertile parents, and any predestined child in Greco-Roman culture with its intercourse between a human and a divine parent. "Virginal conception" is a theological claim about Jesus and not a biological claim about Mary and the only thing sillier or sadder than taking "virginal conception" literally is opposing it literally. It is the claim expressed in that parable that is worth faith or at least debate.

Third, the dying-rising gods have nothing to do with the resurrection of Jesus—at least not for Paul. He comes from a basis in Pharisaic Judaism to announce that the general resurrection has *already begun* with that of Jesus—that is why he can argue in 1 Corinthians 15:12-20 that no Jesus resurrection means no general resurrection; no general resurrection means no Jesus resurrection. They stand or fall together for Paul, and he could never even imagine that "resurrection" is some special privilege for Jesus on the analogy of a dying-rising divinity.

Finally, if I may use the term "Jesus-parable" rather than the more prejudicial "Christ-Myth," what if Jesus exists *only* as do the prodigal son and the good Samaritan? Presuming no early Christian intention to deceive, what if we have a purely parabolical Jesus and not an historical Jesus? What would be lost to Christianity? *Only the incarnation*, the in-flesh-ment, the claim that the character of God is revealed in the factual life of a historical person and not in the fictional life of a parabolic person. Only, in other words, the heart of Christianity itself. If Jesus were only a parable, one could simply deny its actual human possibility. One could reply: a lovely story but nobody could ever live nonviolent resistance even unto martyrdom. But what a human person has done can be done, and can be done by others as well. Or, as Gandhi said in that overture, "my life is my message." Or, as John did not say, "God so loved the world that God sent us a story."

My main purpose in this response, however, is not so much to argue negatively against Price's position as to explain, positively, what persuades me of my opposing viewpoint. I have two arguments, one minor and external, the other major and internal.

The first argument is from a convergence between one late first-century text from the Jewish historian Josephus (*Jewish Antiquities* 18.63-64) and one early second-century text from the Roman historian Tacitus (*Annals* 15.44). And, by the way, Price's comment, "Let me leapfrog the tiresome debate over whether the *Testimonium Flavianum* is authentic" is not an acceptable scholarly comment as far as I am concerned.

Both those authors agree on four sequential points. First, there was a *movement* started by Jesus or Christ. Second, there was an *execution* by Pilate. Third, there was a *continuation* despite that attempt to end it. Fourth, there is still an ongoing movement of "Christians." That is the external argument, and I deem it minor because one could argue—but I would not—that both those authors were just copying uncritically from Christian sources. I think, on the other hand, that they were expressing common knowledge about "Christians" as followers of "Christ"—like Platonists of Plato, et cetera, et cetera.

The second argument is internal and major for me. It is why I am historically convinced that Jesus existed as a still quite reconstructable historical figure. What strikes me most powerfully about Jesus is that—*even or especially within the New Testament itself*—there is a glaring discrepancy between his first (past) and second (future) coming, between incarnation and apocalypse, between the Jesus who announced and lived nonviolent resistance based on the very character of God (Matthew 5:38-48 // Luke 6:27-36) and the Jesus who will return and wade through slaughter to that magnificent consummation in Revelation 21.

Furthermore, it is not as if that apocalyptic transformation were suddenly added on at the very end of the New Testament. Even within the Gospel versions themselves there is a steady escalation of threats from Jesus, a steady incline in punitive and avenging aspects to his discourse. It seems that the more a Gospel version derives from discrimination or persecution, the more violent is the rhetoric of Jesus within it. In case after case, the same unit of tradition from, say, Mark or Q is more violently threatening in Matthew, Luke or John. This process is all the more evident when one accepts—as I do—the interdependence of those Gospel versions. Here are a few examples.

One example. In Mark 6:11 Jesus advises this response to rejection: "If any place will not welcome you and they refuse to hear you, as you leave, shake off the dust that is on your feet as a testimony against them." That and no more. But the parallel version in Q/Matthew 10:14-15; 11:20-24; Luke 10:10-15 is replete with threats of punishment:

> But whenever you enter a town and they do not welcome you, go out into its streets and say, "Even the dust of your town that clings to our feet, we wipe off in protest against you. Yet know this: the kingdom of God has come near." I tell you, on that day it will be more tolerable for Sodom than for that town. Woe to you, Chorazin! Woe to you, Bethsaida! For if the deeds of power done in you had been done in Tyre and Sidon, they would have repented long ago, sitting in sackcloth and ashes. But at the judgment it will be more tolerable for Tyre and Sidon than for you. And you, Capernaum, will you be exalted to heaven? No, you will be brought down to Hades.

Another example. Q/Matthew 8:12; Luke 13:28 has a warning that "there will be weeping and gnashing of teeth when you see Abraham and Isaac and Jacob and all the prophets in the kingdom of God, and you yourselves thrown out." But Matthew creates five more examples of that punitive threat at the end of various parables (Matthew 13:42, 50; 22:13; 24:51; 25:30).

Such examples could be multiplied so that Jesus' own injunction against violence to one's enemies (on the model of God) becomes steadily negated on his own lips across the growth of the Gospel versions themselves. None of this negates, for me, the terrible human consequences for evil. But, as I understand Jesus, those internal consequences from evil should not be described as external punishments from God. Divine punishment, forgiveness and mercy are simply bad theology for the fact that there are consequences for what we do, there is always the possibility of changing what we do, and there is a time before it is too late to change.

It is, in summary, that clash between the nonviolent historical Jesus and the violent apocalyptic Jesus that convinces me that the former was an actual and factual person. If those earliest Christians were inventing him as a parable person, they would not have needed to invent two divergent parable persons. What they needed to do was to invent a nonhistorical Jesus, namely that violent and apocalyptic Jesus, who would return soon and rescue them (us) from their (our) inability to live by, with and like that historical Jesus.

RESPONSE TO ROBERT M. PRICE

Luke Timothy Johnson

Robert M. Price gets Jesus to the vanishing point by the simple expedient of denying all the evidence that makes him visible. He concludes his essay by proposing that only a myth, not a historical figure supports Christian faith. If there was a historical Jesus, "irretrievably lost behind the stained glass curtain of his own glorification," Price asserts, "the burden of proof lies with the one who would affirm such a Jesus."

Although I would not adopt his phrasing—"stained glass curtain" is a bit strained—I do not disagree that the burden of proof lies with those affirming the figure of Jesus as a specific historical character. But I think the burden of proof has been met well enough to counter Price's own act of historical prestidigitation.

I find responding to his essay difficult because, although I do not agree with his conclusion, I share Price's unease with the manner in which Christian apologists, as well as some critics of Christianity, have too easily made assertions about the historical Jesus. Readers of my own contribution in this volume will recognize the severe limitations I place on the ability of grown-up history to speak of Jesus.

I especially appreciate Price's candid statement of methodological principles, and his willingness to follow those principles where he thinks they lead. He recognizes that in a volume such as this one, his essay will stand out as "controversial," and he rightly wishes his argument to be taken seriously and not answered in terms of "tired stereotypes."

In the spirit of sober historiography, then, I take up some aspects of his argument, beginning with his statement of principles. As my own essay makes clear, I agree completely with three of his premises. I agree that historiography is necessarily a revisionist art and that the consensus of historians does not indicate anything more than the social construction of reality. I agree that the principle of analogy is important for any historical inquiry; thus I state that the historical study of Jesus must proceed on exactly the same basis as the study of Napoleon or Caesar. Price does well also to note that the principle of analogy has its limits and cannot by itself exclude the unexpected things that do occur in human experience—children sprout horns and saints have stigmata. But analogy nudges us toward the more probable explanation in any specific case.

Two of Price's methodological premises are more questionable, and in some ways, go hand in hand. He first erects the criterion of dissimilarity into the supreme test for Jesus traditions, ignoring the criterion that is of even greater significance, namely that of multiple attestation (and what I call in my essays points of convergence among sources). Although he acknowledges that there are logical problems with dissimilarity, he quickly dismisses concern about these problems as a failure of nerve among those who fear its ability to consume all putative Jesus traditions, without carefully taking into account the places where dissimilarity actually yields something historically significant.

Price's second problematic premise is not really a premise or methodological principle at all, but another way of asserting the primacy of analogy. The "ideal type" is nothing else than an appeal to a preexistent pattern to explain the appearance of something that (by Price's reckoning) lacks any historically specific cause. Thus, if all positive evidence for a specific figure named Jesus as the source for the movement that arose in his name is eliminated, then the shape of that movement must be explained by the mythic pattern of "dying-and-rising gods."

In short, Price uses the criterion of dissimilarity to demolish any trace of specific evidence for a historically discernible figure named Jesus, and then appeals to analogy/ideal type to account for the rise of the Christ cult.

Price knows that his approach has a long history of its own, and he cheerfully acknowledges that for many, it is considered one of "extreme, even crackpot, theories." But he does not examine the reasons why such appeals to the ideal type of dying-and-rising gods came to be so regarded by sober historians. It was not, as Price intimates, out of a failure of nerve among the apologetically inclined. Rather, it was the failure of such theories to adequately account for the specific character of the Christian movement and its cult figure, as well as the stubborn resistance of certain historical facts to being wished away.

Two interrelated historical facts require explanation. The first is the sudden appearance of a cult devoted not to a "dying-and-rising god" but to a "crucified and raised Messiah." The Christian movement did not exist before Jesus, and when it appeared across the Mediterranean world of the first century, the "Lord" who was believed to be present in the cult worship was not an Egyptian or Persian deity, but a failed Jewish Messiah who was executed under Roman authority in the time of Tiberius. In short, appeal to an "ideal type" fails to account for the specific contours of the religion. The second historical fact is the composition of at least twenty-seven distinct compositions within a fifty year period by members of this religious movement, all of which, despite their diversity of literary genre, social setting and theological perspective, have the same Jesus as their point of focus, and the same generative matrix, namely the death and resurrection of the human person Jesus. Such highly specific historical phenomena do not arise out of generalized social conditions, psychological laws or religious types. Their necessary and sufficient cause is the death and (proclaimed) exaltation of Jesus.

There is not space in this short response to take up in detail Price's demolition of the evidence concerning Jesus as a historical figure. Partly this is due to the difficulty of demonstrating the presence of an object to someone who insists that whatever you bring forward as evidence cannot count. Partly it is due to the difficulty of the evidence itself—here again, while I am sympathetic to Price's resistance to easy affirmation concerning history, I think he goes much too far in the direction of historical skepticism. But I do want to make three simple observations.

First, the outsider evidence concerning Jesus is more significant than Price allows. He dismisses the passage concerning Jesus from Josephus's *Jewish Antiquities* 18, against the very careful arguments of scholars such as John Meier. But he does not consider the passage in *Jewish Antiquities* 20, where Josephus refers to James, "the brother of Jesus who was called Christ." Nor does he mention the important passage in Tacitus *Annals* 15. These references are particularly important because they are, in all probability, not derived from knowledge of the New Testament, but from observation, reports and rumors. Such notices—and one can add Lucian's *Peregrinus* 11-13—do not describe the cult of a dying-and-rising god, but a superstition based on a "crucified sophist."

Second, Price's effort to remove evidence of Jesus from Paul's letters amounts to an unconvincing tour de force. I mention only three examples. (1) He leaves aside the evidence in Paul's letters that Jesus was Jewish (Gal 4:4)—indeed, descended from David (Rom 1:3)—and was regarded as Messiah (Rom 9:4). (2) He does not acknowledge that Paul's reference to a command of the Lord concerning divorce in 1 Corinthians 7:10 provides multiple attestation for Jesus' prohibition of divorce in the Synoptic Gospels (Mk 10:2-8; Mt 5:31-32; 19:3-9; Lk 16:18) and shows how the criterion of dissimilarity—for all its problems—actually yields positive evidence concerning Jesus' teaching, for the very struggles found in Matthew and Paul to provide some exceptions to the command testify to its being a received tradition, and one contrary both to Greco-Roman and Jewish practice. (3) He does not recognize how Paul uses the proper name Jesus with specific reference to the human person: two noteworthy examples are Paul's statement in Romans 3:26, that God makes righteous the one who "shares the faith of Jesus" (*ton ek pisteos Iesou*; compare *to ek pisteos Abraham* in Rom 4:16), and his declaration in 1 Corinthians 12:3, that no one speaking in the spirit of God says "cursed be Jesus" (*anathema Iesous*).

Third, Price spends a considerable amount of space showing how stories told about Jesus appear to be based on, contain elements of and provide allusions to stories in Torah. This is an exercise that has been carried out repeatedly since initiated in 1835 by the first great historical Jesus critic, D. F. Strauss. No responsible student of the New Testament would deny the shaping effect of the symbols of Torah on the story of Jesus—not least on that part of the story presenting the greatest scandal, his passion and death. But most responsible critics take seriously two further realities: (1) For the most part, there is considerable difference between the Gospel passage and the texts of Torah to which it alludes. However cunningly John (chapter 6) suggests a link between Jesus' multiplication of the loaves and walking on the water in the season of Passover, for example, there is actually little resemblance between John's account and the Exodus account of the people crossing the sea and the gift of Manna in the wilderness. (2) More important, one could read Torah forever and never reach the specific portrait of Jesus as a suffering, dying and exalted Messiah such as we find in the canonical Gospels. It is not that Isaiah 52–53 provided the "ideal type" of a Messiah to which the Christian Evangelists conformed Jesus, but that the specific character of Jesus' death and resurrection stimulated first a rereading of Isaiah 52–53, and then the use of its imagery in the Gospels.

Price provides a stimulating perspective on the figure of Jesus by eliminating specific historical evidence found in the sources that is pertinent to the subject and replacing it with an appeal to a Joseph Campbell–like universal archetype. His writing lacks nothing in clarity or color. But it does lack the capacity to convince any but those who despair of history altogether that his alternative serves to account for the shape of the Christian movement or the compositions that it inspired.

RESPONSE TO ROBERT M. PRICE

James D. G. Dunn

Gosh! So there are still serious scholars who put forward the view that the whole account of Jesus' doings and teachings are a later myth foisted on an unknown, obscure historical figure. The Arthur Drews and G. A. Wells versions have been responded to sufficiently, one would have thought. But, no! Robert Price raises the banner once again. "It is quite likely that there never was any historical Jesus"—the term, "historical Jesus," being used once again for an actual historical figure, rather than the historian's reconstruction. For Price the historian can find nothing, at most a *Das* without any *Was*.

He places prime value on the "principle of analogy." It works well with regard to the traditional question of miracle, though Price recognizes that the principle cannot be related solely to our own current experience, and that particularly in the ancient world many will have experienced miracles, that is, events that they could only understand as miracles. As I will note in my response to Bock, this could provide a perfectly viable explanation for the initial formulation of at least many of the miracles attributed to Jesus. Price extends the principle to the multiplication of the hadith attributed to Muhammad without taking any account of the evidence of the Gospel tradition that the teaching of Jesus was already in writing within about forty years of his (alleged) death (the consensus date for Mark's gospel), with a significant oral tradition already in circulation before that.

A second criterion is the familiar criterion of dissimilarity. Price takes up the early form-critical observation that for the Jesus tradition to have been preserved it must have been of some pragmatic value, and he uses it to make the criterion of dissimilarity "all devouring." If every bit and piece of the Jesus tradition had a home in the early church, then "*all* must be denied to Jesus by the criterion of dissimilarity." Such an extension of the criterion of dissimilarity simply undermines what value it has. It is so a priori obvious that an influential teacher's teaching would influence his disciples and shape their own teaching and lives in substantial degree that the dissimilarity criterion does not help us to distinguish the one from the other. And that is the point of the criterion. It was framed not so much to determine authenticity as to provide confidence in authenticity. It did not rule out the authenticity of sayings that failed the test (too like the teaching of the early church); it simply indicated that the quester for the historical Jesus could not demonstrate the saying's authenticity, could not be confident that it did go back to Jesus. The distinction is quite a fine one, but important, and it undermines Price's use of the criterion. This is all the more important if we follow so-called third questers in looking for a Jewish Jesus, rather than a distinctively non-Jewish Jesus, and for a Jesus who almost certainly did influence his followers rather than one whose mission and message left no discernable mark on his followers and those who became the first believers in him.

I will say little more on the other three principles which Price frames. On the principle of the ideal type perhaps all I need point out is that any motivation to conform a man who lived recently to an ideal type of mythic hero (or whatever) most likely presupposes that the man in view had made a significant impact on at least some. The alternative—a man who recently lived but who made no lasting impact or had no influence of any significance—is, to say the least, far more implausible than almost any view that the New Testament Gospels contain (and are themselves) clear evidence of the impact made by the historical figure Jesus of Nazareth. This is always the fatal flaw with the "Jesus myth" thesis: the improbability of the total invention of a figure who had purportedly lived within the generation of the inventers, or the imposition of such an elaborate myth on some minor figure from Galilee. Price is content with the explanation that it all began "with a more or less vague savior myth." Sad, really.

Otherwise, with the other "principles"—"consensus is no criterion" and "scholarly 'conclusions' must be tentative and provisional"—I have no particular quarrel.

Where I begin to become irritated by Price's thesis, as with those of his predecessors, is his ignoring what everyone else in the business regards as primary data and his readiness to offer less plausible hypotheses to explain other data that inconveniences his thesis. Why no mention of 1 Corinthians 15:3—generally reckoned to be an account of the faith that Paul received when he was converted, that is, within two or three years of the putative events—"that Christ died. . . ." Why no reference to Paul's preaching of Christ *crucified* (1 Cor 1:23), his preaching as openly portraying Christ as crucified (Gal 3:1)? How can Price actually assert that "we should never guess from the Epistles that Jesus died in any particular historical or political context," when it is well enough known that crucifixion was a Roman political method of execution characteristically for rebels and slaves? I could go on at some length— "seed of David" (Rom 1:3), "born under the law" (Gal 4:4), "Christ did not please himself" (Rom 15:3). Yet Price is able to assert that "the Epistles . . . do not evidence a recent historical Jesus," a ludicrous claim that simply diminishes the credibility of the arguments used in support.

The implausible arguments are almost as disappointing. The name "Jesus" is hardly to be classified as "the name that is above every name" (Phil 2:9-10), so it hardly provides evidence that the name Jesus first emerged in relation to the putative exaltation of some previously unknown figure. On the contrary, it confirms that Jesus was the well enough known name of the one now widely recognized (in Pauline circles) as the Messiah. As often noted, the fact that Christ was more or less a proper name (Jesus Christ) by the time of Paul (within twenty to twenty-five years of Jesus' death) must indicate that messianic status had already been ascribed to this Jesus for such a long time that the titular significance of Christ (Messiah) had largely faded. To argue both that the reference to James as "the brother of the Lord" (Gal 1:19—an episode which can be dated to 35 or 36) need only mean that James was a member of a missionary brotherhood and that "the commands of the Lord" (1 Cor 7:14; 9:14) might be "midrashically derived inferences from Old Testament commands of Adonai in the Torah," despite the clear reference points in the Jesus tradition, indicates an argument that is scraping the barrel and has lost its self-respect. Nor is it at all fair to dismiss the probability of various allusions to Jesus tradition in the Pauline letters, as though in each case Paul were trying to settle a question by appeal to the words of Jesus. Not so. Most are simply like the echoes and allusions that a well-read Shakespearean scholar might make to the words of the bard in lectures or letters without always being fully aware of the bard's own words.

I should make at least passing reference also to the Acts of the Apostles, which is blithely ignored by Price. There is no need to argue for a high level of historical value in all the information offered in Acts about the beginnings of Christianity. It is sufficient to observe that Acts gives good evidence of beliefs about Jesus' mission, life and death, which almost certainly were circulating among the earliest Christians through the middle decades of the first century.

When it comes to the Gospels, Price's argument is really quite unbalanced. There is a lot to be said for the view that many of the Gospel narratives are a kind of haggadic midrash on the Old Testament. But such data are open to a variety of interpretations as to their origin. There is no necessary implication that the Gospel narratives were created solely from the Old Testament material. On the contrary it is entirely possible (much the more likely, I would say) that the data can be explained by the hypothesis that early Christian narrators were telling stories about events in Jesus' mission but were doing so in order to bring out such Old Testament echoes and parallels as they discerned.

Where the evidence is ambiguous, one way forward, which Price totally ignores, is to take account of the data in the Jesus tradition that are not readily explained by creation from Old Testament precedents and building blocks—a modest application, I suppose, of the first criterion of dissimilarity. There are quite a few of these. For example, that the single main motif of Jesus' preaching and teaching was the kingdom of God. Which Old Testament prophet is that modelled on? Or Jesus' apparent self-reference as "the Son of Man"—very difficult to explain from such Old Testament precedents as there are, or from a subsequent Son of Man christology (markedly lacking in the early churches). Or the quite unheard-of introduction of several of Jesus' sayings with a prefixed "Amen." What was the inspiration to portray Jesus as a "parabolist" and a successful exorcist? The most obvious answer is that he was remembered as such, his parables treasured and passed around groups of believers, and his exorcisms well-known beyond their ranks. To ignore such data or to be content with much less plausible possibilities in the face of such probabilities is a tactic of the Christ-Myth proponents, but not one that does them much credit or gives their thesis much credibility.

Similarly the appeal to the confused dates for Jesus' crucifixion as similar to the occasional speculations about the "historical" Hercules or an "historical" Osiris, an appeal that, once again, ignores the much more substantial data of the New Testament writers, writing within a generation or two of Jesus himself, simply smacks of some desperation.

In short, if Price's essay is a true expression of the state of health of the Jesus-myth thesis, I can't see much life in it. His essay would be better retitled "The Jesus Myth—a Thesis at Vanishing Point."

RESPONSE TO ROBERT M. PRICE

Darrell L. Bock

As Price himself notes, his position is the most controversial of the options presented about Jesus. If his position is correct, then an incredible amount of effort has been expended throughout the centuries to understand a figure who should be relegated to the realm of myth alone. Price seemingly explains his view by saying if there were no Jesus, human desires are such that he must have been created to meet those needs. In fact, at one point in the essay, Price posits that Jesus might have existed, but not in a way that left any real deposit of his memory, nor did the early church really care to remember him as he truly might have been. This lack of interest Price argues for is unlike most of history's greats, but for him Jesus' exalted story is like that of several other expressions of ancient religious hope. The key question is where the starting point for any such move to exalt Jesus resides: in historical roots or in the creative desire of humans to reach for God.

I want to first focus on the framework for this discussion because Price begins by arguing that the "historical" principle of analogy alone is enough to disqualify what is presented about Jesus. Price's definition of reality on which this idea is based reflects a very circumscribed, selectively Western Enlightenment mindset. Many people do believe there is a Creator who acts in the world. Granted, being able to show it is a debated point, but the possible existence and activity of God cannot be ruled out by a kind of fiat. When Price speaks of contemporary assessment standards, he excludes many of his counterparts' views because he rules out that God or any other transcendent spirits, for that matter, exist in our world.

More importantly, this claim actually ignores many features we can consider historically, such as a figure's impact on his contemporaries or their testimonies that this impact is not a matter of myth. First-century Christian documents clearly claim this distinction, which means they are aware of the difference and reject a tie to myth for Jesus. This puts Jesus and his historical reality on the table. In addition, Price interestingly at times appeals to the testimony of revelations of a risen Lord who never seemingly existed. What was the first step to that explanation? Where did the impetus for a risen Lord come from? Did it come from an ex nihilo origin, from a very modest great-healer existence or something more profound? A modest origin seems very unlikely given the impact and descriptions we have of Jesus, even in nonbiblical sources. Price dismisses Josephus far too easily, but even more he ignores the fact that Jesus' Jewish opponents never argue that he did not exist. There seems to be an extant figure for the disputants on both sides of the Jewish-Christian debate. Thus, whether we look to Justin Martyr's *Dialogue with Trypho,* Josephus or what Tacitus and Suetonius describe in terms of the origins of the church, the idea that Jesus did not exist at all is historically quite unlikely.

From such general principles, Price moves to a discussion of orality. I agree with his observation that there is a range for orality in the ancient world: from quite disciplined to quite loose. This is what Dunn's essay covers as well. What we can see from our sources is that the Gospel tradition has an element of both fixity and flexibility. That direct evidence does not limit us to the all or next-to-nothing options that Price provides as our choices. Proceeding one saying at a time, as Price contends we should, is something many Jesus scholars have done, with most having confidence that many sayings do go back to Jesus even on standards that require corroboration. Even the Jesus Seminar saw around 20 percent of the Jesus material as going back to Jesus, using a very skeptical employment of such principles.

Price's handling of the criteria of authenticity, such as the criterion of dissimilarity, has the same "heads I win; tails you lose" tone that much of his essay carries. Analogy plus dissimilarity is what is commended, but the search for other criteria was dismissed. No, what made scholars look for principles to go with dissimilarity was the historical observation that great figures do interact with and reflect their cultures even if they do so in creative ways. (An exceptional Jesus, or the exceptional in any other historical figure, is not always the only facet to such a figure.) Such a culturally displaced figure makes no sense (even as a creation!). This criterion as the key does too much. It detaches Jesus far too much from his context.

The main part of Price's essay is the defense of the Jesus-as-myth model. Price makes several claims in this section: (1) There is no miracle-working Jesus in the secular sources. Now to make this claim, he must dismiss the evidence that Josephus gives *as well as* the Jewish tradition, which marked Jesus as a sorcerer—evidence he does not discuss but that shows up in major second-century sources that debate Jesus.[1] Obviously we disagree on Josephus, but the *Jewish Antiquities* 18 text does not stand alone, nor does he note how there is an allusion to the "Christ" in *Jewish Antiquities* 20.200, which suggests that Josephus had discussed the Christ earlier in his work. This points to the likelihood that *Jewish Antiquities* 18.63-64 was a part of Josephus's material. In sum, Price's claim that there is no miraculous Jesus in the sources does not reflect claims that Jesus did unusual works (Josephus) or that he was a sorcerer (elements of Jewish tradition).

(2) Price argues that the New Testament Epistles do not evidence a historical Jesus. Where is the proof of this claim? Look at what it ignores. The Last Supper tradition (called a possible interpolation by Price, but Paul did not write this tradition) is assumed in practically all early Christian communities, not just the ones that originated due to Paul's preaching (see the four Gospels, Jude and even the *Didache*). It also shows up in the practice of memory in the church. What do we say about the resurrection tradition Paul defends in 1 Corinthians 15? This tradition gives little evidence of being made up since it mentions appearances to Cephas (Peter), and yet there is no detailed, "created" story

---

[1]G. Stanton, "Jesus of Nazareth: A Magician and a False Prophet Who Deceived God's People," in *Jesus of Nazareth Lord and Christ: Essays on the Historical Jesus and New Testament Christology* (Grand Rapids: Eerdmans, 1994), pp. 164–80, details the relevant ancient texts (b. *Sanhedrin* 43a; Justin Martyr *Dialogue with Trypho* 69).

of such an appearance. This is an amazing fact if the church was indeed making things up as easily as Price suggests. The tradition of Romans 1:2-4 assumes the death and resurrection of an earthly Jesus. Where do we get Jesus according to Price? We must run to his frequently invoked risen-Lord revelations or appeal to midrash for its roots. We must even posit Jesus as a postmortem name! I repeat, then, why is there not a challenge from the Jews that Jesus never existed? When we can dismiss these portraits, we are playing with evidence, playing "heads I win; tails you lose." Even more incredulous is Price's view that James, the brother of the Lord, is not evidence of Jesus' existence. Would not people in the region have known of James's origin and challenge such a claim if it had been fabricated? Price argues for James's appellation being shared by a missionary brotherhood. This is very unlikely given that such an association could then pertain to hundreds of disciples. Paul also cites Jesus in 1 Corinthians 7. And Jesus' teaching runs through units of Romans 12–16. Jesus is far more present in the Epistles than Price suggests.

(3) Price maintains that a key appeal for the Jesus story is rooted in the parallels that exist with other religions on important themes, especially dying-and-rising gods. This approach has been common since the rise of the history of religions school in the late nineteenth and early twentieth centuries. There is no core experience of a resurrected Jesus, just the expression of hope rooted in a human desire to experience God. However, is this Jesus who challenges the world about sin and calls for suffering and rejection by the world a god of human fabrication made to make us feel good? Is Jesus really just like the Attis analogy or some other type of ancient religious conglomeration, rising from the ashes like a phoenix from hero myths? A closer look at such parallels shows they are not really parallel. Attis in the most popular form has a very limited "resurrection." His body will not be corrupted (i.e., not decay), his hair grows, and he can move one finger (Arnobius *Against the Nations* 5.7)! As Klauck, a scholar of Greco-Roman religion, says, "One can scarcely call this a 'resurrection' of Attis."[2]

---

[2]Hans-Josef Klauck, *The Religious Context of Early Christianity: A Guide to Greaco-Roman Religions* (Edinburgh: T & T Clark, 2000), p. 122. A look at Klauck's survey of these ancient

So again a question emerges: Where does this spontaneous genera-tion of Jesus come from? Why create him if many of these elements already exist in the culture? It is far more likely that something caused this particular set of emphases, as well as the distinctives, that would not have been a part of the kind of religion humans would have created. Remember we are not dealing with a figure who was centuries removed from the era in which he is placed, but a largely contemporary figure. This is another feature that makes Jesus different from these other ex-pressions of religious hope.

The hero archetype also suffers from a lack of specifics about the origins of its characteristic traits. Where do the twenty-two different elements come from? Are they an amalgamation of themes from dispa-rate sources? Would these have been in play in a Jewish setting? Beyond this problem, some elements within the list are suspect: unusual birth (pretty vague, generic category), reared by foster parents (does this par-allel Jesus when it is not clear how much Joseph raised him?), no details of childhood (by the way, Luke 2:40-52 is an exception) and marries a princess (I do not believe the accounts of Mary Magdalene make her a princess). These supposed associations are just too loose to count for anything.

These problems in Price's presentation show that the path of the other essays is far more helpful in thinking about who Jesus is and how to discuss him historically.

---

religions as a whole shows how they really do not apply as the foundation for such ideas in Christianity.

2

JESUS AND
THE CHALLENGE OF
COLLABORATIVE
ESCHATOLOGY

John Dominic Crossan

"God made you without you. . . . he doesn't justify you without you."
AUGUSTINE, BISHOP OF HIPPO, *SERMON* 169.13 (416)

"St. Augustine says, 'God, without us, will not;
as we, without God, cannot.'"
DESMOND TUTU, ARCHBISHOP EMERITUS OF CAPE TOWN,
SERMON AT ALL SAINTS, PASADENA, CALIF. (1999)

PROLOGUE

The historical Jesus was *a Galilean Jew within Judaism within the Roman Empire.* That, for me, has always been the necessary methodological *matrix* rather than the unnecessary historical *background* for any discussion of that first-century figure. You can see that three-layer matrix, for example, in the subtitle to my book on *The Historical Jesus.* It is: *The Life of a Mediterranean Jewish Peasant.* Those three terms—and that specific sequence—were intended quite deliberately to emphasize, first, the Roman Empire, then the Jewish faith and finally the historical Jesus. That same triad and that same sequence reappears in the book's major divisions: part one, "Brokered Empire" (Rome); part two, "Embattled Brokerage" (Judaism); and part three, "Brokerless Kingdom" (Jesus).

The first step in my own methodological process does not begin with the words or deeds of Jesus himself from the earliest Christian data but—trying to imagine *as if* Jesus had never existed—I begin with the Roman Empire and the Jewish tradition in interaction with it. Furthermore, even from non-Christian sources, we can locate Jesus as a Galilean from the time Pilate ruled Judea—that is, as a Jew living in the territory of Herod Antipas between 26 and 36 C.E. So, bracketing Jesus initially (as best I can—with some integrity), I try to reconstruct the interaction between Roman imperialism and Jewish tradition in Antipas's Galilee by the mid-20s C.E.

Then, and only then, do I take the next step. What is, within my theory of sources, relationships and dates, the earliest layer of the Jesus tradition, and does that layer cohere within the matrix already established in the first step? For example, in terms of the life of Jesus, I accept the existence of the *Q Gospel* and the independence of the *Gospel of Thomas*. For me, therefore, the *Common Sayings Tradition*—the thirty-seven units common to both those Gospels—is the earliest identifiable large-scale stratum of Jesus sayings. (If I am wrong on those presuppositions, my reconstruction is methodologically invalidated. But, of course, if I am right, then any reconstruction that denies them, is also methodologically invalid.)

I am also utterly aware that "early" does not guarantee accuracy and that "later" does not prove inaccuracy, but if "early" fails, we must then explain if and why "later" succeeds. Unless, of course, the traditional Jesus has nothing at all to do with the historical Jesus and any linkage is lost forever. I explained that process with greater detail a decade ago in chapter ten on "The Problem of Methodology" in *The Birth of Christianity*, pages 139-49.

My purpose here is not to repeat the arguments of those pages but, presuming their validity—at least for me and at least until I see a more persuasive alternative—to outline as clearly and fully as I can how I now see Jesus as a Galilean Jew within Judaism within the Roman Empire as those two traditions confronted one another in the territories of Herod Antipas in the 20s of that first common-era century.

THE FIFTH AND FINAL KINGDOM OF EARTH

In his *Works and Days* from around the year 700 B.C.E., the poet Hesiod took a rather jaundiced view of human history. It was composed, he wrote, of five generations, eras, ages, world-kingdoms or people types which had steadily declined from the Golden and Silver Ages, through the Bronze and Heroic Ages, to his contemporary Iron Age in which, "strong of hand, one man will seek the city of another" and "right will be in the arm" (174-201). But half a millennium later, in the middle of the second century B.C.E., two very different visions of earth's fifth and final kingdom were proposed to the west and east of Hesiod's Greece. One was the imperial kingdom of Rome, the other was the eschatological kingdom of God.

THE IMPERIAL KINGDOM OF ROME

The fifth kingdom. Soon after 30 C.E., Caius Velleius Paterculus, legionary general and imperial administrator, wrote a two-volume *Compendium of Roman History* starting with the fall of Troy and ending around the year 29 C.E. As he begins his account of how the gods "exalted this great empire of Rome to the highest point yet reached on earth" to become "the empire of the world" (2.131), he gives us this quotation:

> Aemilius Sura says in his book on the chronology of Rome: "The Assyrians were the first of all races to hold world power, then the Medes, and after them the Persians, and then the Macedonians. Then through the defeat of Kings Philip and Antiochus, of Macedonian origin, followed closely upon the overthrow of Carthage, the world power passed to the Roman people." (1.6)

Aemilius Sura, otherwise unknown, penned that serene assertion of Rome's global imperialism sometime after 146 B.C.E. The first four kingdoms of world history had already come and gone, and now

Rome was the fifth, final and climactic kingdom of earth. There was, in other words, a certain inevitability, a certain manifest destiny in all of this.

The first century. Rome's next century, however, would see a hundred years of class struggle and social unrest culminating in twenty years of savage civil war. Then, on a serene Mediterranean afternoon, September 2, 31 B.C.E., it all ended out in the Ionian Sea off Cape Actium in northwestern Greece. It was the last great naval battle of antiquity, and never had so much been gained for so many by so little. With their forces sapped by a summer of disease, desertion and despair, Antony and Cleopatra fled to double suicide at Alexandria leaving their troops to survive and surrender as best they could.

The victorious Octavian, grandnephew and adopted son of the deified Julius Caesar, would soon be titled in Latin *Augustus*, the One-Who-Is-Divine, or in Greek *Sebastos*, the One-Who-Is-to-Be-Worshiped (from *sebomai*, to worship). Roman imperial theology was now incarnated in him and diffused outward from him. Immediately, the site of his own command tent on the Michalitsi foothills became sacred ground and its dedication was inscribed in large Latin uncials above the projecting line of thirty attack rams as a tithe from the conquered fleet of Anthony and Cleopatra.

Many of the great blocks of that inaugural Augustan inscription are still extant to the east of the tent-site platform and contain the basic structural sequence of Roman imperial theology as incarnated in Augustus: *Religion* → *War* → *Victory* → *Peace*. The "Imperator Caesar, Divi F" dedicates the monument to the sea-god Neptune and the war-god Mars in gratitude that the "war which he waged for the republic in this region" resulted in "victory" with the result of "peace established on land and sea."

By the way, the lapidary Latin of Augustus's first inscription on stone, *victoriam . . . pace parta terra marique*, reappears over forty years later in his final one on bronze at the gates of his Roman mausoleum as *terra marique parta victoriis pax*. You can summarize Roman imperial theology, therefore, in this mantric motto: peace through violent victory. And that program for global peace was incarnated first in Augustus, then in his dynasty and eventually in every Roman emperor.

Before Jesus existed, in other words, and even if Jesus never existed, there was a human being in that first century B.C.E. Mediterranean world with these titles: Divine, Son of God, God and God from God; Lord, Redeemer, Liberator and Savior of the World. As the Augustan poet Horace noted in his *Epistles*, Greco-Roman humans were normally deified for extraordinary gifts or transcendental benefits to the human race *but* only after their deaths. "Upon you [Augustus], however, while still living among us, we already bestow divine honors, set up altars to swear by in your name, and confess that nobody like you will arise hereafter or has ever arisen before now" (2.1). The human Augustus was divinity incarnate.

THE ESCHATOLOGICAL KINGDOM OF GOD

The adjective *eschatological* (from the Greek *eschata* or last things) refers to God's vision for that fifth or final kingdom of earth, for how the world would be run if God were its direct ruler (we might ask: what would a divine budget look like?). The *eschaton* denotes, in other words, the kingdom of God.

Eschatology is not about the destruction of the earth but about its transfiguration, not about the end of the world but about the end of evil, injustice, violence—and imperialism. I think of the *eschaton* as the Great Divine Clean-Up of the World. It is clear, I hope, that the kingdom of God is 100 percent political and 100 percent religious all together and inextricably intertwined at the same time. It is ultimately about who owns this world and how, therefore, it should be run.

The fifth kingdom. Daniel 7 begins with a dream-vision in which there is, once again, a sequence of four great empires—those of Babylonia, Medea, Persia and Greco-Macedonia. But those imperial powers are described not as human forces arising from the orderly land but as feral animals arising from the disorderly ocean. "I, Daniel, saw in my vision by night the four winds of heaven stirring up the great sea, and four great beasts came up out of the sea, different from one another" (Dan 7:2-3) and "these four great beasts [are] four kings [that] shall arise out of the earth" (Dan 7:17).

The Greco-Syrian Empire of the 160s B.C.E. is not even counted as another empire. It is but a subempire of Alexander's. It is only one of the horns of that Macedonian beast. It is, indeed, only "a little horn." (Dan 7:8). But then comes Daniel's vision of the fifth, final and climactic empire of earth, the eschatological kingdom of God.

The earthly empires are symbolized and personified as beasts from the depths of the disordered sea. The fifth and final kingdom is symbolized and personified as a human being from the ordered heights of heaven. As they were "like" eagle, bear, leopard or some ultra-animal, it is "like a son of man," that is, "like a human being." (As in English-language male chauvinism, *humanity* often appears as *mankind,* so, in Semitic-language male chauvinism, *human being* often appears as *man* or *son of man*.) But what is at stake in Daniel is this: the first four empires are inhuman beasts, only the fifth and final empire is truly human.

Just as those individual beast-like ones represent and contain an entire community, so also here, the individual human-like one represents and contains an entire community. Hence the world's climactic kingdom is first given to that "one like a human being" in heaven: "To him was given dominion and glory and kingship, that all peoples, nations, and languages should serve him. His dominion is an everlasting dominion that shall not pass away, and his kingship is one that shall never be destroyed" (Dan 7:14).

It is, however, given *in* heaven but *for* earth: "The kingship and dominion and the greatness of the kingdoms under the whole heaven shall be given to the people of the holy ones of the Most High; their kingdom shall be an everlasting kingdom, and all dominions shall serve and obey them" (Dan 7:27). The kingdom of God is given to "him" (Dan 7:14) for "them" (Dan 7:27). But, despite the confrontation between imperial kingdoms and eschatological kingdoms, Daniel's final kingdom is not specified in any great detail.

The first century. So there is still this question: how exactly is that final and eschatological kingdom of God different from the final and imperial kingdom of Rome? Each claimed to be divinely decreed, eternally mandated and transcendentally guaranteed. Each claimed to be universal and everlasting, to be unlimited by time and space. Each offered a magnificent vision for global peace here below on this earth. What then was the difference between them?

Here is at least one answer from the Jewish *Sibylline Oracles*, a type of eschatological prophecy that first Judaism and then Christianity borrowed from Rome and used against it:

> The earth will belong equally to all, undivided by walls or fences. It will then bear more abundant fruits spontaneously. Lives will be in common and wealth will have no division. For there will be no poor man there, no rich, and no tyrant, no slave. Further, no one will be either great or small anymore. No kings, no leaders. All will be on a par together. (2.319-24)

For that ultimate vision, by the way, the model is not modern expectations, democratic hopes or universal human rights. It is the extended family. God is *Householder*—named *Father*, with time-place prejudice in a patriarchal world—who must provide fairly and equitably for all the Earth-Family, who must insure that all have enough in the World-Home.

The program of Roman imperial theology was "Religion, War, Victory, Peace" or, more succinctly, "Peace Through Violent Victory." Was the program of Jewish eschatological theology exactly the same except that Yahweh replaced Jupiter, the Messiah replaced the Augustus and eschatological violence replaced imperial violence? Or was there to be an alternative program whose structural sequence was *Religion → Nonviolence → Justice → Peace?* Was there, beside and even against the Roman vision of "Peace Through Violent Victory," a Jewish vision of "Peace Through Nonviolent Justice"?

EMPIRE, ESCHATON AND A GALILEAN LAKE

Roman imperialism—or any other imperialism before or after it—is about ownership and control of this earth. If the eschatological kingdom of God is about heaven rather than earth, empire and eschaton can live happily together no matter how divergent their programmatic visions may be. But what happens if and when the eschatological kingdom of God is *from* heaven but *for* earth, is not *of* this earth but *on* it? What happens if the clash between them is about who owns this earth and how, therefore, our world is to be run? And, to be much more specific, what if those general and global questions focus on one very specific and local example? What if the question *who owns this lake?* becomes the focal point and chosen case for the question *who owns this world?* Finally, what happens when the God of the Jewish tradition proclaims in Leviticus 25:23 that "the land is mine; with me you are but aliens and tenants," and that tradition responds in Psalm 24:1 that "the earth is the Lord's and all that is in it, the world, and those who live in it"?

In the prologue of our coauthored 2001 book, *Excavating Jesus: Beneath the Stones, Behind the Texts*, Jonathan Reed and I asked these two questions: "Why did Jesus happen when he happened? Why then? Why there? Sharpen the question a little. Why did two popular movements, the Baptism movement of John and the kingdom movement of Jesus happen in territories ruled by Herod Antipas in the 20s of that first common-era century? Why not at another time? Why not in another place?"

I now add another and more specific question: Why is Jesus so often found around the Sea of Galilee, the Lake of Tiberias, the harp-shaped Lake Kinneret? In the concluding paragraph of his magnificent 1906 book *The Quest of the Historical Jesus*, Albert Schweitzer said of Jesus that "He comes to us as one unknown, without a name, as of old, by the lakeside, he came to those men who did not know who he was."[1] It is almost discourteous to interrupt that soaring peroration and ask: what was Jesus doing "of old, by the lakeside"? Why precisely there? Why precisely then?

Since Nazareth was Jesus' native village, and he was always called "Jesus of Nazareth," why this relocation in Matthew 4:13: "He left Nazareth and made his home in Capernaum by the sea" that is, by the inland Sea or Lake of Galilee? He moved not just from a very tiny village to a somewhat larger one but he moved from a hillside village to a lakeside one.

---

[1]Albert Schweitzer, *The Quest of the Historical Jesus*, trans. J. R. Coates, Susan Cupitt and John Bowden (Minneapolis: Fortress, 2001), p. 487.

Or again: why were Jesus' two most famous disciples closely connected with lakeside fishing villages. Mary was from Magdala, the most important town on the lake before Herod Antipas built Tiberias around 19 C.E. Its Hebrew name comes from *migdāl*, a tower, that is, presumably, a lighthouse. Its Greek name, *Tarichaeae,* means salted fish. Peter also came from one fishing village, Bethsaida (Jn 1:14), and then moved to another one at his wife's house in Capernaum (Mk 1:31). Think also of Philip and Andrew (Jn 1:14) or James and John (Mk 1:16). Jesus in Galilee is seldom far from lake and boat and net and fish. Why?

The imperial program of *Romanization by urbanization for commercialization* struck Galilee forcibly not under Herod the Great in the generation *before* John and Jesus but under his son Herod Antipas in the generation *of* John and Jesus. Herod the Great undertook world-class and state-of-the-art construction projects in creating the city Caesarea and its port Sebastos on the coast and in enlarging the plaza of the temple in Jerusalem to five football fields long and three across. But that was outside Galilee, and his three temples to Rome and Augustus were also all outside Galilee.

For whatever reason—be it punishment or prudence—Herod the Great controlled but did not Romanize Galilee. That project fell to Herod Antipas, but he also had a far wider ambition—a lifelong desire to be, like his father, the Rome-appointed King of the Jews, the *monarch* of the whole Jewish homeland and not the *tetrarch* of a mere part. And in that project he was to plan carefully and lengthily but also to fail ultimately and dismally. Think of that life as a drama of acute disappointment over six sequential acts.

The *first act* took place as Herod the Great was close to death. His will designated Antipas heir to his throne as King of the Jews. But then he changed his mind and designated Antipas's older brother Archelaus as heir to both title and kingdom. When Herod finally died in 4 B.C.E., both Antipas and Archelaus appeared before Caesar Augustus in Rome to plead their opposing cases. The Herodian family members preferred direct rule by a Roman governor but, failing that, they supported Antipas over Archelaus. Augustus, however, compromised on all sides. He gave half the Jewish homeland—Idumeaea, Judea and Samaria—to

Herod Archelaus but entitled him ethnarch (people ruler) and not monarch. He divided the rest between two tetrarchs (quarter rulers) with Herod Antipas getting Galilee and Peraea on either side of the Jordan and Herod Philip getting the far northern reaches of the country. Antipas began his rule sorely disappointed.

The *second act* began immediately as, in the words of Josephus's *Jewish War*, "Herod fortified Sepphoris to be the ornament of all Galilee, and called it Autocratoris" (18.27). *Autocrator* is the standard Greek translation for the Latin term *Imperator* and is *the* first-mentioned title of Augustus in official inscriptions. It is best translated into English not just as "Emperor" but as "World Conqueror." Sepphoris, of course, was nowhere near the world-class level of Herod the Great's construction projects but, still, Antipas began his program of Romanization by urbanization for commercialization when he dedicated his rebuilt capital city to Augustus. Thereafter he stayed very quiet as long as Augustus was alive and maybe especially after Archelaus was ordered into exile in 6 C.E. and a Roman governor took over direct control of his territory in the southern half of the country. Luke 13:32 had Jesus call Antipas—quite accurately—"that fox."

The *third act* began in 14 C.E., when Augustus died and Tiberius became emperor. At that point, Antipas made his second move to become King of the Jews. To replace his older capital city Sepphoris he started to create a new one about twenty miles to the east on the western shore of the Sea of Galilee. He named it Tiberias in honor of the new emperor Tiberius. But why a new capital and why a new one there and not somewhere else? Antipas could have renamed Sepphoris as Tiberias and built, say, a major new basilica there to celebrate Tiberius's ascension to the throne. Once again, then, why build a new capital city and why built it there on the lake?

If you were Antipas and wanted to become King of the Jews, you would have to increase your tax base in Galilee so that Rome might grant you that royal promotion. If Antipas did this as *tetrarch* of Galilee and Peraea, Rome might think, what would he not accomplish as *monarch* of the entire Jewish homeland? Antipas could not squeeze more taxation from his peasant-farmers without risking resistance or even revolt. But, having learned, as it were, how to multiply loaves in the valleys around Sepphoris, he would now learn how to multiply fishes in the waters around Tiberias.

The *fourth act* was the necessary tandem step to that preceding one. It was Antipas's second, internal or home-directed step toward kingship. He needed Roman approval but he also needed Jewish acceptance and for that he needed to forge a Herodian-Hasmonean connection. The Hasmoneans were a native dynasty who had ruled the Jewish homeland for a hundred years before the Romans arrived in the middle of the first century B.C.E. and appointed the Herodians in their place. Herod the Great, for example, had first chosen the Hasmonean princess, Mariamme, as his queen but had later executed her—rightly or wrongly—for conspiracy against him. Antipas obtained his Hasmonean consort by divorcing his Nabatean wife and marrying Herodias, wife of his own half-brother Philip, and granddaughter of that murdered Mariamme.

To jump ahead for a moment, consider these two texts, one from John and another from Jesus, and imagine how these two accusations could have derailed Antipas's hope for a popularly applauded Herodian-Hasmonean marriage alliance. First, in Mark 6:18, John the Baptist "had been telling Herod, 'It is not lawful for you to have your brother's wife.'" And later, in Mark 10:11-12, Jesus announced that "whoever divorces his wife and marries another commits adultery against her; and if she divorces her husband and marries another, she commits adultery." Criticism of his marriage by two popular prophets was not exactly part of Antipas's plan.

The *fifth act* was supposed to establish Antipas as a major player on the world stage of high imperial politics. When the Roman governor of Syria met the Parthian ruler Artabanus to discuss peaceful relationships, Antipas gave a great feast for them on the river Euphrates and immediately—but unwisely—got his report of that meeting back to Rome before that of the governor himself.

The *sixth act* ran Antipas out of time. Herod Agrippa (I), grandson of that murdered Mariamme, grew up from childhood in Rome's imperial palace. Then, in 37, after the death of Tiberius, Caligula gave him the territories of the dead Philip but with the title of king rather than tetrarch. Next, in 39, Antipas and Herodias hastened to Rome to plead their case, this time against Agrippa as earlier against Archelaus, but instead of becoming King and Queen of the Jews, they both ended up in exile. Finally, in 41, after the murder of Caligula, Agrippa I persuaded the praetorians to appoint and the senators to accept Claudius as their new Emperor. For that achievement—by a Herodian prince!—the grateful Claudius made him "King of the Jews" with the title and territory of Herod the Great. Despite forty-three years of patient and careful planning, it was Agrippa I and not Antipas who finally became the second—and last—Herodian "King of the Jews."

The saga of Antipas the would-be king concluded over a decade after the time of John and Jesus, but I have given it in full to understand that *third act* when he was founding Tiberias to commercialize the lake and its fishes in the name of Rome's empire and both John and Jesus clashed with him in the name of Israel's God. Who owned the lake and how it was to be used was but a microcosm question to the macrocosm question of who owned the earth and how it was to be used. It was not about salted fish and fish sauce in Rome's world but about equality and justice in God's world.

JOHN AND ESCHATOLOGY

Imminence. John was an apocalyptic eschatologist who proclaimed the imminent arrival of God's kingdom—not of Jesus' advent but of God's kingdom. Any day now but certainly very soon, God would come to purify and justify an earth grown old in impurity and injustice. John's program presumed the validity of that Deuteronomic theology in which oppression by Roman power was a punishment for Israel's communal sinfulness which alone impeded the promised advent of God's transformative power.

What was needed, therefore, was a great sacrament of repentance, a popular repetition of ancient Israel's coming out of the desert, crossing the Jordan, and entering the Promised Land. And in that process they would repent of their sins as they were "baptized" or immersed in the Jordan with their moral cleansing symbolized by the physical washing. Once a critical mass of repentant people had "retaken" their promised land, that would at least prepare or possibly even hasten the start of God's Great Clean-Up.

We know about John from both the New Testament and Josephus's *Jewish Antiquities* 18.116-19, but each source has one major difficulty. On the one hand, Josephus never wants to admit that Jewish apocalyptic eschatology was a powerful first-century force and so explains John's execution very vaguely. "Eloquence that had so great an effect on mankind might lead to some form of sedition," he informs us, "for it looked as if they would be guided by John in everything that they did." The content of that eloquence is never mentioned.

On the other hand, the canonical Gospels insist that John's message was about the imminent advent of Jesus and not about the imminent advent of God. Mark 1:7-8, for example, has John announce that "the one who is more powerful than I is coming after me; I am not worthy to stoop down and untie the thong of his sandals. I have baptized you with water; but he will baptize you with the Holy Spirit." Also, in this next section, notice that John's description of God's advent is quite inappropriate for Jesus' program.

Violence. My point is emphatically not that John's vision advocated a violent revolution. If Antipas considered John a violent threat, he would have also rounded up as many of his followers as he could catch. By executing only John, Antipas was responding to somebody who opposed the Roman system but did so nonviolently. Later, Pilate would act similarly with Jesus.

The question, therefore, is not about human but about divine violence. Does God's kingdom involve divine—even if exclusively divine—violence? And to that the Baptist's reply is very clear. The imminent advent is of a punitive, avenging and violent God, as you can see in these metaphors:

> John said to the crowds that came out to be baptized by him, "You brood of vipers! Who warned you to flee from the wrath to come? Bear fruits worthy of repentance. . . . Even now the ax is lying at the root of the trees; every tree therefore that does not bear good fruit is cut down and thrown into the fire." (Lk 3:7-9)

That language in Luke 3:7-9, 16 comes from John himself, but it is humanely softened by Luke's own editorial insertion in Luke 3:10-14:

> And the crowds asked him, "What then should we do?" In reply he said to them, "Whoever has two coats must share with anyone who has none; and whoever has food must do likewise." Even tax collectors came to be baptized, and they asked him, "Teacher, what should we do?" He said to them, "Collect no more than the amount prescribed for you." Soldiers also asked him, "And we, what should we do?" He said to them, "Do not extort money from anyone by threats or false accusation, and be satisfied with your wages."

Monopoly. John was "the Baptist" or "the Baptizer." That was his nickname in both Josephus and the New Testament. There were not lots of baptizing stations all up and down the Jordan and you simply went to the one nearest your own home. You went to John and only to John. Otherwise you were not operating within the great sacramental and repentant reenactment of the exodus. You might be simply crossing the Jordan on your own business. To stop his movement, therefore, Antipas had only to execute John. It might linger on in memory, nostalgia and sorrow for one or two generations, but since it depended on John's life, it ended with John's death.

A PARADIGM SHIFT WITHIN ESCHATOLOGY

Before I turn from John to Jesus, I want to raise one very significant question. The proclamation of John about the imminent advent of an avenging God fits well enough within the general Jewish apocalyptic eschatology of its time. But is Jesus' vision of God's kingdom basically the same as that of John, or does it represent a paradigm shift within the general Jewish eschatology? By a paradigm shift I mean an unexpected swerve within a religious, political or indeed any other type of human process.

You will recognize, of course, that I have taken that phrase, *paradigm shift,* from Thomas Kuhn's 1962 book *The Structure of Scientific Revolutions.* The term works just as well for eschatological revolutions. And, by the way, the first century was filled with paradigm shifts—from, say, imperial rulers replacing republican consuls in Rome at its start to Pharisaic Torah replacing Sadduceean Temple in Judaism at its end.

To prepare for my positive answer on that paradigm shift from John to Jesus, I first look at two recent comments on the messianic eschatology of Jesus.

Violent and nonviolent. In his book *The Scepter and the Star*, John J. Collins gives a thorough and very helpful survey of, as its subtitle says, *The Messiahs of the Dead Sea Scrolls and Other Ancient Literature.*[2] He focuses, despite other "minor" understandings of the term *messiah* around the time of Jesus, on this "common core" or "dominant note":

> This concept of the Davidic messiah as the warrior king who would destroy the enemies of Israel and institute an era of unending peace constitutes the common core of Jewish messianism around the turn of the era. . . . There was a dominant notion of a Davidic messiah, as the king who would restore the kingdom of Israel, which was part of the common Judaism around the turn of the era.[3]

The Davidic Messiah as a warrior king is not, therefore, just one option among many messianic understandings and expectations. It is rather the basic one. And that, of course, raises this immediate problem:

> Although the claim that he [Jesus of Nazareth] is the Davidic messiah is ubiquitous in the New Testament, he does not fit the typical profile of the Davidic messiah. This messiah was, first of all, a warrior prince, who was to defeat the enemies of Israel. . . . There is little if anything in the Gospel portrait of Jesus that accords with the Jewish expectation of a militant messiah.[4]

We cannot explain that discrepancy by taking the "common core" or "dominant note" of a violent Davidic Messiah as "Jewish" and that of a nonviolent Davidic Messiah as "Christian."

[2]John J. Collins, *The Scepter and the Star: The Messiahs of the Dead Sea Scrolls and Other Ancient Literature* (New Haven, Conn.: Yale University Press, 2007).
[3]Ibid., pp. 68, 209.
[4]Ibid., pp. 13, 204.

At least for some Jews at the start of the first century C.E., that warrior understanding of the Davidic Messiah underwent a profound paradigm shift in interaction with their experience of Jesus himself. *For some Jews, in other words, Jesus was a nonviolent Davidic Messiah.* In the light of that swerve, I turn next to what happens when another scholar attempts to interpret Jesus' eschatology without any acceptance of a paradigm shift within the more general Jewish eschatological and messianic expectation.

Future and present. In discussing the kingdom of God, John P. Meier's ongoing four-volume project, *A Marginal Jew: Rethinking the Historical Jesus,*[5] draws three major conclusions from the Gospel materials. But he himself also drastically undercuts his own conclusions in his *Volume 2: Mentor, Message, and Miracles.*[6]

First—and it comes first—Meier finds "Jesus' Sayings Concerning the Future Kingdom" in four major places: (1) "Your Kingdom Come" in Q/Matthew 6:10 // Luke 11:2; (2) "Drinking Wine in the Kingdom of God" in Mark 14:25; (3) "Reclining at Table with Abraham in the Kingdom" in Q/Matthew 8:11-12 // Luke 13:28-29; (4) "The Beatitudes" in preQ/Matthew 5:3,4,6 // Luke 6:20-21 (pp. 291-336).

But, on the other hand, Meier argues that the next three sayings are *not* original with Jesus: (1) Matthew 10:23 is "not from Jesus but from the early church" (p. 341); (2) Mark 9:1 is "likewise the utterance of a first-generation Christian prophet" (p. 344); and (3) Mark 13:30 has its "origin in the early church" (p. 348). Meier therefore answers negatively his initial question: "Did Jesus Give a Deadline for the Kingdom?" (pp. 336-48).

But all of that seems dangerously close to a distinction without a difference. On the one hand, "Jesus himself thought of the kingdom's coming as imminent" (p. 337). On the other hand, there is, from Jesus, "a notable absence of phrases that state explicitly that the coming of the kingdom is very imminent" (p. 337). Imminent, in other words, does

[5]John P. Meier, *A Marginal Jew: Rethinking the Historical Jesus*, vol. 1, Anchor Bible Reference Series (New York: Doubleday, 1991).
[6]John P. Meier, *A Marginal Jew: Rethinking the Historical Jesus: Volume 2: Mentor, Message, and Miracles.* Anchor Bible Reference Series (New York: Doubleday, 1991), pp. 235-506. Page numbers from this source are cited parenthetically.

not mean very imminent? And, in any case, "how imminent is imminent?" (p. 338).

I myself cannot see much difference between phrases like "imminent" or "soon" or "within this generation." And, while "imminent" or "soon" may be a little vague "within this generation" strikes me as clear enough. None of those phrases, at least, means two thousand years and counting. If "the future, definitive, and imminent arrival of God's kingly rule was central to Jesus' proclamation" (p. 398), then Jesus' central proclamation was quite simply wrong and misguided. And neither special pleading nor semantic evasion can rectify that situation.

Next—and it is next—Meier finds "The Kingdom already Present" for Jesus in six major places: (1) "The Baptist-block" in Q/11:12-13 // Luke 16:16; (2) "Jesus' Exorcisms" in Q/Matthew 12:28 // Luke 11:20; Mark 3:24-27; Q/Luke 11:21-22; (3) "The Kingdom of God is in Your Midst" in Luke 17:20-21; (4) "The Kingdom of God Has Drawn near" in Mark 1:15; (5) "The Beatitude on Eyewitnesses" in Q/Matthew 13:16-17 // Luke 10:23-24; (6) "The Question about Fasting" in Mark 2:18-20. In other words, for Jesus, "the kingdom of God had already arrived—however partially and symbolically—in his own words and actions" (p. 398).

But Meier's presentation of the kingdom's presence is repeatedly and consistently undercut by phrases such as these: "somehow" (p. 429), "in some way" (p. 450) and especially, "in some sense" (pp. 398, 399, 400, 403, 423, 449, 454). Could Jesus' proclamation of God's present kingdom have been that vague, unclear and uncertain to his first audience?

Finally, Meier is quite aware that his imminently-future-yet-somehow-already-present interpretation of Jesus' kingdom proclamation requires some further explanations, and he gives three of them. I find their tone as significant as their content since he becomes more and more rhetorically truculent as he moves from one to the other.

First, "the kingdom of God that [Jesus] proclaims for the future is in some sense already present. How this coheres—or whether it coheres—with what Jesus says about the kingdom soon to come remains an open question. But that further problem should not lead us to suppress or twist some of the evidence that creates the problem, all for the sake of a neat systematization that was not a major concern of Jesus" (p. 423).

Second, he claims that Jesus saw an "organic link between his own ministry in the present and the full coming of God's eschatological rule in the near future." But, he continues, "in my view this is all that we can say. To go beyond this minimal explanation of the kingdom present yet future is to leave exegesis and engage in systematic theology" (p. 453).

Third, there is an excuse or explanation that is repeated three times and which I take as Meier's primary one. Here are its three repetitions in fuller context, and I find them not only absolutely unconvincing but incredibly condescending. A first time: "Recently some critics have objected that a kingdom both future and present is an intolerable contradiction in terms. One might reply that the Semitic minds behind a good part of our biblical literature were not overly troubled by our Western philosophical principle of non-contradiction" (p. 11). A second time: "the kingdom that [Jesus] promised for the near future was paradoxically, in some strange way, already present in his work. To some modern minds such a paradox may seem an intolerable contradiction. . . . The ancient Semitic mind, not unlike the outlook of many third-world people today, was not overly concerned with the principle of non-contradiction, however revered the principle may be by Western logic" (p. 399). A final time: "the problem of logical consistency that the Western mind may raise with regard to the systematic writings of a Spinoza may be beside the point when dealing with an itinerant Jewish preacher and miracle-worker of 1st-century Palestine. Our concern about the principles of non-contradiction might have been greeted with a curious smile by the Nazarene and his audience" (p. 452).

Within the space constraints of this article, my point is not to debate *for or against* the originality of those thirteen sayings. I admit that I have always been much more convinced of the original historicity of present-already emphases than of future-imminent from Jesus. But, for here and now, my point is that Meier's four-volume project is in tatters after that debacle in his second volume.

Furthermore, I think it is both possible and necessary, *precisely within the acceptance of Meier's own data*, to explain the historical Jesus' kingdom of God without taking defensive refuge with "in some sense" or offensive refuge with "the outlook of third-world people." Meier might even have glimpsed that better explanation had he begun with the *presence* of Jesus' kingdom before considering its *future*. But, be that as it may, I propose in the next section to understand Jesus' proclamation as a paradigm shift within the general Jewish expectation of the kingdom of God.

JESUS AND ESCHATOLOGY

I interpret Jesus' vision of God's kingdom on earth against those same three categories used above for John's proclamation. My purpose in making those three major comparisons between John and Jesus is not to exalt one martyr over another and certainly not to exalt Christianity over Judaism. Jesus owed so much to the Baptist that easy superiority is precluded. But John promised the advent of God, for example, and all that came was Antipas's cavalry. John died and still God did not come. Jesus watched, learned and changed his vision of God. Also, John's execution protected Jesus until if and when Herod Antipas felt safe enough to kill another popular but dissident prophet.

Presence. One of the surest things we know about Jesus is that he was baptized by John. What makes it so sure is the growing nervousness that fact evokes as you move from Mark, through Matthew and Luke, into John.

Mark's Gospel is quite matter of fact in Mark 1:9: "In those days Jesus came from Nazareth of Galilee and was baptized by John in the Jordan." But that baptism is immediately overshadowed by this vision for Jesus in Mark 1:10-11: "Just as he was coming up out of the water, he saw the heavens torn apart and the Spirit descending like a dove on him. And a voice came from heaven, 'You are my Son, the Beloved; with you I am well pleased.'"

Matthew's Gospel is much more defensive. Jesus arrives for baptism in Matthew 3:13, but this interaction ensues in Matthew 3:14-15: "John would have prevented him, saying, 'I need to be baptized by you, and do you come to me?' But Jesus answered him, 'Let it be so now; for it is proper for us in this way to fulfill all righteousness.' Then he consented." Thereafter, as in Mark, the heavenly vision and revelation overshadow the baptism.

Luke's Gospel is almost evasive and unless you are reading carefully you might miss any mention of Jesus' own baptism in Luke 3:21: "Now when all the people were baptized, and when Jesus also had been baptized and was praying, the heaven was opened." In this case, however, the revelation from God is not accompanied by any vision for Jesus.

John's Gospel has the final solution in John 1:26-33. He omits any mention of John's baptism of Jesus and insists instead on the Baptist's testimony to Jesus as "Son of God" and "Lamb of God." John the Baptist explicitly identifies Jesus (and not God) with the one greater than himself he had foretold as coming soon. The heavenly vision now assists the Baptist to identify Jesus instead of assisting Jesus to recognize his own identity:

> John testified, "I saw the Spirit descending from heaven like a dove, and it remained on him. I myself did not know him, but the one who sent me to baptize with water said to me, 'He on whom you see the Spirit descend and remain is the one who baptizes with the Holy Spirit.'"

But all of that only emphasizes that John baptized Jesus and that therefore Jesus had *at least originally* accepted John's message of the imminent advent of an apocalyptic and avenging God. That would explain, for example, Jesus' defense of John, the desert-hardened prophet, in contrast with Antipas, the wind-shaken reed, in Luke 7:24-27, quoting from Malachi 3:1:

> Jesus began to speak to the crowds about John: "What did you go out into the wilderness to look at? A reed shaken by the wind? What then did you go out to see? Someone dressed in soft robes? Look, those who put on fine clothing and live in luxury are in royal palaces. What then did you go out to see? A prophet? Yes, I tell you, and more than a prophet. This is the one about whom it is written, 'See, I am sending my messenger ahead of you, who will prepare your way before you.'"

But the very next verse in Luke 7:28 both reiterates that accolade in its first half and then drastically downgrades it in the second part: "I tell you, among those born of women no one is greater than John; yet the least in the kingdom of God is greater than he."

Since I consider that both those statements came from the historical

Jesus, I think that Jesus started by accepting John's theology of God's *imminence* but, precisely because of what happened to John, he changed from that to a theology of God's *presence*. John expected God's advent but instead John was executed and God still did not come as an avenging presence. Maybe, thought Jesus, that was not how God acted because that was not how God was? Jesus' own proclamation, therefore, insisted that the kingdom of God was not imminent but present, was already here below on this earth and, however it was to be consummated in the future, *it was a present-already and not just an imminent-future reality.*

But Jesus could hardly have made such a spectacular claim without immediately appending another one to it. One can speak forever about the *future-imminence* of the kingdom and, unless one is foolish enough to give a precise date, one can hardly be proved right or wrong. We are but waiting for God to act and, apart from preparatory faith, hope and prayer, there is no more we can do. When God acts it will be, presumably, like a flash of divine lightning beyond all categories of time and place. But to claim an *already-present* kingdom demands some evidence, and the only such that Jesus could have offered is this: it is not that we are waiting for God, it is that God is waiting for us. The present kingdom is a *collaborative or participatory eschaton*, an eschatological dialectic between the human and divine worlds. The Great Divine Clean-Up is an interactive process with a present beginning in time and a future (short or long?) consummation. Would it happen without God? No. Would it happen without believers? No. To see the presence of the kingdom of God, said Jesus, come, see how we live, and then live likewise. And thence, of course, the radical ethics of Jesus came not as unnecessary *preparation for* but rather as necessary *collaboration with* the advent of God's kingdom.

Violence. The motivation given by Jesus for human nonviolence is quite simply divine nonviolence—even or especially when dealing with one's violent enemies. In Matthew, Jesus commands his hearers to "love your enemies and pray for those who persecute you," and the reason given is so that "you may be children of your Father in heaven; for he makes his sun rise on the evil and on the good, and sends rain on the righteous and on the unrighteous" (Mt 5:44-45). And Luke's version says to "love your enemies . . . and you will be children of the Most High; for he is kind to the ungrateful and the wicked" (Lk 6:35).

Furthermore, the conclusion in Matthew is very striking. "Be perfect, therefore, as your heavenly Father is perfect" (Mt 5:48). That sounds impossible, for how could the human be as perfect as the divine? But in Greek, that verb "to be perfect" can also be translated as "to be finished"—for example, with Jesus' dying words, "It is finished," in John 9:30. In other words, we humans are perfected, finished, fully completed in our humanity, when we are nonviolent in imitation of and participation in the nonviolent God.

Franchise. There was, however, a third major difference between John and Jesus, and it was almost a necessary concomitant to those two former distinctions. I put it this way: *John had a monopoly but Jesus had a franchise.* As we saw above, John's nickname in both Josephus and the New Testament was "the Baptist" or "the Baptizer," and, therefore, to stop the Baptism movement, Antipas had only to execute him. Once again, I think, Jesus watched and learned. And here is how his strategy differed from that of John.

First of all, recall this from above. Jesus announced the presence of the kingdom of God by inviting all to come and see how he *and his companions* had already accepted it, had already entered it and were already living in it. To experience the kingdom, he asserted, come, see how *we* live and then live like us. But that presumes a *communal* program, presumes that Jesus did not just have a vision or a theory but a praxis and a program—and a program not just for himself but for others as well. What was it?

Basically, this: *heal the sick, eat with those you heal and announce the kingdom's presence in that mutuality.* That program is still quite visible in the *Q Gospel* at Luke 10:1-12, in Mark in 6:7-13 // Luke 9:1-6, and combined in Matthew 10:1, 5-15. It is also reflected by Paul in 1 Corinthians 9 and in the *Gospel of Thomas* 14b. Furthermore, it avoids the necessity of giving priority to either the words or the deeds of Jesus since that program involves a saying about doing, a word about a deed.

But notice some unusual features of those texts. First, Jesus himself does not settle down at Nazareth or Capernaum and send his companions to bring people to him as monopolist of the kingdom. Second, he tells others to do exactly what he himself is doing—healing the sick, eating with the healed and proclaiming the kingdom's presence. Third, he does not tell them to heal in his name or even to pray to God before they heal—nor does he himself pray before he heals. That is actually quite extraordinary and can only be explained by the kingdom's presence and their participation in it—if you are in the already-present kingdom you are already in union with God and can act accordingly.

That logic of Jesus' kingdom program is a mutuality of healing, as the basic spiritual power, and eating, as the basic physical power, shared freely and openly. That process built *share* community from the bottom up as a positive alternative to Antipas's Roman *greed* community established from the top down. That food is the material basis of life and that the control of eating controls all else is clear enough. Even if we are normally well fed, we realize our absolute dependence on food before all else. After that is furnished, there is much else needed but, first and foremost, no food, no life. So eating as basic physical power is relatively clear but healing a spiritual power is much more difficult to understand.

It is quite clear that Jesus was a great healer and, however we explain that capacity, its actuality seems securely certain. In his famous book *Patients and Healers in the Context of Culture*, Arthur Kleinman emphasized that

> a key axiom in medical anthropology is the dichotomy between two aspects of sickness: disease and illness. *Disease* refers to a malfunctioning of biological and/or psychological processes, while the term *illness* refers to the psychosocial experience and meaning of perceived disease. Illness includes secondary personal and social responses to the primary malfunctioning (disease) in the individual's physiological or psychological status (or both). . . . Viewed from this perspective, illness is the shaping of disease into behavior and experience. It is created by personal, social, and cultural reactions to disease.[7]

[7]Arthur Kleinman, *Patients and Healers in the Context of Culture* (Berkeley: University of California Press, 1980), p. 72.

And *curing* goes with disease while *healing* goes with illness. Some-times a disease can be cured but very often the best that is possible is to heal the illness that surrounds it. That was especially true for ancient medicine but is still very often true today especially for chronic or ter-minal pain.

When I tried to explain that distinction between *curing disease* and *healing illness* to my undergraduate students at DePaul University, they usually understood that disease/illness complex in psychosomatic terms and interpreted healing as a mind-over-matter phenomenon. They were seldom able to comprehend it as what I called a sociosomatic complex until they saw the movie *Philadelphia* in 1993. You will recall that Tom Hanks played Andrew Beckett, a gay lawyer fired by his law firm be-cause his AIDS infection came from homosexuality. My students all understood that Beckett's *disease* could not be *cured* but, as the story unfolded, they could also see that his *illness* was being *healed* by the sup-port of his partner, his family and his lawyer's successful suit against his law firm's illegal discrimination. *Curing* was not available, but *healing* was still possible. Not everything, to be sure, but not nothing either.

Here is an example from another book by Arthur Kleinman, his 1988 study, *The Illness Narratives*. It concerns one "Lenore Light . . . an intense twenty-nine-year old internist who comes from an upper mid-dle class black family and works in an inner-city ghetto clinic." She works with, in her words, "our black underclass: the poorest, the most miserable, the most chaotic, the oppressed and oppressive reminder of where we have all of us come from." The result, she admits, is that "it has radicalized me: it is a revolutionary encounter with the social sources of mortality and morbidity and depression. The more I see, the more appalled I am at how ignorant I have been, insensitive to the social, economic, and political causes of disease."[8] Here is her specific example:

> Today I saw an obese hypertensive mother of six. No husband. No fam-ily support. No job. Nothing. A world of brutalizing violence and pov-

---

[8]Arthur Kleinman, *The Illness Narratives: Suffering, Healing, and the Human Condition* (New York: Basic Books, 1988), pp. 216-17.

erty and drugs and teenage pregnancies and—and just plain mind-numbing crises, one after another after another. What can I do? What good is it to recommend a low-salt diet, to admonish her about control of her pressure: She is under such real outer pressure, what does the inner pressure matter? What is killing her is her world, not her body. In fact, her body is the product of her world. She is a hugely overweight, misshapen hulk who is a survivor of circumstances and lack of resources and cruel messages to consume and get ahead impossible for her to hear and not feel rage at the limits of her world. Hey, what she needs is not medicine but a social revolution.[9]

She is right that "what we need is prevention, not the Band-Aids I spend my day putting on deep inner wounds."[10] Healing is what happens within a community of concern, support and assistance and that is a sociosomatic and not just a psychosomatic reality.

The healing of illness by Jesus and his companions must be understood in a framework of a preventive social revolution, in Light's terms, and in a framework of the kingdom of God's Great Cosmic Clean-Up of the World, in their own even more radical terms. Do not be surprised, of course, if a great and famous healer, like Jesus or Asklepios, is reputed to raise the dead, that is, to bring life emphatically and triumphantly out of death. Do not be surprised if you find it in the advertisements of their followers, but be very surprised if you find it in the testimonials of their patients. It comes from a healer's department of public relations and not from a healer's department of medical records. But you only get claims of raising the dead about transcendentally great healers so that they simply and serenely certify the presence of extraordinary powers of healing.

THE FUTURE OF COLLABORATIVE ESCHATOLOGY

As I noted above, John Meier began his analysis of Jesus' eschatological kingdom of God as imminently future ("but how imminent is imminent?"), then proceeded to it as already-present ("in some sense") and finally reconciled that future-present tension by noting that "Semitic

---

[9]Ibid., p. 217.
[10]Ibid., p. 217.

minds" and "third-world people today" lack our Western concern for "principles of non-contradiction." That leaves—to my mind—the core of his four-volume project in a shambles of ethnocentric condescension.

My own analysis begins with Jesus' message of God's eschatological kingdom as already present, that is, of God's Great Clean-Up of the World as already underway—but only insofar as it involves an interactive collaboration between divine challenge and human response. The radical ethics of Jesus and his companions are not *negative preparation* for what is coming soon but *positive participation* in what is already here. (That, of course, is true for Paul as well.) Furthermore, that proclamation represented a paradigm shift within the more standard Jewish view of any eschatological consummation.

First, that traditional consummation was absolutely future—even if possibly imminent. Second, that consummation was exclusively divine—even if mediated by an appointed messiah. Communal cooperation could exist at most as preparatory prayer, purity or martyrdom—even if such piety might facilitate or expedite God's transforming advent. Third, nobody asked how long it would take God to transform the world from the human normalcy of injustice to the divine radicality of justice. It would be, presumably, like a flash of divine lightning, outside of all human time or sequence.

But the mutational swerve introduced by Jesus changed that general eschatological advent of God from a moment to a process, from an instant outside time to a sequence inside time. And that changed any question about the future from *when will it start?* to *when will it end?*

John proclaimed the imminent beginning of the end of evil. Jesus proclaimed it as already but only collaboratively present, so the only question left about Jesus is this: granted he did not speak about *the imminent beginning of the end*, did he speak about *the imminent end of the beginning?*

On the one hand, I am not convinced that Jesus showed much concern about the future consummation of the already-present kingdom of God—be that consummation imminent or distant. On the other hand, from Paul of Tarsus to John of Patmos there is a consistent expectation of imminent consummation—however diversely that is imagined. And, indeed, whenever a paradigm shift occurs in any area of life we tend to persuade ourselves that it is only a minor deviation from normalcy—automobiles were just horseless carriages—no great change, just no more horses!

For me, in other words, the first and most important discussion about the historical Jesus should be on his vision of collaborative eschatology—for then and now. If, however, Jesus expected that collaborative eschatology to end soon, he was wrong—as were all others with similar proclamations ever since. And, quite frankly, I see little value in saying more about it than that. If Jesus thought the consummation of collaborative eschatology was imminent in the first century, he was wrong.

EPILOGUE

In a magnificently climactic scene in John's Gospel—a scene parabolically true rather than historically accurate—Pilate confronted Jesus about the kingdom he proclaimed. "My kingdom," said Jesus in the King James Version of the incident, "is not of this world" (Jn 18:36).

First, Jesus opposes the kingdom of God to the kingdoms of "this world." That is simply another way of opposing eschaton to empire, the eschatological kingdom of God to the imperial kingdom of Rome—or to any other empire before or after it.

Second, Jesus is condemned to death by Roman Pilate, in Roman Judea, in the eastern reaches of the Roman Empire. But Jesus never mentions Rome as such, and he never addresses Pilate by name. He opposes something incarnated in but also far greater than Rome or any other empire. He condemns imperialism as the normalcy of "this world."

Third, we sometimes stop after saying that "my kingdom is not of this world," in quoting Jesus before Pilate, as I myself did quite deliberately above. In that case, the phrase would be utterly ambiguous. "Not of this world" could mean: never on earth, but always in heaven; not now in present time, but off in an imminent or distant future; not a matter of the exterior world, but of the interior life alone. Jesus spoiled all those possible misinterpretations by continuing with this: "if my kingdom were of this world, then would my servants fight, that I should

not be delivered" up to execution. Therefore, repeats Jesus, "my kingdom [is] not from hence" (Jn 18:36).

Fourth, then, Pilate is the most important commentator on Jesus in
the New Testament. By executing Jesus, officially, legally and publicly,
he certified that Jesus was a lower-class subversive of Roman law and
order. But by executing Jesus alone, that is, by not attempting to round
up his companions, Pilate certified that Jesus and his companions represented nonviolent rather than violent resistance. Had Pilate considered them a violent threat, he would have acted as he did with Barabbas's group. In that other story—also parabolically true but not
historically accurate—"Barabbas was in prison with the rebels who had
committed murder during the insurrection" (Mk 15:7).

Finally, the crucial difference—and the only one mentioned—between the eschatological kingdom of God and the imperial Kingdom
of Rome is Jesus' nonviolence and Pilate's violence. Your soldiers hold
me, Pilate, but my companions will not attack you even to save me from
death. Your Roman Empire, Pilate, is based on the injustice of violence,
but my divine kingdom is based on the justice of nonviolence.

RESPONSE TO
JOHN DOMINIC CROSSAN

Robert M. Price

I was privileged to be present on the day Robert W. Funk and the Jesus Seminar presented to Dr. Crossan the David Friedrich Strauss medal for distinguished scholarly work on the life of Jesus. He deserves it. His books on the aphorisms of Jesus and the Cross Gospel underlying the canonical Passion Narratives are my favorites among his work. But I have always felt ill at ease with certain, I think fundamental, assumptions and moves in his Jesus books and not entirely absent from the essay in this book.

First, I believe I detect in Dr. Crossan's work a tendency to reduce Jesus to a function of the categories and methods through which he has decided to study him. He does not seem to find any particular avenue unfruitful. Jesus will always be there waiting for him at the end, whether as an anachronistic Zen master who coined all the koans contained in the parables as Crossan interprets them or the community organizer (something of a combination of Mahatma Gandhi and E. F. Schumacher) who practices "commensality" and serves somehow as the broker of a "brokerless kingdom." He is a magician and a healer, but only in the sense that he does not shun the disintegrating leper and welcomes the contagious. As early Christians are imagined to have borrowed Christological titles/categories from surrounding worldviews (Logos from Philo, Son of Man from apocalyptic, Kyrios from mystery religions), so Crossan creates modern Christologies patterned after patronage studies, honor and shame cultures, peasant sociology and economics, Hellenistic magic, feminism, et cetera.

Dr. Crossan is genuinely critical of the Gospel materials, weighing whether they go back to Jesus or not. But very often I find myself thinking he is jumping from skepticism to fideism, as many scholars do: if you can't prove Jesus didn't say it, we are free to assume he did. How dare one go beyond a toss up? And Crossan too often does. For instance, in this article he credits to the historical Jesus the sayings in Luke 7 on John the Baptist, for example, "Of men born of women, no human being has appeared who is greater than John." Isn't it equally plausible that this saying stems from the sect of John the Baptist and that a Christian writer is here (Q, Matthew, Luke) trying to co-opt it, having Jesus cite it but spoil it: "but the lowest on the totem pole in the kingdom is John's superior." Damning with faint praise, is it not? Sectarian propaganda, is it not? Sounds enough like it to me to suspect the saying originated in a later period of sectarian rivalry between Baptists and Jesus believers.

These two tendencies, to feed Jesus through the grinders of the latest research trends at the SBL, coupled with an inconsistent skepticism toward very much of the Gospel tradition, leave Dr. Crossan with an odd and arbitrary approach (or so it seems to me, and I have tried to read his books closely). His authentic Jesus sayings float like the last leaves of autumn on the surface of a rain pool. There is more water between them, holding them up, than there is of them. And Crossan begins stirring up the water in the puddle. When he likes the emerging Rorschach pattern, he takes a snap shot, and that is the "historical rain puddle."

In the essay we are reviewing, take the example of Jesus' embracing nonviolence on the basis of God's omitting to deliver the Baptist and to slay the enemies of righteousness. Albert Schweitzer[1] made a similar move. He judged that Jesus believed God had preserved John (the eschatological Elijah) and himself (the hidden Son of Man) for epic martyrdoms at the hands of the antichrist, all in Technicolor. When John met instead with a mundane, secular death, and with no Great Tribula-

---

[1]Albert Schweitzer, *The Mystery of the Kingdom of God: The Secret of Jesus' Messiahship and Passion*, trans. Walter Lowrie (New York: Schocken Books, 1964), pp. 219-36.

tion on the horizon, Jesus retreated to take stock of things. He decided God would spare the world at large and instead place the full weight of the tribulation on his own cross-gouged shoulders. That is pretty speculative, but it allowed Schweitzer to harmonize all manner of seemingly inconsistent gospel verses. Crossan, like Schweitzer, is positing a crucial development *nowhere actually stated in the text* and using it to align the texts with notions equally invisible there.[2]

Put it this way: Crossan's case would be much stronger if he could show us a verse like, "You have heard it said to the men of old, 'I the Lord am a jealous God, visiting the iniquities of the fathers upon the children to the third and fourth generations,' but I say to you that God is love and forgives men their sins." But there isn't any. And so where *is* any suggestion that Jesus repudiated the violent judgment of God in the Last Days? Whence the urgency of repentance? Oh, I know that all texts become a marshy bog once all are equally subject to the back and forth parsing of scholars. But that's the way it is, and scholars have no right simply to pretend they have evidence they lack and then just to keep going. One can disregard the "thin ice" sign on the lake and go skating anyway—but one will still crash through. I am surprised Dr. Crossan finds enough brick chips left to build with. I don't think he does, in fact. That's why most of his edifice is speculative cement.

Time and again amid the deliberations of the Jesus Seminar, I found myself puzzled, shaking my head at the group's decisions to vote as red (= surely authentic) sayings that Bultmann wouldn't have touched with a ten-foot pole in his *History of the Synoptic Tradition*. He argued, quite soundly as I view it, that the narrative lead-ups to Gospel pronouncements were secondary attempts to interpret the sayings by providing a plausible but fictive context: "Well, suppose he was referring to *this*?" Lead-ins like Jesus being invited to a Pharisee's house for dinner, or being stuck in the middle of a crowd, or having healed a demoniac, or dining with tax collectors: all of it was dramaturgical guesswork, and

---

[2]The ubiquity of the "Son of Man as Suffering Servant," early posited by Rudolf Otto (*The Kingdom of God and the Son of Man: A Study in the History of Religion* [London: Lutterworth Press, 1937; rev. ed., Boston: Starr King Press, 1957], pp. 244-55), is another memorable example. What Gospel text was not interpreted in light of that theological dialectic, yet it is everywhere conspicuous in its absence from the Gospel database.

not all of it fit too well on closer examination.[3] Yet Funk said it was probably in Jesus' habitual behaviors, as described in these lead-ins and generalized summaries based on them, that we are liable to find the real data about Jesus. I remain stunned; that is absurd. And that is also the basis of Crossan's central picture of Jesus as the broker of a brokerless kingdom of potluck suppers to which all the outcasts were invited. (I realize Luke 14:12-14 advises hearers to invite the street people instead of one's relatives, but that singly attested saying is patently as Lukan as the day is long.)

Similarly, it seems clear to me that the main reason for Crossan's seeing Jesus and John as revolutionaries (albeit nonviolent ones) against Herod Antipas is the huge superstructure Crossan erects from first-century history and sociology connected with Herod and his motives of self-advancement—exactly none of which is set forth in the text. Jesus and the Baptist turn out to be tiny barnacles clinging tenuously to this hull. It might be that John the Baptist saw as shrewdly as Crossan does what Antipas was really up to by divorcing his wife and marrying his sister-in-law, but this is not what the Gospel says that he said. As we read it, the Baptizer was just upset about some Levitical traffic jam. Maybe that is a cover up for an originally political version—who knows?

And can we picture Herod even understanding (I'm not sure I do) what some guy organizing a soup kitchen for lepers has to do with hopes of overthrowing Roman and Herodian rule? I think we are, as so often in the study of the Gospels, transforming a theological or homiletical abstraction into a piece of history. Such niceties of social etiquette and Torah reinterpretation would have been about as threatening to the secular powers as the theological hairsplitting for which the indifferent Gallio dismissed Paul's accusers (Acts 18:12-16). Another tempest in an SBL ballroom.

I will go further and venture that Dr. Crossan's mighty attempts to create a vast socioeconomico-historical tapestry into which to stitch a tiny Jesus figure appear to me to be the latest in the long series of at-

---

[3]Rudolf Bultmann, *History of the Synoptic Tradition*, trans. John Marsh, rev. ed. (New York: Harper & Row, 1972), pp. 56-61.

tempts to "euhemerize" Jesus by making him, originally a pure and powerful myth-deity, plausible as a historical figure. I believe Dr. Crossan is not filling in the historical air Jesus breathed on earth centuries ago. He is rather trying to pump historical breath and life into a mythic character that never lived on earth at all. One might read Crossan's exhaustive research and come away saying, "How can anyone doubt the existence of Jesus? Crossan has shown Jesus' place in history." Instead, I suspect, Crossan has assigned Jesus a place in a history into which he never set foot, not having one to set.

As for Dr. Crossan's sophisticated analysis of how one may heal without affecting physically the sufferer's physical malady, perhaps it is all quite true. But to suppose that this sort of "empowerment" is what Jesus was about and that he was talking about that in the Synoptic Mission Charge ("Heal the sick, raise the dead, cast out demons.")—well, there, on display, is the peril of modernizing Jesus.[4] For Crossan, Jesus did not heal lepers; he just declared them ritually clean as far as he was concerned and welcomed them to lunch. If I understand him correctly, Dr. Crossan has returned to something surprisingly like the infamous Rationalism of the eighteenth century. Neither Jesus, nor his contemporaries, nor the Gospel writers nor their first readers believed in "fantasy" (as he calls it), that is, literal miracles. But since multiple attestations will not let him dismiss the healing stories *en masse* as legendary fabrications, he must rationalize them in the manner we have seen. I will only say that it seems unfair for Barbara Thiering[5] to be ridiculed for reintroducing such Rationalism while Dr. Crossan seems to be making the same suggestion.

Though he is more erudite than all the old liberal questers for the historical Jesus put together, I cannot help thinking that John Dominic Crossan has fallen into their trap of creating a liberal Jesus in his own image.

---

[4]Henry J. Cadbury, *The Peril of Modernizing Jesus* (New York: Macmillan, 1937).
[5]Barbara Thiering, *Jesus the Man: A New Interpretation from the Dead Sea Scrolls* (London: Corgi Books, 1993), p. 133.

RESPONSE TO
JOHN DOMINIC CROSSAN

Luke Timothy Johnson

John Dominic Crossan has written widely and effectively on the topic of the historical Jesus. His work has been marked by methodological self-consciousness, cross-cultural imagination and highly effective writing. His work is studded with eye-catching aphorisms like the one he crafts in the present essay, "John had a monopoly but Jesus had a franchise."

His essay in this collection advances basically the same construal of Jesus as his more substantial treatments: Jesus is set within the context of competing kingdoms, and against the violent rule of the world exercised by the Roman Empire; Jesus' ministry enacts a vision of God's rule that is peaceful, present, inclusive, collaborative and healing.

This is an intensely appealing construal, particularly for a generation that has been schooled to detest all forms of political hegemony, that uses "imperial" only as a term of abuse and that considers all things colonial as intrinsically evil. To imagine Jesus as consciously opposing an ancient oppressive empire through a politics of inclusion is, Crossan claims, not only to perceive him most accurately in historical terms, but also to receive him most profoundly in religious terms, for Jesus' struggle is still there for others to pick up and continue, against all the oppressive regimes still active in the world today.

The construal is so appealing to contemporary readers, indeed, that the historian's instinct is to suspect that it may be the force of the ideological framework that makes Crossan's argument appear to work, more than the actual historical evidence. In this response, I touch on several aspects of Crossan's argument that tend to support such a suspicion.

Crossan gets considerable mileage from putting opposites into juxtaposition. Thus, even though the Gospels address Roman rule only indirectly, Crossan delights in making Jesus' proclamation of God's rule, which, within the narratives themselves appears as the opposite of the reign of Satan over human persons, into a direct challenge of the Roman Empire. Thus, in this essay, Crossan takes the Gospels' placement of a part of Jesus' ministry along the Sea of Galilee as a direct challenge to the commercial plans of Herod Antipas on the Sea of Galilee.

Such juxtapositions, however, are the work not of the ancient actors or even of the ancient sources but are entirely due to Crossan himself. Even if Jesus had a collaborative ministry centered along the lake, in other words, and even if Antipas actually did seek to raise taxes through intensifying fish production, neither Jesus nor Antipas would have thought of themselves as actors within a script that pitted (good) socialism against (bad) capitalism. I take it that this is what Crossan suggests when he describes Antipas's effort as a Roman "greed community established from the top down."

In short, not unlike N. T. Wright, Crossan consistently commits the historical fallacy of having ancient characters act and think in virtue of realities that can be known and named only by the present-day historian. Crossan also claims privileged access to the thought processes of the ancient figures he discusses, even when no evidence for such motivations or reactions are provided by the sources. In the case of Antipas, he elaborates precisely the mental machinations the tetrarch employed in pursuing his ambition to become a favorite of Rome and a king of the Jews. Crossan knows precisely Antipas's motivations for his actions. Similarly, Crossan claims access to Jesus' mental development as well. Jesus sees and learns from the fate of John, and changes his eschatological program. He states, "Jesus watched, learned and changed his vision of God."

Crossan's anti-imperial reading is so strong, indeed, that it overrides the explicit evidence provided by the ancient sources. Both Josephus and the Gospels, for example, are perfectly clear on the reasons why

John was killed by Antipas, although they differ in their explanations. Josephus states that John gathered such popular approval for his moral exhortations—"the Jews [should] lead righteous lives, to practice justice toward their fellows and piety towards God, and so doing to join in baptism"—that Herod feared the possibility of sedition because of his power to gather crowds, and he put him to death (*Jewish Antiquities* 18.118-19). The Gospels, in contrast, attribute Antipas's imprisonment and subsequent execution of John to the prophet's criticism of his marriage to Herodias, the wife of Antipas's brother Philip (Mk 6:17-29; Mt 14:3-12; Lk 3:19-20). But neither Josephus nor the Gospels connect the prophet's criticism to Antipas's taxation or building program. Yet Crossan confidently states that John "opposed the Roman system," even though there is little reason to suppose that John had much of an idea what "the Roman system" might have been.

What is perhaps most disappointing to a reader who has enjoyed and even been impressed by Crossan's early efforts, even when disagreeing with his conclusions, is the way this essay plays fast and loose with the sources, with logic and with his own painstakingly elaborated methodological principles.

Josephus devotes relatively little attention to Antipas. As Crossan notes, Josephus (*Jewish Antiquities* 18.29) states that Antipas gave the name *Autocratoris* to the city of Sepphoris—the inference that this was a nod to imperial favor is certainly possible and perhaps even probable, but not absolutely necessary: the name could also indicate "self-governing." Josephus also tells of Antipas's founding of Tiberias in honor of the emperor Tiberius (*Jewish Antiquities* 18.36-38). But Josephus says nothing about the commercialization of the fishing industry or taxation in connection with this founding. Instead he focuses on Antipas's need to people the city with a mixed population, since pious Jews avoided a place that had been built over graves—and was thus considered by them to be unclean.

How does Crossan connect Tiberias to the commercialization of fishing as a means of increasing taxes and thus advancing Antipas's ambitions? He does so through the happy proximity to Tiberias of the town of Magdala. Through the Greek name used by Josephus *(Tarichaeae),* and through the Rabbinic designation "Magdala of fishes," Crossan not unreasonably concludes that Magdala was a center for processing the fish caught in the Sea of Galilee. It should be noted that although Josephus mentions this town frequently as a site for armed conflict during the Jewish War, he does not discuss it as a center for the fishing industry (see, e.g., *Jewish War* 2.596-597, 608-635). Nevertheless, the region's pickled fish were widely known (see Strabo *Geography* 16.2.45).

What Crossan does not—indeed cannot—explain is why the founding of an expensive city in honor of the emperor should have in any way increased the production of fish or the taxation derived from that production. Indeed, if that were Antipas's aim, would he not have more logically expanded operations at Magdala and changed its name to honor the emperor? In fact, the creation of an expensive new city would have had the logical effect of depleting Antipas's revenues rather than increasing them. The entire thesis of "Romanization by urbanization for commercialization" is a product of Crossan's imagination rather than a conclusion demanded by the reading of Josephus. He has not demonstrated that Antipas founded Tiberias "to commercialize the lake and its fishes in the name of Rome's empire," and therefore fails to show that "both John and Jesus clashed with him in the name of Israel's God" on this score.

The same carelessness characterizes Crossan's reading of the Gospels. He would like us to see Jesus' moving from Nazareth to Capernaum on the Sea of Galilee (citing Mt 4:13) as having a significance connected to Antipas's imperialistic project. But the Gospels do not suggest or support any such suggestion. In contrast, what the Gospels do tell us about fishing and the sea, Crossan neglects entirely.

Should we find significance in the description of Peter and the sons of Zebedee as *metochoi* ("partners") and *koinōnoi* ("sharers") in a small-time fishing enterprise (Lk 5:7, 10)? On one hand, this would present readers with a small "guild" of workers that could stand in contrast to "Romanization by urbanization for commercialism." On the other hand, Jesus encourages them to abandon their fishing nets to follow him and become "fishers of humans" (Lk 5:10). Does this indicate that Jesus found even small trade guilds as inconsequential compared to his larger mission? I am not suggesting either option. But if Crossan wants to make a point about Jesus, the lake and fishing, he ought at least to include the relevant data.

More telling is the fact that all of the details concerning Jesus' movements near or away from the lake are drawn precisely from those narrative portions of the Gospels that Crossan's methodological principles—established and elaborated in his earlier writings—have already removed from the historian's available database. Such an abandonment of his own basic principles suggests that Crossan's commitment to an anti-imperialist construal of Jesus has moved far beyond the bounds of sober historiography to dwell in the regions of a certain kind of theology.

RESPONSE TO
JOHN DOMINIC CROSSAN

James D. G. Dunn

There is always a fascination with Crossan's contributions to "historical Jesus" research. He likes to set the scene in a broad context—the Roman Empire—and draws on an interesting sequence of sources to characterize that setting. Here his pen sketch of Herod Antipas, while inevitably speculative, provides a nice foil for what he wants to say about John the Baptist and Jesus, though how far Galilee (even with moderately Hellenized cities like Sepphoris and Tiberias) could be regarded as examples of Roman rule or as typical of a generalized Mediterranean peasantry are questions whose answers cannot be assumed, as Crossan tends to do. But he also likes to seize on a particular motif, to sum it up in ear-catching phrases, and to pose sharp antitheses. No matter that the motif is selective, that the phrases use the language of the twenty-first century and that the antitheses are overdrawn for greater effect—so long as the chosen motif can be represented as truly deriving from or illuminating the mission of Jesus, that is sufficient justification. Other motifs and emphases, also present in the Jesus tradition, can be sidelined or ignored, or set in contrast to the (s)elect(ed) motif to their disadvantage, and the spotlight shone ever more brightly on the chosen motif, casting all the rest in a shadow that deepens as it stretches further away from the epitomizing motif.

Here the motif is Jesus' message of the kingdom of God in contrast to that of John the Baptist's. Jesus' message marks a paradigm shift from that of the Baptist. John proclaimed the imminent arrival of

God's kingdom, the beginning of "God's Great Clean-Up," "the imminent advent . . . of a punitive, avenging and violent God." Jesus, Crossan infers from the fact that Jesus was baptized by John, must initially have accepted John's message—of the imminent advent of an apocalyptic and avenging God. But when John's expectation was unfulfilled ("John died and still God did not come"), "Jesus watched, learned and changed his vision of God." (Crossan here displays the old liberal confidence of being able to access Jesus' inner thoughts, the neoliberal equivalent of the late nineteenth-century confidence regarding Jesus' "messianic consciousness.") He went on to announce the presence of God's kingdom. He changed "John's theology of God's *imminence* . . . to a theology of God's *presence*." The present kingdom is a collaborative or participatory eschaton. "To see the presence of the kingdom of God, said Jesus, come, see how we live, and then live likewise. And thence, of course, the radical ethics of Jesus came not as unnecessary *preparation for* but rather as necessary *collaboration with* the advent of God's kingdom," "not *negative preparation* for what is coming soon, but *positive participation* in what is already here." This involves a nonviolent and communal program, summed up as "Heal the sick, eat with those you heal and announce the kingdom's presence in that mutuality."

Where this all becomes frustrating is in exaggeration of what seems indeed to have been a major point of contrast between John and Jesus. According to our sources, John did focus on future/imminent events, and a characteristic emphasis in Jesus' mission was on the already active rule of God; "if it is by the Spirit/finger of God that I cast out demons, then the kingdom of God has come upon you" (Mt 12:28 // Lk 11:20). But by focusing exclusively on that contrast, by sharpening that contrast, and by ignoring other features of both the Baptist and the Jesus traditions, the whole becomes lopsided, like a zeppelin where all the helium has gone to one end leaving the whole unbalanced and unable to take off completely.

At various points in Crossan's essay I found myself demurring.

1. The presentation of the Baptist's preaching. Crossan is very confident that the Baptist proclaimed the advent of God. That is cer-

tainly possible, though most infer that the image of unloosing the Coming One's (God's!) sandals would be so absurdly inappropriate to the situation as to be highly unlikely. Nor can we assume that the Baptist referred to the coming of the kingdom of God; only Matthew 3:2 sums up his message in such terms. And the fierce and frightening imagery of ax, winnowing fork and fire should be balanced by the positive implications of a baptism of repentance, which offers a way of escape from the coming wrath, of fruit-bearing and wheat gathered into the granary. The Evangelists were not without justification in placing the mission of John the Baptist as the beginning of the Gospel.

A curious element of Crossan's presentation is his contrast between the Baptist as exercising a monopoly whereas Jesus exercised a franchise. I confess I don't really understand the contrast, but it seems to refer to the fact that John expected people to come to him to be baptized, whereas Jesus did not settle in Capernaum or expect people to come to him but sent his disciples to the villages of Galilee. Here again the contrast is overdrawn and posed in oddly chosen terms which hardly reflect the accounts of many people coming to Jesus, in Capernaum and on the shores of the lake. Quite why the contrast has to be drawn out in this way remains for me something of a puzzle.

2. The debate about Jesus' kingdom preaching will never end, I suppose. Crossan belongs to that school that is so confident that Jesus preached the kingdom's *presence* that it dominates all else. Unlike those who banish any future emphasis from the Jesus tradition, Crossan is more open on the point, though he is "not convinced that Jesus showed much concern about the future consummation of the already-present kingdom of God." But that really is not good enough. The selective acceptance of one sequence of texts, and effective dismissal or denigration of others (including the second petition of the Lord's Prayer and various parables) is poor scholarship. When both emphases are characteristic within the Jesus tradition, then the most obvious conclusion is that *both* emphases were characteristic of Jesus' mission. An overemphasis on the already-present aspect leaves such a presentation open to the jibe that the kingdom of God can hardly be said to have come

when Antipas and Tiberius still ruled the roost. Certainly the case can be made that the presence of God's rule was evident in Jesus' table fellowship with sinners and tax collectors. But was such communion the complete fulfillment of the hope and prayer for God's kingdom to come? Crossan seems willing to accept a rather modest (in extent) communal program as the complete coming of the kingdom—Jesus' message of the kingdom of God reduced to people being healed and eating together. And that is a crucially important dimension of Jesus' mission, I wholly agree. But is it the whole? And by reducing the whole to that, are we losing sight of other important aspects of Jesus' mission and message?

Here I have to protest at Crossan's critique of J. P. Meier. In order to defend his own exclusive focus on the already-present strand of the kingdom preaching in the Jesus tradition, Crossan ridicules Meier's attempts to make sense of both strands, the future and the present. Why is it so unacceptable that both strands were characteristic of Jesus? And why is it so ridiculous to offer possible explanations of how the one message could contain both? Most astonishing, and quite unacceptable, is Crossan's conclusion that the "debacle" of Meier's offering of possible explanations leaves the rest of his four-volume study of Jesus "in tatters," "a shambles of ethnocentric condescension." Given Crossan's own attempt to portray a Jesus who can fit more effectively into a twentieth or twenty-first century context of realpolitik, his cavalier setting aside of tradition, which does not fit so readily, and his tendentious interpretation of tradition, which does so fit, the critique of Meier is a rich case of a pot calling a relatively polished kettle black.

I don't want to lose, or lose sight of, the important aspects of Jesus' mission that Crossan highlights. But he does seem to me to fall into the old trap of selecting the features of the Jesus tradition that he finds most amenable and most adaptable to his modern life-setting. In particular, is Jesus' proclamation, including its repeated warnings and calls to repentance, really summed up as the invitation to "come, see how we live, and then live likewise"? That's a much easier message to translate into the twenty-first century—much less offensive, much less challenging—but it leaves us back with the modernizers of the nineteenth-century quest, with a Jesus who is far too nice to be worth crucifying. Crossan quotes Albert Schweitzer with some approval, but he would be wiser to take more seriously another of Schweitzer's famous obiter dicta: "the historical Jesus will be to our time a stranger and an enigma."

RESPONSE TO
JOHN DOMINIC CROSSAN

Darrell L. Bock

Few writers have stimulated more discussion about the historical Jesus than John Dominic Crossan. Almost omnipresent on television treatments about Jesus, his work placing Jesus in his sociopolitical context has made him one of North America's most important conversation partners about Jesus. His approach to Jesus is a classic example of trying to get back to the earliest layers as the best place to ground this discussion.

Crossan begins by placing Jesus in the sociopolitical context of Judaism before the Roman Empire, a starting point shared by most. The question here is the nature of the interaction between these two spheres and to what extent Jesus focused on this interaction in relation to the interaction with the believing community of the people and kingdom of God.

Key to his method is Crossan's confidence in being able to peel back layers to reveal the earliest level of Jesus tradition. This actually is very hard to do because we have to reconstruct the full range of sources (and, even harder, try to reconstruct from them alleged earlier forms). It also must come to grips with the oral level of the tradition as well as the itinerant nature of Jesus' ministry, which allowed Jesus to address many topics on frequent occasions. A key starting point for the earliest sources according to Crossan involves Q plus the *Gospel of Thomas*. This results in a "sayings as primary" approach to Jesus. Seeing the sayings as primary for the earliest Jesus tradition is a heavily debated point, especially when for most scholars the *Gospel of Thomas* is seen as an early second-century text.[1] As Crossan notes, if he is wrong here, then his reconstruction has problems. The early-later dilemma is also complex. The fact is that different streams of tradition existed, and some showed up earlier than others. But when a tradition surfaces as a written record by itself, it does not establish the age of the tradition it reflects. This starting point is a problem for the emphasis Crossan gives to the materials as a whole.

Another distinctive in Crossan's approach is his placing Jesus in a Roman context. We might call it the Roman-emperor-versus-Jesus model. Crossan is correct to note that between the emperor and Jesus we find differing claims of divine vindication (one through power, the other through dependence on God and service). There also is the difference between seeking peace through violent victory (emperor) and peace through nonviolent justice (Jesus). But there is something clearly missing when the main emphasis is placed here. Jesus' teaching, even his multiply attested teaching, issues calls for discipleship and personal piety. This emphasis pointed not so much to the global politics of empires, but to relationships at a more grass-roots level and in terms of loving God and one's neighbor. Moreover, the elaborate sociopolitical emphasis of Crossan, including his explanation of why Jesus moves from Nazareth to Capernaum, raises a major problem if Jesus is focused on confronting empire. The problem is that the tradition never shows Jesus in Sepphoris or Tiberias, the most important regional locales to challenge and engage Rome on a sociopolitical level. Neither does Jesus go to Caesarea Maritima to challenge Rome, but he heads to Jerusalem. And when in Jerusalem, Jesus goes to the temple to discuss the proper orientation to God in the context of Judaism, not Rome. In addition, why does Jesus challenge customs associated with the Sabbath or ritual cleanliness if Rome is his central concern? These controversies, also multiply attested, stand at the center of Jesus' actions and suggest that his major concerns lie elsewhere. Jesus is less concerned about who owned the lake than who owned the heart of people who claimed to be God's within Israel. These points also indicate how important the

---

[1]Fred Lapham, *An Introduction to the New Testament Apocrypha* (London: T & T Clark, 2003), p. 120; Hans-Josef Klauck, *Apocryphal Gospels: An Introduction* (London: T & T Clark, 2003), p. 108.

events and controversies are in pointing to how Jesus presented himself and his authority to explain his ministry.

Despite my critique, I agree that Jesus portrayed himself (at least in the context of his earthly ministry) as a nonviolent Davidic messiah, which is one of the reasons those who looked for a militaristic messiah may have been disappointed in what Jesus seemed to offer. Jesus left the decisive judgment and reckoning to God by appealing to a timing left in divine hands through a return by the Son of Man in glory. Jesus' kingdom teaching was a paradigm shift from Jewish expectation in this regard but not in a direction that took on Rome directly. Rather, Jesus portrayed his battle in more cosmic terms, with his acts of healing and exorcizing directed at a battle that transcended Rome.

So was there a paradigm shift from Judaism in Jesus' kingdom teaching, as Crossan claims? Yes, to a degree, but living in the context of a brokerless community is not Jesus' central point. Yes, Jesus called disciples to share and not be greedy, but this was because they were also called to reflect the character of God as his children (Luke 6:27-36). Crossan's emphases understate the accountability to God that precedes a future form of the kingdom, an idea more widely attested in the materials than Crossan mentions. I do not accept the notion that Jesus reflected a franchise as opposed to a monopoly because it is *the* Son of Man through whom all of God's activity is realized and who is uniquely vindicated by God. Alongside a Jesus of wisdom, justice, social and political critique, we need to see an apocalyptic Jesus, preaching the arrival of a long-promised kingdom. When it comes in fullness, God will decisively vindicate the righteous as that kingdom that hope had always promised. However God does so through a singular figure, the Son of Man, who one day will ride the clouds as the vindicated and vindicating one. Jesus was about more than social revolution and condemnation of imperialism. He was about internal transformation and the condemnation of a life detached from honoring God.

Now, when he critiques Meier's work, Crossan takes on this alternative model of a kingdom that is imminently-future-yet-already-present. Crossan is correct to say that Meier has given us too little here. However, rather than going in the direction Crossan takes, I prefer to argue that the texts stress a view of the kingdom that calls people to turn in faith with a renewed humility and dependence on God. The call is to carry out his will and reflect God's presence and rule as one loves and serves in the world. The present-future tension Crossan highlights as remaining unresolved in Meier is addressed by understanding that the community Christ seeks to form is called to reflect God's way and will in a manner that anticipates the future kingdom of God. This is part of what Jesus' Sermon on the Mount seeks to urge. Be a light that gives honor to God, reflecting the virtues of a character formed by values in which God delights. I agree with Crossan that Jesus argued for a present kingdom and presented a radical ethic in terms that emphasized nonviolence and participation in a collaborative walk toward the realization of the eschaton. However, this was not at the expense of a future kingdom to come, as his treatment argues, nor does it carry the implication that such a walk puts us on a march to the eschaton, as if we can bring the consummation.

I do not see quite the distance between John the Baptist and Jesus that Crossan does. Vengeance and vindication are left to God while the community engages in the mission of reflecting what it is to live in the world while honoring God. Even in the pursuit of that mission, the world is still so fallen that God will once again be forced to intervene more directly to bring the ultimate resolution.

Let me further illustrate the point by looking at one detail of how Crossan handles the text. I have in mind the example of John the Baptist's baptism of Jesus. Crossan's suggestion that Luke is evasive about who baptized Jesus is overstated. He does suggest a careful reading rids one of this impression. But how careful must that reading really be? Luke places the event in the section where John the Baptist is being discussed. John's association with baptism in the wilderness was surely well known. Even Josephus notes it, so it was unnecessary to say who baptized Jesus. In addition, later, Luke 7:28 is *not* downgrading John but is exalting the new era, noting how anyone in it is better than the best of the former era, even the previously greatest born of woman (i.e., John the Baptist). The one who participates in the now-present kingdom is part of a truly special time of God's program and activity, performing God's calling until the return that brings a more complete restoration. Crossan's nuanced differences in the readings leave the impression that the gospel traditions have more tension in them than they actually possess.

All of this raises the question of why Rome reacted to Jesus. Did Pilate act because he simply considered Jesus a nonviolent threat? Did Pilate really act unilaterally with little instigation by the Jewish leadership who actually had born the brunt of Jesus' challenge and had been his greatest source of opposition? It seems unlikely that Pilate's actions came out of a strict concern for Roman interests or a sense of a need to stop Jesus for Rome's sake. Jesus had no army. Our texts suggest Pilate hardly took Jesus very seriously as a threat to Rome, and for obvious reasons, because in standard political terms Jesus had little he could use to challenge Roman power. Our texts suggest that Rome hardly would have acted without the influence of the debate Jesus had stirred up with the Jewish leadership. It was this catalyst to social chaos that raised a public challenge to the public peace, especially after Jesus' acts in Jerusalem. Events at the temple and other incidents like it involving Jewish practice point to concerns other than those Crossan raises. In other words, to get to the historical Jesus, we must keep a careful eye on Jesus' Jewish roots and concerns and not look so much at the Roman context.

Crossan's portrait of Jesus seems to lack an appropriate focus on Jesus' view of God and his promised people's relationship to him. Emphasizing how we relate to each other as a kind of ethical example narrows down the message of Jesus too far. It ignores issues raised by the start of the great commandment: love God with all of your heart, soul and mind. It severely underplays the disputes Jesus had with the Jewish leadership over genuine covenantal faithfulness. Crossan's Jesus does reflect the concerns Jesus did have about justice and proper community, but it misses far too much of his message about what the kingdom of God brings to the inner being of God's people, both individually and collectively. Jesus was about more than the injustice of violence and the justice of nonviolence. Jesus was about lives receiving the grace of a restored relationship to God. This involved God receiving the honor due to God of lives reflecting his character, creatures giving appropriate allegiance to him, and humans acknowledging his presence and rule in the world through what God had done through Jesus.

3

LEARNING THE
HUMAN JESUS

Historical Criticism and Literary Criticism

Luke Timothy Johnson

In the contemporary controversy over the historical Jesus—a controversy that, like a virus, tends to reoccur in Christianity under conditions of stress—there are some areas of agreement as well as areas of sharp disagreement. All participants in the discussion agree, for example, on the importance of knowing the human Jesus. Simply as the pivotal figure in the shaping of Western culture, the human being Jesus must be engaged. Ignorance of Jesus when studying the character of European or American civilization is as inexcusable as omitting consideration of Muhammad in seeking to understand the culture of the Middle East, or skipping over Confucius when trying to grasp Chinese culture.

All agree as well that Jesus demands engagement as the founding figure of Christianity, the largest world religion numbering some two billion members, and growing with particular impressiveness in Asia, Africa and Latin America, a lively corpse indeed despite all premature obituaries pronounced over it. Within the many rival parties that make up Christianity, furthermore, all agree that the humanity of Jesus somehow functions as the model and measure for Christian discipleship. Getting Jesus right, they agree, matters.

The persistence of the controversy both within and outside the church, furthermore, has made all participants agree that people are hungry to know Jesus. I mean ordinary people, those usually referred to as lay people by academic and ministerial professionals. As a human being, Jesus is compelling, fascinating and elusive; for believers and unbelievers alike, the man from Nazareth is worthy of serious consideration. Both seek to find out about Jesus through publications available at Borders and Barnes & Noble more than in preaching from Christian pulpits. For non-Christians, this is a natural reflex, since the church has long since lost a substantial portion of its intellectual and moral credibility. For Christians, it is a necessary tactic, since preaching seldom takes up the humanity of Jesus in a manner that actually leads to real knowledge. To a remarkable extent the current stage of the controversy, despite generating some substantial scholarly efforts,[1] has been characterized by the production of publications directed to a lay audience.[2]

The main point of disagreement concerns the best way of getting to know Jesus. One position holds that Jesus is best learned through the

---

[1]Particularly deserving of respect for the clarity and rigor of their methods and for the degree of real historical knowledge they bring to bear on the subject are John Dominic Crossan, *The Historical Jesus: The Life of a Mediterranean Jewish Peasant* (San Francisco: HarperSanFrancisco, 1991), and J. P. Meier, *A Marginal Jew: Rethinking the Historical Jesus*, 4 vols. (New York: Doubleday, 1991, 1994, 2001, 2009).

[2]In addition to the two books I will mention below, my own thoughts on the issue can be found elsewhere in *The Creed: What Christians Believe and Why It Matters* (New York: Doubleday, 2003), and in the following articles: "The Humanity of Jesus: What's at Stake in the Quest for the Historical Jesus," in *The Jesus Controversy: Perspectives in Conflict*, with John Dominic Crossan and Werner Kelber (Harrisburg, Penn.: Trinity Press International, 1999); "A Historiographical Response to Wright's Jesus," in *Jesus and the Restoration of Israel: A Critical Assessment of N. T. Wright's* Jesus and the Victory of God, ed. Carey C. Newman (Downer's Grove, Ill.: InterVarsity Press, 1999), pp. 206-24; "The Search for the Wrong Jesus," *Bible Review* 11 (1995): 138-42; "Who Is Jesus? The Academy vs. the Gospels," *Commonweal* 122 (1995): 12-14; "The Jesus Seminar's Misguided Quest for the Historical Jesus," *Christian Century* 113 (1996): 16-22; "Response to Criticism of *The Real Jesus*," *Bulletin of Biblical Research* 7 (1997): 249-254; "Learning Jesus," *The Christian Century* 115 (1998): 1142-46; "Is History Essential for Christians to Understand the Real Jesus?" *The CQ Researcher* 8 (1998): 1089; "Learning Jesus in Liturgy," *Theology, News and Notes* 46 (1999): 20-23; "Knowing Jesus Through the Gospels: A Theological Approach," *The World of the Bible* 3 (2000): 19-23; "The Eucharist and the Identity of Jesus," *Priests and People* 15 (2001): 230-35; "The Real Jesus: The Challenge of Contemporary Scholarship and the Truth of the Gospels," in *The Historical Jesus Through Catholic and Jewish Eyes*, ed. B. F. LeBeau et al. (Harrisburg, Penn.: Trinity Press International, 2000), pp. 51-65.

practices of faith in the church: through prayer, worship, the reading of Scripture, and encounters with saints and strangers. This position is based on the premise that Jesus is not a dead man of the past but a living Lord of the present, and that the tradition of the church, beginning in the Gospels, got Jesus right when they viewed all of his story from the perspective of his resurrection and exaltation, for that is who he now truly is. The "real Jesus" in this perspective is not a figure of the past but of the present, not an object of scholarly research but the subject of obedient faith. Critical to this position is the conviction that faith itself is a mode of cognition that makes contact with what is real even if empirically unverifiable.[3]

Such a strong position simply rejects the adequacy of historical study for getting at Jesus as he truly is. Not surprisingly in a world where even Christians are defined by the categories of modernity, not least in the assumption that only what is in principle verifiable can be the object of real knowing, it is a position that is seldom explicitly stated, although I think it fundamentally correct and have argued it in another place. To be more precise, I think it the correct position for those who claim to be Christian in any meaningful sense of the term, for it is difficult to understand why the name Christian should continue to be claimed by anyone who did not confess Jesus as exalted Lord present in the Spirit. The main objection to the position, indeed, is that although it may be satisfying to Christians, it appears to close the conversation concerning Jesus for those who do not share such faith. It does so by unacceptably expanding the notion of "human" beyond ordinary usage. Perhaps it is appropriate for believers to speak of the "living Jesus" in the present, but it is difficult for those outside such faith to accept that Christians are still speaking about the human being, Jesus of Nazareth.

An equally strong position directly opposes the first by claiming that the human Jesus is knowable only through historical reconstruction. The premise here is that Christian tradition got Jesus wrong from

---

[3]These are the positions I argued first in *The Real Jesus: The Misguided Quest for the Historical Jesus and the Truth of the Traditional Gospels* (San Francisco: HarperSanFrancisco, 1996), and more positively in *Living Jesus: Learning the Heart of the Gospel* (San Francisco: HarperSanFrancisco, 1998).

the beginning, above all in the Gospels, especially because they interpreted Jesus from the perspective of faith in his resurrection and exaltation even in recounting his human ministry. The Gospel accounts, and for that matter, all New Testament testimony concerning Jesus of Nazareth, must be corrected by critical historiography. In effect, if one is going to speak of the human Jesus in a manner that makes sense to all participants, he must in effect be regarded solely as a dead man of the past rather than as an active subject in the present. In the classic form found in Christianity's cultured despisers, more than a historical correction is involved: the recovery of the "real" (= "historical") Jesus serves to discredit Christian claims concerning Jesus.

These strong and intellectually self-consistent positions, with their clear points of difference, are, alas, less often articulated today than are a variety of fuzzy mediating positions espoused by those calling themselves Christian yet seeking to ground their convictions concerning Jesus in some form of historical inquiry, either by way of confirming those convictions (by more conservative scholars) or by way of correcting them (by more liberal scholars). Such intellectually fuzzy positions are possible because the most fundamental critical questions concerning the nature of historiography (its goals, possibilities, limits) and the treatment of the sources (above all, let's face it, the four canonical Gospels and secondarily the letters of Paul) are either bypassed or dealt with in careless fashion.

Thus we find "histories" of Jesus that are, on one side, little more than retellings of the Gospels of Matthew and John[4] or the Gospel of Luke[5] that offer no reflection on what the term *historical* might mean when applied to Jesus, and lacking even a rudimentary discussion of the literary relationships of the four Gospels. On the other side, we find reconstructions of the "historical Jesus"[6] that proceed with blithe over-

---

[4]See Adolf Schlatter, *The History of the Christ: The Foundation of New Testament Theology*, trans. A. J. Köstenberger (Grand Rapids: Baker Books, 1997 [1923]).

[5]N. T. Wright, *Jesus and the Victory of God* (Minneapolis: Fortress, 1996).

[6]See especially Robert W. Funk and Roy W. Hoover, eds., *The Five Gospels: The Search for the Authentic Words of Jesus* (New York: Macmillan, 1993); and John Dominic Crossan, *The Historical Jesus: The Life of a Mediterranean Jewish Peasant* (San Francisco: HarperSanFrancisco, 1991).

confidence in source criticism to dismantle the Gospel narratives in order to salvage certain "authentic" pieces, yet show little awareness of the dominating effect of ideological commitments (not least to the implicit image of Jesus found in the Gospel of Luke) in the subsequent reassembling of the pieces into a portrayal supposedly more historical than the Gospel narratives.

In this essay, I address the question of knowing the human Jesus apart from faith in his resurrection, that is, totally and completely as a historical figure. In so doing, I state what I consider the most responsible way of employing the Gospels as sources for that knowledge. I take up the legitimate uses of history for learning Jesus, arguing for a distinction between historical study that enables a fuller and more responsible engagement with the literary figure of the Gospels called Jesus, and a project of historical reconstruction of Jesus that involves the deconstruction of the Gospels. Finally, I make the argument that a literary-critical engagement with Jesus in the Gospels actually leads to a fuller knowledge of him in his human character.

THE USES OF HISTORY FOR LEARNING JESUS

I begin by straightforwardly asserting the legitimacy and importance—even for believers—of studying Jesus historically, for all of the reasons stated in the opening paragraphs of this essay. My assertion is especially vigorous because I have been understood by my critics to be an opponent of historical inquiry, whereas my concern has been only with the scholarly integrity of such inquiry. Jesus can and should be interrogated historically because he is a historical figure, a real human being whose mortal life covered roughly the first thirty years of the Common Era. As someone who occupied time and space in the past, he is the legitimate subject of the discipline that inquires into events and persons in the time and space of the past.

If Jesus is the subject of historical inquiry, furthermore, he should be treated in precisely the same way as other human figures of the past, such as Socrates or Napoleon or Christopher Columbus. Historiography cannot be redefined because Jesus is its subject. If historiography cannot declare concerning the divine claims made for a Roman emperor such as

Augustus, neither can it declare concerning Jesus as the incarnate one. If historiography cannot adjudicate claims to miracle-working by Apollonius of Tyana, neither can it adjudicate such claims in the case of Jesus. On this point, I agree wholeheartedly with the first great historical Jesus quester, David Friedrich Strauss: history must concern itself only with what falls within time and space as potentially verifiable.[7]

I also willingly agree that when appropriate historiographical methods are used, important things can be said about Jesus as a historical figure. By appropriate methods I mean those that are used by critical historians in the study of other events and figures: the identification of all plausible sources as primary and secondary, and firsthand and secondhand; the testing for bias; the evaluation of specific points of information; and finally, on the basis of the lines of convergence among all the sources, reaching tentative conclusions concerning the event or figure in question. The ideal, to be sure, is the construction of a narrative, especially one that contains motivations, but sometimes the evidence does not allow more than a set of probable statements. In all cases, the limits of the verifiable evidence must be respected. I consider as inappropriate the methods of source criticism that seek earlier sources within literary compositions and use such putative earlier sources as leverage against the literary compositions; the results yielded by such procedures are far too circular and arbitrary to be considered legitimate.

In the case of Jesus, the very slender evidence provided by outsider sources (the Roman historians Suetonius and Tacitus, the Jewish historian Josephus, the indirect polemic of the Jewish Talmud)[8] are important above all as providing some controls for insider sources (those written by Christians); the information provided by Paul and the letter to the Hebrews, in turn, is important both in itself and as providing further controls for the later Gospel compositions. As everyone acknowledges, the most problematic sources are the narrative Gospels, because of their distinctive combination of literary interdependence (among the Synoptics)

---

[7]David F. Strauss, *The Life of Jesus Critically Examined*, ed. with an introduction by P. C. Hodgson, trans. G. Eliot (Philadelphia: Fortress, 1973 [1835/1846]).

[8]For the evidence, see F. F. Bruce, *Jesus and Christian Origins Outside the New Testament* (Grand Rapids: Eerdmans, 1974).

and independence (in John as well as in the distinctive portraits of Matthew, Mark and Luke). It is simply impossible fully to harmonize these accounts while still retaining any credibility as a historian. Nevertheless, when read within the controls provided by the other sources, the narrative Gospels also offer points of genuine convergence at the level of historical facts about Jesus that the historian can affirm with varying degrees of probability—probability being all that any history can yield.

The historian can assert, for example, with the highest degree of probability that Jesus existed as a Jew in the first century, that he was executed by Roman authority in Palestine, that a movement arose in his name and proclaiming him as risen Lord spread across the Mediterranean world within twenty-five years and finally, that beginning in that same time span and continuing for some decades, the writings that came to be called the New Testament were composed by believers in an effort to interpret their experiences and convictions concerning Jesus. All these assertions but the last are confirmed by converging lines of outsider and insider sources. The final assertion is a historical statement about the human Jesus because the production of such literature is incomprehensible if one denies the first three propositions, and it follows logically (and as a matter of verifiable fact) from the first three propositions.

There is more: the historian can affirm with a very high degree of probability some of the basic patterns of Jesus' activity: that he proclaimed God's rule as connected to his own words and deeds, that he performed healings; that he taught in parables and interpreted Torah, that he associated with marginal elements in Jewish society, that he chose twelve followers. The historian can even affirm with considerable probability that certain specific events reported in the Gospels occurred, for example, his baptism by John the Baptist, or his performance of a prophetic act in the Jerusalem temple, perhaps also that he interpreted a final meal with his disciples in terms of his impending death. This is not an insignificant yield of historical information concerning Jesus, but it reaches the limits of what proper historiographical method allows.

The significance of these results is considerable, even for believers. They show first that Christian faith is based in a real human person, rather than being based in nothing more than a sheer invention. They show second that this human person had very specific characteristics. One cannot assert that Jesus was a Gentile rather than a Jew, for example, or a female rather than a male, or that he died comfortably in bed of old age rather than violently by execution, and remain within the bounds of historical plausibility. Insofar as the Christ symbol is attached to the historical person Jesus, about whom specific historical assertions can be made, that symbol is not infinitely malleable. And although Christians must, if they are to stay true to their convictions, use mythic language when they speak of Jesus —God was in Christ, he ascended into heaven—such language is applied to an actual historical figure, who "was crucified under Pontius Pilate"— rather than to the figment of individual or collective fantasy.

There is another way in which historical study is important for learning about the human Jesus. The more we know the historical circumstances of the first-century Mediterranean world, and in particular, the circumstances of Jews in Palestine during an uneasy period of Roman rule, the better readers we can be of the Gospel narratives. Although Jesus appears at the most in one paragraph of Josephus, for example, knowledge of Josephus's *Jewish Antiquities* and *Jewish War* are invaluable for the light they throw on the characters in the Gospels and the historical tensions within which they lived. Similarly, although Jesus has no demonstrable connection with the Essenes, knowledge of them gained from Josephus and Philo, not to mention the library of their writings discovered at Qumran, tremendously enriches the reading of all the Gospels. The greater one's historical knowledge, the greater is one's capacity to read the Gospels responsibly. Indeed, the refusal to engage such historical study amounts to a refusal to take the specific, culturally determined symbols of the Gospels seriously and, one might even say, a refusal to take the incarnation seriously.

I repeat the distinction I made earlier: such historical study is in service of the fuller appreciation of the Gospel narratives, rather than in service of the dismantling of the Gospel narratives in order to reconstruct a "historical Jesus." In contrast to the slender amount of genuine historical fact that is available on the specific figure of Jesus, there is an abundant mass of historical data available to shed light on the meaning of the Gospel narratives.

THE LIMITS OF HISTORY

One of the disappointing aspects of recent historical Jesus research is the tendency in some quarters to trade on the self-designation of "scholar" and "historian" while at the same time failing seriously to take up the entire difficult issue of history and the making of history (historiography), instead speaking loosely as though history were simply "the past" or "what happened in the past." Those who do this simultaneously provide academic respectability to their reconstruction of Jesus while camouflaging the all-too-human process of reaching that reconstruction. At least four limitations inherent in any attempt to write history must be noted.

1. History is not simply "the past" or "what happened in the past" or a place that exists and to which the historian has access. It is the result, rather, of a human process of critical analysis and creative imagination. Historians construct history rather than simply find it. There are at least two stages to the process. The first consists in the critical evaluation of evidence from the past contained in sources; the second is the effort to provide a narrative account of events based on that critically assessed evidence. The fuller the evidence, the better is the chance of constructing a coherent narrative. The opposite is also the case: the more meager the evidence, the more difficult it is to provide more than a tentative sketch.

Because of its constructive character, historiography is also properly revisionist. I do not mean that the historian simply imposes his or her views on the past; good historians always allow the evidence to push against such projection. But an appropriate revision occurs when new evidence comes to light that fundamentally affects an earlier portrayal. More subtly, the changing perspectives created by present circumstances (themselves always changing) inevitably cause the past to be seen in new light. The most obvious example is the evaluation of U.S. presidents: Truman left office among the most excoriated of chief executives; subsequent events as well as the evaluation of those events have led to a much more positive assessment of Truman among presidential historians.

2. History is inherently limited in its way of knowing (past) reality. Its subject is human activity (or events) in time and space, but only as these are made available to observation and recording. A history of Broadway musicals up to 1950, for example, must rely on diaries, advertisements, playbooks, memoirs, theater receipts, reviews and scores. It cannot convey the actual music, the sense of drama, the excitement in the theater, the smell of greasepaint, the roar of the crowd. Even if the history takes the form of a documentary film that manages to use old recordings or pictures, the events cannot be summoned as they were, as they occurred. To show further what a clumsy instrument history is, the very phrase "as it occurred" obscures the complexity of sensation, movement, perception, that goes into any event. And the noun *event* itself obscures the fact that, like a copyeditor snipping out a paragraph for analysis from a manuscript, or like a movie editor snipping out a frame of film for study, the historian also "creates" an event by constructing a frame that sets off certain elements in the constant flow of human activity in time and space.

In one sense, there is simply too much happening for history to encompass. Even the most voluminous history of the American Civil War must restrict itself to battles sufficiently major to receive a name, and leave aside the countless skirmishes, sniper attacks and forays in which men died but in insufficient bulk to demand a historical plaque. In another sense, history's own subject matter—human events in time and space—leaves out much that is "real" but not "historical." This is so for the lower end of human existence: men in the civil war continued to shave and cut their nails and eat and sleep, but although part of each man's existence, and possibly also a major part of every company's conversation during the war, such realities seldom rise to the level of historical scrutiny. Likewise for the upper end of human existence: neither can history properly address the human states of alienation, reconciliation, compassion, forgiveness, loneliness and grief that were also most real to men separated from family and sometimes fighting former friends. It is simply not the case that "the historical" equals "the real."

3. Historiography is limited most obviously by its total dependence on sources. The construction of a satisfactory narrative requires suffi-

cient evidence resulting from the critical analysis of shared human memory preserved from the past. But how fragmentary and fragile are the sources bearing those memories! For ancient history in particular, sources are always partial. In many cases, our knowledge of an event or person depends on a single source. Sources are, in addition, inevitably biased. The bias may be a matter of physical perspective only, but it may also be ideological: demonstrators and policemen would give widely various accounts of the events at Chicago's Grant Park in the 1968 Democratic Convention. What is critical to grasp, however, is that all present-day knowledge of the past is based on the subjective judgment of witnesses: somebody saw and had reason to preserve what they saw in a manner that could be transmitted to a later time.

Such testimonies, especially from the distant past, are also unevenly preserved; the great Library of Alexandria was not the only storehouse of knowledge destroyed over the centuries. Single rather than multiple manuscripts are the norm for many great literary, religious and philosophical works of the past. The historian, in short, is dependent on what was perceived in the first place, what was then recorded, what was saved and what is still available for scrutiny. A colleague who is a student of Indian religion once expressed amusement at the willingness of Western scholars to make sweeping generalizations about the religious practice of the subcontinent. He observed that at best a tenth of what had happened was recorded, and at best a tenth of what was recorded was preserved, and at best a tenth of what was preserved has been edited, and at best a tenth of what was edited has been translated for Western consumption! There are good reasons for historians to be modest about their craft.

4. A final limitation on history is that it can only describe (or construct) the past; it cannot prescribe for the future. Even though histories and biographies from the start have provided examples for imitation and thereby hoped to affect the present, their capacity to guide decision making in the present is severely limited. Arguments from analogy go just so far. Politicians are fond of citing the "lessons of history," but good historians know that such lessons are more obscure and ambiguous than sometimes supposed. History by itself is simply not

normative for the present. No Englishman in 1945 would have dis-
agreed with the proposition that Winston Churchill had saved the nation, the empire and possibly Western civilization. But that universal
agreement did not keep the British electorate from dismissing him
from the prime ministry and beginning the dissolution of the empire.
Even when communities agree on their past, that is only one of the factors involved in their discernment of present need or future goals. Indeed, the better history is as a descriptive science ("what the war between the states was all about") the worse it is at providing norms.

THE LIMITS OF HISTORY CONCERNING JESUS

All these limitations are present to such a degree as to make any scien-
tifically respectable effort at constructing a "historical Jesus" daunting
in the extreme. Take the problem of history's scope: the insider sources
are replete with accounts of "events" that in principle fall outside the
ability of the historian to declare: virgin birth, voices from heaven, exorcisms, healings, transfiguration, resurrection. Speaking of the resurrection, all of the insider sources are deeply biased because of their conviction that Jesus is the present and powerful Lord within Christian
communities. The resurrection is not only a historically unverifiable
"event" within the Gospel narrative, it is the perspective from which all
of the earliest letters and all the Gospels were composed. When Jesus
teaches in the Gospel of Matthew, for example, it is not as a dead rabbi
of the past, but as the living Lord of the church who is "with them"
through the ages. In this respect, the discovery of Gnostic gospels at
Nag Hammadi offers no help, for in them, the humanity of Jesus virtually disappears altogether in favor of the divine revealer.[9]

The importance of the resurrection perspective for the historian is
that it affects not only the shaping of stories (such as the controversies
between Jesus and the Pharisees and Scribes), but their very selection.
Everything said about Jesus in the narratives of the Gospels derives (at
least in principle) from some witness, and is therefore already a subjec-

[9]See Luke Timothy Johnson, "Does a Theology of the Canonical Gospels Make Sense?" in
The Nature of New Testament Theology: Essays in Honor of Robert Morgan, ed. C. Rowland and
C. Tuckett (Oxford: Blackwell, 2006), pp. 93-108.

tive report, limited in its perspective and comprehension by the nature of human witnessing. But in addition to that, such witness accounts have been shaped by years of oral transmission in the preaching and worship of early churches, as well as interpretation through the lens of Scripture, and are finally selected and arranged by the individual Evangelists. On top of the individual subjectivity of the original witness—interpretation is inevitably present even if it were possible to determine "the earliest stage"—the explicit resurrection perspective (and engagement with the symbolic world of Torah) is at work in the second and third stages of transmission. Freeing a specific saying or story from its narrative context, in short, does not eliminate the resurrection bias that was at work in the entire process of selection and shaping.

Since the outsider sources available to the historian are so sparse and have their own bias, dependence on the narrative Gospels of the New Testament is both inevitable and problematic. The Gospels are most obviously limited in their scope. They cover at best one to three years of Jesus' public life, with only two of the Gospels touching—in dramatically different ways—on his childhood. A "history" of a figure that deals only with one to three years is obviously severely limited. But their status as historical sources is complicated as well by the literary interdependence of Mark, Matthew and Luke. However one solves the "Synoptic Problem," it remains the case that, strictly as sources for a history of Jesus, they represent on the major points one witness with variations rather than three independent sources.

If the majority view on this issue is accepted (and I do accept it), then Matthew and Luke have used the Markan plotline—extending from John the Baptist to the empty tomb—as the framework for their own narratives. At the level of plot, the variations each introduces (Matthew's blocks of discourses, Luke's long journey section) do not erase the fact that they share the same basic "story" they have derived from Mark. Thus, at the level of plot, the historian is presented with two starkly divergent witnesses, the Gospels of Mark and John. These witnesses disagree on the most basic points: the length of Jesus' ministry, the main location where it took place, the sequence of critical events—quite apart from differences in specific deeds and modes of speech that are impossible simply to harmonize. The majority of historical Jesus scholars have chosen to privilege the Markan (Synoptic) version of the storyline over the Johannine, reducing John to a minor source for specific information rather than as a competing witness to the shape of the entire story. Yet close examination of the Markan narrative makes clear that it also is more a theological construction than a historical report; thus Mark clusters temptations, healings, parables and teachings on discipleship topically rather than, we must assume, chronologically.

Such discrepancies at the level of plot are more than matched by an overwhelming number of smaller differences in the available sources. Even leaving aside the deeds and words of Jesus found only in John, close synoptic comparison reveals the impossibility of the historian asserting with confidence concerning any specific formulation, "Jesus said this." The same applies to determining the historicity of any specific healing or exorcism, much less their occasion or sequence. Even in that part of the story where we find the greatest degree of agreement among all four Gospels—the passion accounts—the differences are sufficiently numerous and important to make the careful scholar to assert as historically plausible only the bare bones of the event. These same factors, together with the degree to which stories about Jesus are also shaped by reflection on Scripture (not least in the passion narratives), make it impossible for the historian responsibly to declare on Jesus' intentions or motivations, much less his internal states of mind. The state of the sources simply does not allow such access. Can inferences be drawn from verifiable facts, such as Jesus' choice of the Twelve? Yes, but only with great care, and only to a limited extent.

Given the impediments presented by the factors I have enumerated—and I do not think I have overstated the case—it is all the more remarkable that historians can assert the not insignificant set of statements concerning the historical Jesus that I listed earlier in this essay. Although modest in scope, these statements are supported by the most stringent analysis and do not overreach what the sources can support. It is also clear that this set of statements does not constitute a narrative. It is a set of historical facts rather than a historical account. Restricting oneself to such a set of statements may frustrate the historian's longing for narrative, but it preserves the historian from a narrative that is not responsibly historical.

The consequences of pushing beyond such limitations in order to construct a historical Jesus are evident in many contemporary publications that regularly distort historical methods and as a result distort the sources as well. The consequences are evident in the multiple images of Jesus offered in such publications, all claiming to be based on historical-critical methods, yet projecting the authors' own ideals so powerfully on the ancient figure that their portrayals tell the reader far more about them than about Jesus. Finally, such publications consistently fall prey to the fallacious supposition that a historical reconstruction has normative force, so that a "recovery" of the historical Jesus should work to reform Christianity. Historical Jesus research all too frequently turns out to be not historical research at all, but a theological agenda wearing the external garb of history.

ANOTHER APPROACH TO LEARNING THE HUMAN JESUS

By no means does history's inability to adequately know the human Jesus mean that real knowledge of him is impossible. There is in fact another approach to the human Jesus—through the careful and critical literary engagement with the Gospel narratives as narratives—that is accessible to all who are capable of such close reading. It does not require knowledge of data or methods available only to specialists, but it does require intelligence, critical awareness, discipline and sensitivity to literary art. It does not, above all, require the elimination, harmonization or deconstruction of the Gospel narratives. Just the opposite, this approach requires that each Gospel be considered in its full literary integrity. It is controlled by the evidence offered by the Gospel narratives themselves, which means that it is constrained by evidence that is available to all other readers, so that conclusions can be established or challenged on the basis of a shared analysis of those shared texts.

In this approach, the Gospels are treated not as limited and problematic sources for historical reconstruction but as invaluable witnesses to and interpretations of—precisely in their integrity as narratives—the human person, Jesus. The Gospels are read literarily rather than historically. Rather than ask first concerning a word or deed of Jesus, "did Jesus really do this or say that?" the reader asks first, "what does attributing this saying or that deed" do to shape the meaning of the character of Jesus within the narrative? The reader respects the narratives as the medium of meaning regarding Jesus and engages the Gospel narratives in the way that literary critics engage other such narratives, with specific attention to the literary elements of plot, character and theme. Historical knowledge, not necessarily of specific events but certainly of social, cultural and linguistic possibilities, serves to enrich such a literary reading and to provide certain controls to the imagination. In sum, such a disciplined reading engages the human Jesus as a literary character in the narratives written about him within fifty to seventy years of his death.

If each of the narrative Gospels of the New Testament is read individually with attention to its use of the symbolic world of Torah, and its portrayal (through the narrative) of Jesus and his followers, the reader is immediately impressed by the marked diversity of their interpretations. I do not mean simply all those points of divergence in sequence and wording that have always impressed critics. I mean that such plot and verbal differences are parts of a larger deliberate literary crafting. Each narrative shapes a portrayal of Jesus and his followers that, when taken with full seriousness, is not reducible to the portrait found in any of the others. In this essay, I cannot develop a complete interpretation of each with supporting textual evidence, but I can offer only a thumbnail sketch by way of reminder and an invitation to read.[10]

NARRATIVE AS INTERPRETATION

In the Gospel of Mark, the larger historical world is barely evident before the passion account. The narrative is almost claustrophobically focused on the drama in which Jesus is the central character: his battle against cosmic forces at work in human distress, his conflicts with Jew-

---

[10]For a fuller development of the literary art and portrayal of Jesus and the disciples in each Gospel, together with specific and detailed textual support for the assertions made here, see Luke Timothy Johnson, *The Writings of the New Testament: An Interpretation*, 2nd ed. (Minneapolis: Fortress, 1999), pp. 155-257, 521-57, and *Living Jesus*, 119-94.

ish religious leaders, his call and instruction of followers. The narrative focuses above all on the drama of discipleship and on the portrayal respectively of Jesus and those he summons as his followers. Because of the compression and tension built into Mark's narrative, and because of the complex compositional techniques he uses to construct that narrative, Mark's is not the easiest and most accessible Gospel to read, but the most difficult and deflecting.

Mark's Jesus is a complex combination of power and weakness. On one side, his proclamation of God's rule is enacted by powerful deeds of exorcism and healing that demonstrate the imminent collapse of Satan's captivity of humans. On the other side, Jesus is himself captive to the machinations of his human opponents, who finally have him arrested, tortured and executed under imperial authority. He is himself the *mysterion* of God's rule, who simultaneously attracts and repels even as it reveals power in weakness and weakness in power. In Mark's narrative, Jesus' teachings are correspondingly compressed and cryptic: his parables serve as much to confuse as to enlighten; his demands turn away followers as much as draw them; his declarations concerning his own destiny create fear rather than hope.

The depiction of the disciples in Mark's Gospel is, in turn, almost completely negative. Although they are summoned to carry forward his activities and to "be with him," they prove both mentally incompetent and morally deficient. Jesus declares that his parables are intended for insiders, yet these insiders do not grasp his parables; indeed, they react to his plain speech as though it was parabolic! They are as "hard of heart" and slow to understand as outsiders. Above all, they refuse to accept Jesus' declarations on the demands of discipleship. Their failure to understand is perhaps explicable because of Mark's portrayal of Jesus as *mysterion*. Their moral failure is more serious. They had been called to "be with" Jesus, yet as he moves toward his destined suffering and death, he is betrayed by Judas, denied by Peter and abandoned by all the rest. In their disloyalty, they fail in their most fundamental responsibility. In Mark's Gospel, readers are not to look to the disciples to learn but are rather to look to Jesus: "this is my beloved Son, listen to him."

Matthew follows the Markan storyline from the Baptist to the empty tomb, thus expressing a fundamental level of agreement with Mark's narrative. Both by the inclusion of extensive bodies of sayings material, however, and by the shaping of the narrative around the discourses arranged by the Evangelist, Matthew has opened Mark's narrative up to a larger world. Matthew's Gospel shows unmistakable signs of a church in conversation and conflict with a formative Judaism that was organizing itself around the convictions of the Pharisees and the expertise of the Scribes into a religion centered in the symbol of Torah. Matthew retains the complex elements of Mark's portrayal of Jesus as one who is both powerful and weak, who conquers evil forces yet suffers from evil men. But in Matthew, Jesus not only teaches more extensively—and much less paradoxically—than in Mark, but his narrative portrays Jesus as the teacher of the church who fulfills Torah, who definitively interprets Torah and who personifies Torah.

The portrayal of the disciples in Matthew's Gospel corresponds to the portrayal of Jesus. They are no less morally problematic than the disciples portrayed in Mark: Judas betrays, Peter denies (with an oath that Jesus expressly forbids) and all abandon Jesus. Matthew characteristically has Jesus call them "you of little faith." In striking contrast to the disciples in Mark's narrative, however, those in Matthew are portrayed as intelligent. They are nonironically the insiders who understand the parables; when Jesus asks them, "Do you understand these things?" they respond, "Yes," and the narrator does not deny that assertion. The reason for this change is also clear: Matthew's disciples must carry on Jesus' teachings in the world, as Jesus commissions them, "Go make disciples of all nations, teaching them all that I have commanded you." To carry out this mission, however morally flawed they are, the disciples must have intelligence.

The Evangelist Luke also takes over the Markan narrative and follows it even more closely than does Matthew both in sequence and wording. But Luke opens up that narrative even more fundamentally than does Matthew, in two ways: he extends the Gospel narrative into an entire second volume that continues the story of Jesus in the acts of his disciples, to form a single, two-volume work (Luke-Acts); and he opens the story of Jesus and the church to the larger story of Israel within the world history then dominated by Greek culture and Roman rule. In the Gospel portion of his story, Luke's infusion of sayings material and his narrative redaction works to portray Jesus as the spirit-filled prophet who brings God's visitation to the people of Israel and, by his good news to the poor (enacted by his powerful deeds of liberation), divides the people from within, so that the marginal elements in society come join the people constituted by faith in the prophet, while the powerful and pious find themselves excluded. It is small wonder that virtually every "historical Jesus" on offer today bases itself on Luke's narrative; for this public, prophetic and political Jesus is one most deeply appealing to contemporary sensibilities.

As for Luke's portrayal of the disciples, in the Gospel they appear as prophets-in-training. They are not as unintelligent or as faithless as the disciples in Mark, nor as puny in faith but intelligent as the disciples in Matthew. They are, rather, those who are prepared by Jesus to continue his mission of service after his death and resurrection, when they will be empowered by the Holy Spirit. It is in the second volume that his portrayal of Jesus' disciples is fully shown: filled with the Holy Spirit after Jesus' resurrection, they continue Jesus' prophetic mission within Judaism and in the wider Greco-Roman world, exemplified above all by extending Jesus' provocative fellowship with sinners and tax collectors to the inclusion of Gentiles within the people.

I noted above how John's Gospel diverges from the synoptic pattern in dramatic fashion. It does not follow the Markan storyline. As a result, Jesus' ministry lasts three years rather than two, it is centered in Judea rather than in Galilee, and the cleansing of the temple occurs at the start rather than at the end of his ministry. Even more fundamental is the way John portrays Jesus. He does none of the exorcisms that dominate Mark's account and performs only a few healings. Jesus' manner of speech is even more divergent. Instead of short aphorisms and parables, he characteristically delivers long monologues that follow upon extended exchanges with his opponents. All of Jesus' teaching of his disciples takes place at the Last Supper, which is notably lacking in any of the symbolic words found in the Synoptics.

As Matthew and Luke "open up" Mark's story respectively to the larger social contexts of formative Judaism and Greco-Roman culture, so John also opens the story of Jesus to an explicitly cosmic dimension. John certainly affirms Jesus' humanity as the word "made flesh": his Jesus experiences fatigue and thirst, disappointment, friendship and grief; he asks for and receives love; he enters into real conflict with his human adversaries. Yet John's concern to show that Jesus is also the "Word" made flesh makes him portray Jesus above all as the Man from Heaven, the revealer whose deeds and words shines the light of God's judgment into the darkness of the world's sin, and who therefore experiences the hatred and rejection of the world that does not want to walk in the light. In the fourth Gospel, individual disciples act as their counterparts in the Synoptics: Judas betrays Jesus and Peter denies him. But John includes "the disciple whom Jesus loved" as an example of one whose friendship with Jesus enabled fidelity even to the cross. As a whole, the portrayal of the disciples corresponds to John's depiction of Jesus: they are his friends for whom he prays they be consecrated in the truth so that they can bear witness in the world as he has borne witness, even though they will experience the hostility of the unbelieving world just as Jesus has.

These brief sketches have suggested that the narrative Gospels of the New Testament present richly textured and distinctive portraits of Jesus. Each constructs a narrative world that is recognizably that of first-century Palestine. Each displays characters that fit within that province during the time of its Roman occupation. In each, the portrayal of Jesus fits within that constructed world. The portrait of Jesus in each Gospel fits within its narrative but would not fit within the narrative of another Gospel. In each Gospel, finally, the portrayal of the disciples corresponds to the depiction of Jesus: Mark's unintelligent and faithless disciples are not the same as Matthew's weak but intelligent disciples; the prophetic successors-in-training found in Luke are different from the friends of Jesus in John. The "literary character" Jesus whom the reader engages in each narrative is highly specific and distinctive to that Gospel.

NARRATIVE AS WITNESS

Precisely because of their obvious divergence in their interpretations of
the human Jesus, the Gospels are all the more valuable as witnesses on
those points where they agree—even if their understanding of the point
differs. This is a principle of testimony basic to the demonstration of a
case in law. If four neighbors offer distinct explanations for something
they saw or heard the previous night, that difference in explanation (it
was a thunderclap around 11:45, it was a gunshot exactly at midnight,
it was a dog barking at 11:50, it was a truck backfiring at around midnight) tends to confirm the fact that there was a loud noise in that area
between 11:45 and midnight.

I have already stated that the convergence of the Gospel narratives
confirms only a few of these facts concerning Jesus. But there is another
question of divergence and convergence on which they offer the most
important sort of witness, namely the question of Jesus' character *(ethos)*.
The question of character—what *kind* of person is this?—is at the heart
of historical inquiry at the level of the individual, that is, of biography.
Even when all the available facts concerning a figure have long been
available, new studies can be written precisely because the question of
character remains open. Is the subject good or evil, a positive presence
among other humans or negative, and in what fashion? It is a question
that narrative is distinctively capable of addressing. Narratives, indeed,
can get character right even when they get some facts wrong. It is possible, for example, to get every biographical fact about Mother Teresa
correct, yet ascribe her life of (apparently selfless) service to nefarious
motives. It is also possible to be mistaken on one or another biographical fact, yet accurately estimate and communicate Mother Teresa's
character. As it happens, the four Gospels, which disagree on so many
specific facts concerning Jesus of Nazareth, show a remarkable level on
convergence in their witness concerning his character.

The character of Jesus as depicted in all four Gospels is not complex
or filled with ambiguities. It is profoundly simple and straightforward,
and is clearly displayed within the gospel story. I do not mean to suggest that it is an abstraction. The opposite is true: the Gospels agree on
the factual elements identified earlier: he is a Jewish male of first-

century Palestine who chooses twelve followers, who performs healings, proclaims God's rule, who teaches in parables and interprets Torah, and who is crucified by order of the Roman prefect Pontius Pilate.
He is baptized by John and he "cleanses" the temple. Each of the Gospels, furthermore, renders Jesus still more concretely by using the symbols drawn from Torah, such as Son of Man and prophet. The depiction of Jesus' character lies within all the dense specificity of description
of him in each Gospel.

The most obvious element defining Jesus' human character is his
obedient faith in God, whom he calls Father. Jesus is defined above all
by his relationship with God. Negatively, this can be described in terms
of the sorts of allegiance available to all humans that he eschews. Jesus
is clearly not captive to the classic appetites for pleasure (although neither is he portrayed as an ascetic like John), possessions and political
power. Neither is he driven by the need to meet the expectations of his
followers or to thwart the hopes of his opponents. He responds rather
to what he perceives to be God's will, as disclosed in the specific circumstances of his life. The decisive expression of Jesus' obedience is
found in the acceptance of his death as his Father's will even when,
filled with anguish, he desired to live.

The second major element in Jesus' character as depicted in all the
Gospel narratives is his self-disposing love toward other people. Because he is defined above all by obedience to the will of God, and that
will is disclosed moment by moment in the needs of others, Jesus is free
to respond to others with the poverty of accessibility. The degree of
availability ascribed to Jesus by the Gospels is literally astonishing: he
approaches, touches, embraces persons of every status and situation,
just as he is approached by and touched by persons of every sort of affliction and need. Ancient literature offers no real parallel to such human accessibility. Jesus' "meekness" and "lowliness" are not a matter of
self-suppression, but a matter of self-giving without regard to self.

The Synoptic Gospels portray such availability to others through
the narratives themselves—as in the Markan passages in which Jesus is
repeatedly deflected from his own intentions by the needs of others—
as well as by self-referential statements made by Jesus that speak of him

as a servant who gives his life as a ransom for many and that interpret the bread and wine he shared with his disciples before his arrest as his body and blood given for them. In John it is expressed metaphorically in sayings about bread given for the life of the world, and the shepherd laying down his life for the sheep and the seed that must die for the sake of new growth. It is expressed narratively by Jesus' symbolic washing of his disciples' feet at the final meal he shared with them. In the Gospels, Jesus is innocent in the original sense that he does no harm to others and seeks only to do good to them. The depiction of his suffering in these narratives has both poignancy and power precisely because it comes on one who has done nothing to deserve it.

The Gospels also converge in their understanding of the nature of discipleship. I have shown how the portrayal of the disciples within each narrative differs significantly. In what respect, then, do they converge? Although they disagree concerning the degree to which Jesus' followers met the standard, they agree on what the standard is: discipleship is measured by the character of Jesus. To be a follower of Jesus does not mean doing the specific actions he did, or repeating the words he spoke. It means having the same sort of character as a human being, to be radically obedient to God alone and to serve fellow humans unselfishly. There is no hint in the Gospels of an understanding of discipleship as sharing in prosperity or success or power; indeed, these are explicitly rejected in favor of the image of the servant willing to suffer for the sake of others.

What is even more striking is the way in which the same character traits of radical obedience to God (faith) and self-disposing love toward others are ascribed to Jesus by the earliest Christian epistolary literature that speaks of the humanity of Jesus. The letters of Paul, the letter to the Hebrews and 1 Peter all refer to the humanity of Jesus in terms of his character, and the elements they single out are the same ones on which the Gospel narratives converge. In their exhortations to readers to "put on the Lord Jesus" (Paul) or "look to Jesus" (Hebrews) or "follow in his footsteps" (1 Peter), these compositions single out the same qualities for believers: faith in God defined in terms of obedience and loving service toward the other. Despite all the obvious disparity among these compositions, as among the Gospels, the New Testament compositions taken as a whole agree most impressively on the one point concerning the human Jesus we most need to know: what sort of character he had and the sort of character into which Christians seek to be transformed.

CONCLUSIONS

I have argued in this essay that although properly executed historical study can yield significant results—a set of highly probably facts concerning Jesus and a rich context for reading the Gospels more responsibly—history also has severe intrinsic limitations that are exacerbated in the case of Jesus. The effort to bypass or overcome these limitations has resulted in depictions of Jesus that lack historiographical integrity. I have argued further that although the canonical Gospels are problematic as sources for historical reconstruction, they are excellent witnesses to the humanity of Jesus precisely in the way the respective narratives diverge in their portrayal of Jesus and the disciples yet converge on the question of Jesus' human character and the nature of discipleship. I conclude this essay with four observations concerning the advantages offered by this approach to the humanity of Jesus.

1. This approach is publicly accessible to all who can read narratives intelligently and are willing to expose their readings to others in public exchange. It does not require a special methodology beyond attention to the simple and widely known literary categories of plot, character and theme. Most of all, it does not require the dismantling of the narratives that are our earliest explicit interpretations of the human Jesus; rather, it demands that those narratives be treated in their literary integrity and that meaning is sought in the narrative rendering of Jesus as such.

2. Such a narrative reading yields an understanding of Jesus that is far richer and more nuanced than the sociological reductions offered by many "historical Jesus" publications. The interplay of difference and similarity is a positive invitation to contemplate a human being who could give rise to such complex interpretations and, at the same time, draw the reader to the perception of the same "character" within the diversity of each literary representation.

3. Paradoxically, approaching Jesus as a literary character within the Gospel narratives also provides our best access to history with respect to Jesus. It is the case, first of all, that the past two centuries of intensive archaeological research have tended to confirm rather than disconfirm the details provided by the Gospels; indeed, the Gospels remain our best historical source for early information concerning important elements of Palestinian Judaism, for example, the Pharisees, Scribes and Sadducees. Even when the Gospel accounts most conflict with other historical knowledge, such as the dating of the imperial census at Jesus' birth (in Luke) or the intricate legal process recounted in the passion narratives, they are sufficiently in line with that other knowledge to enable serious historical conversation. Most remarkable is the manifest rootedness of the literary character Jesus in the Palestinian Judaism of the first century under Roman dominance. Even though the traditions of Jesus' sayings and deeds were transmitted orally within faith communities for some forty years before the first of these Gospel narratives was composed—passed on for decades, it should be noted, as much outside Palestine as within, for none of our Evangelists seems to have had firsthand experience of that place or time—Jesus' healings and exorcisms, his parables and his aphorisms all make most sense in that setting. Even more, it is impossible to imagine the Jesus of the four canonical Gospels as a character in any other time or place than the one these narratives imagine.

4. Finally, the Jesus whom we engage and come to know as a human character in the canonical Gospels is also the historic Christ. It is this fully rounded literary character that provides the basis for the "Christ-Image" in literature, so recognizable a way of being human that it can be mistaken for no other. More important, it is the Jesus of the Gospels who has caught the attention and won the deepest devotion of the saints and reformers throughout the history of Christianity, a Jesus far more radical and demanding than any conjured by the questers' art. It was not a scholarly historical reconstruction but the Jesus of the Gospels that galvanized Francis of Assisi, Martin Luther, Martin Luther King, Dorothy Day and Mother Teresa. Historically, Christianity has never been renewed or reformed by a historical Jesus, but it has always been renewed and reformed by closer attention to the Jesus of the Gospels.

RESPONSE TO
LUKE TIMOTHY JOHNSON

Robert M. Price

The argument of Luke Timothy Johnson in this essay seems to me to parallel that of Hans Frei in *The Eclipse of Biblical Narrative*.[1] Both minimize the supposed results of attempts to use the Bible as a historical mine to be dredged for evidence of past events. Some bits of the text turn out to be gold, others fool's gold. Scholars debate which is which. Both Johnson and Frei propose that a better use of one's time would be to stick with the surface level, to read the biblical narratives *as narratives* and to let them make their intended literary impact. Then we may be in a position to approach the question of underlying events obliquely and perhaps more profitably.

SECURE ASSUMPTIONS?

Professor Johnson begins with three postulates about Jesus and the sources concerning him. Jesus was a genuine historical figure, he was born in first-century Jewish Palestine, and he died executed by the Roman authorities. His disciples preached his messiahship across the Roman world during the next quarter century, resulting in the production of the various New Testament documents. Had there been no historical Jesus, and had his life not ended in crucifixion, we cannot imagine the propagation of Christianity as we know it. The spread of the Christian faith rules out any other mode of beginning for the faith. I am far from

---

[1]Hans W. Frei, *The Eclipse of Biblical Narrative: A Study in Eighteenth and Nineteenth Century Hermeneutics* (New Haven, Conn.: Yale University Press, 1974).

certain about these "facts." For one thing, it is circular to argue that Jesus cannot have been a mythical figure because the time between his earthly life and the writing of Gospels was too short for myth monger-ing. If the birth is mythical, the connection with Herod the Great bor-rowed from Josephus's version of Pharaoh trying to forestall the infant Moses, then there is of course no terminus a quo. The bottom falls out. I think it quite likely that Jesus is an offshoot of an ancient version of Yahve depicted along the lines of Baal, Osiris, Dionysus or Attis: a heavenly hero or king who won his divine throne by defeating a dragon who initially devoured him, but then yielded to the resurrected savior.[2] At some point, institutional consolidation, factional polemics against spiritualists like the Gnostics, led church officials to historicize their Jesus as a figure of recent history.[3] It had to be recent enough that "our" bishops (or their mentors) had met him and been trained by him: "Shake the hand that shook the hand."

And as for the spread of this gospel all over the ancient world within twenty-five years, we have to ask, again, within twenty-five years of what? Nor is it clear that whatever new element lent Christianity its new nametag must have had much to do with ostensible events in Jew-ish Palestine. One can understand how various Mediterraneans of var-ious nationalities would have been happy enough to add a new name, Jesus, to their portfolio/pantheon of initiation deities. (First Corinthi-ans 8 seems to be trying to stop such ecumenical henotheism, presup-posing its practice.) It is not so easy to picture Gentiles giving a fig over whether a recently executed man named Jesus had really been the theo-cratic king of Israel. What concern was that of theirs? They weren't Jews. Even if they were God-fearing Gentiles who admired Jewish ethical monotheism, messianism would have fallen as far outside their circle of interest as circumcision did. A Jesus mystery religion with its sacramental meal of wine (like the Dionysiac blood) and bread (like the

---

[2]Geo Widengren, "Early Hebrew Myths and their Interpretation" in *Myth, Ritual and King-ship: Essays on the Theory and Practice of Kingship in the Ancient Near East and in Israel*, ed. S. H. Hooke (New York: Oxford University Press, 1958), p. 191; Margaret Barker, *The Great Angel: A Study of Israel's Second God* (Louisville: Westminster John Knox, 1992), pp. 4-5.

[3]Arthur Drews, *The Christ Myth*, trans. C. DeLisle Burns, Oxford: Classics in Religious Studies (1910; reprint, Amherst, N.Y.: Prometheus, 1998), p. 272.

Osirian flesh) required no historical founder, recent or remote, any more than the similar faiths of Isis, Mithras, Attis or the rest.

METHODOLOGY AND MYTHOLOGY

Professor Johnson well understands the methodological challenges that prevent the historian's rendering a verdict of "probable" on very much of the Gospel material. He even seems pessimistic. He is not much bothered by this since, like Raymond E. Brown, he depends on an alternative kind of epistemology, that of faith, for what he believes to be access to realities of the distant past. Personally, I wonder if that amounts to any more than the sheer will to believe, and I doubt if one has the right to make such a leap. But I will not fault Dr. Johnson as long as he keeps straight which hat he is wearing when. He seems to have things pretty clear, as Brown did.

Dr. Johnson offers yet a third epistemological path to Jesus, and this one I am not so sure about. Again like Hans Frei, he recommends that we encounter Jesus as a literary character, even as four literary characters since he admits the four Evangelists draw distinct portraits of Jesus. I agree. A wonderful idea, a completely "clean" means of encounter with a transformative, life-challenging figure. I feel that way also when I am reading Kazantzakis's *The Last Temptation of Christ* or Gibran's *Jesus the Son of Man*. To me it does not matter if there should somehow be an historical basis to the thing. But to Dr. Johnson, I think that it does, and that it matters very much to him. He wants us to identify the Gospel Jesus with Jesus as he really lived in the past. Here, from what little he says at this point in the necessarily short space allotted him, Dr. Johnson strikes me as leapfrogging back over his weighty and credible section on methodology, as if he had never written it. For instance, he says that, given the freedom of the Evangelists as narrators (= writers of historical fiction?), we can once again explain and defend their disagreements as the piddling differences in detail we find between four independent witnesses of a single event. But he has admitted he believes Matthew and Luke are dependent on Mark. How do they become "independent" at this point? If he is saying the Evangelists each felt free to fictionalize the details as he wished,

I should think the historian finds himself in more trouble rather than less.

Then Dr. Johnson tabulates the ethical qualities, hence the overall noble character, of the narrated Jesus, which is pretty consistent throughout the Gospels. He seems to be arguing that such a compelling figure must reflect a real historical individual standing behind them. This, I fear, is a dangerous inference. One might be tempted to believe in a euhemeristic version of Sherlock Holmes or Superman based on the same sort of evidence. The "temporary willing suspension of disbelief" while we are under literature's enchantment is one thing: a permanent suspension of disbelief is another.

At this juncture, Professor Johnson even repairs to the apologetical argument that the gospel "story" is probably basically historical after all because it rings true archaeologically. This is certainly not at all the impression I receive from following the debates over whether archaeology permits us to believe there were synagogue buildings in pre-70 c.e. Galilee, whether scribes were called rabbi before the end of the first century c.e.,[4] whether the "seat of Moses" was a second-century phenomenon,[5] or even whether Nazareth was completely vacant during the decades assigned to Jesus in the story.[6] And the threat of a devastating negative verdict, which would be completely irrelevant to a novel (who requires a geographical location in the ancient world for Gondor or Rohan?), raises the ghost of Old Testament minimalism. I think it is now fair to say, in view of the work of Thomas L. Thompson,[7] Philip R. Davies,[8] Giovanni Garbini[9] and others that biblical epics need bear little or no relation to the ostensible events they seem at first glance to relate. Biblical sagas may be intended to provide a sacred past, a

---

[4]J. Andrew Overman, *Matthew's Gospel and Formative Judaism: The Social World of the Matthean Community* (Minneapolis: Fortress, 1990), pp. 44-45.

[5]Ibid., p. 145.

[6]Rene Salm, *The Myth of Nazareth: The Invented Town of Jesus* (Parsippany, N.J.: American Atheist Press, 2008).

[7]Thomas L. Thompson, *The Mythic Past: Biblical Archaeology and the Myth of Israel* (New York: Basic Books, 1999).

[8]Philip R. Davies, *In Search of "Ancient Israel,"* Journal for the Study of the Old Testament Supplement Series 148 (Sheffield: Sheffield Academic Press, 1992).

[9]Giovanni Garbini, *History and Ideology in Ancient Israel*, trans. John Bowden (New York: Crossroad, 1988).

holy heritage, a "theology of recital"[10] precisely where one had to be fabricated to serve the needs of a new community who had or knew no long history and were forced to make one up, or to receive one from the legitimators of their social and cultic common life. The distance between Mallory's King Arthur and the Romano-British warrior chief he may have been based on is very wide. The same may be said for the gap between Santa Claus and the fourth-century Saint Nicholas of Myra. So again for King David whose mighty kingdom seems to have left no foundation stone on the firm ground of history. And the same will prove true, I think, for Jesus of Nazareth. The tendency of history, disappointing as it is to us at a certain stage, telling us it is time to put away childish things, is that the more a narrative resembles myth and epic, or fiction, the more likely it is. The more brimming with archetypes and artifice the story is, the more probable that it is "just" a story.[11] And as we grow more mature, we stop saying things like "just a story."[12]

---

[10]Gerhard von Rad, *Old Testament Theology*, vol. 1, *The Theology of Israel's Historical Traditions*, trans. D. M. G. Stalker (New York: Harper & Row, 1962), pp. 121-128; G. Ernest Wright, *God Who Acts: Biblical Theology as Recital* (Chicago: Regnery, 1952).

[11]Frank Kermode, *The Genesis of Secrecy: On the Interpretation of Narrative* (Cambridge, Mass.: Harvard University Press, 1979), pp. 62-63. In pointing out the fictive character of Mark's Gospel, Kermode does not mean to denigrate it, though he knows many pious readers would think that is the implication.

[12]Paul Tillich, *Dynamics of Faith*, World Perspectives Series 10 (New York: Harper & Row Torchbooks, 1957), p. 45.

RESPONSE TO
LUKE TIMOTHY JOHNSON

John Dominic Crossan

The first part of Johnson's essay concerns the necessity of reconstructing (my term) the historical Jesus against the background of historiography's dangers and delusions, biases and prejudices, divergences and disagreements. As I read those pages, I kept agreeing with what was said and still wondering if it protested too much. I kept wondering if, after those warnings about reconstructing Jesus, one could and should continue with equal warnings about confessing Christ. There are, to be sure, "the limits of history," and there is also such a thing as bad or even evil history. But there are also the limits of theology and such a thing as bad or even evil faith. Have historians caused more havoc by getting Jesus wrong than theologians have by getting Christ wrong?

To take an ordinary and everyday example, what about trial by jury—specifically for those overly impressed by postmodernist theory? On a jury, one swears to reconstruct what happened based solely on the evidence presented in court. Having heard two narratives, splendidly presented and totally at odds with one another, we claim to be able—most of the time—to decide "beyond a reasonable doubt" on what actually happened, on which story is true and which false. With that example in mind, I find some of Johnson's claims too much like preemptive strikes.

One example.: "If historiography cannot declare concerning the divine claims made for a Roman emperor such as Augustus, neither can it declare concerning Jesus as the incarnate one." On one level, and immediately, I think: of course. But on another level, historiography can and must explain the precise content of those opposing claims within, say, Roman imperial theology and Pauline Christian theology. What were Romans seeing in Augustus as divine, Son of God, and God incarnate, and what (was it low lampoon or high treason?) were Christians seeing in transferring all such titles to Christ? Titles are incarnate programs, and a historian should be capable of accurately delineating those programs and why they were incarnate at this time and place in this rather than that person. In other words, good history should explain why some people chose Christ rather than Caesar, some Caesar rather than Christ, and some finally equated them in an apocalyptic consummation of Christ-as-Caesar.

Another example: "It is simply not the case that 'the historical' equals 'the real.'" Once again: yes, of course. But if the real is everything that has ever happened in the past and present world, one's mind shudders into silence even before one's own life and its limited memories and forgotten happenings. But that "real" is unknowable and comes to us—all of us together in multilateral debate—only as history (including anthropology, sociology and archaeology). To invoke "the real" against "the historical" is either a mere defensive strategy or a disqualification for scholarship—not to speak of jury duty.

Final example: "A final limitation on history is that it can only describe (or construct) the past: it cannot prescribe for the future." Again, and finally, yes and no. But is that a limitation of history or of human life? No interpretation of the past can prescribe the future but those projective interpretations are all we ever have. On the deepest level any interpretation of history is called faith—the trust that this interpretation can serve to prescribe—delicately and carefully—a future.

Let me, then, risk such a prescription. My historical reading of the escalatory growth of human violence since the Neolithic Revolution prescribes the future for me. We will learn to disallow the normalcy of civilization's violence or we are a doomed species, magnificent but—like the saber-toothed tiger—destined for extinction. And we may take the world with us. I admit, of course, to finding that same message adumbrated in Genesis 4 and incarnated in Jesus the Christ. And I can no longer certify which came first as an absolute conviction.

The second and third parts of Johnson's essay come together for me and, since I am in basic agreement with them, my purpose is simply to push each of them a little further toward convergence. If Johnson will allow my "blithe overconfidence," I am much more convinced than he is that it is precisely on what he terms the "character" of Jesus that one can reconstruct—as a historian—that which one can believe in—as a Christian. I also agree with him, by the way, that a Christian is one who confesses "Jesus as exalted Lord present in the Spirit." But, in honor of Matthew 7:21-23 // Luke 6:46, I would add: confesses and lives accordingly. And, as always, I want to see the *content* of that confession before even wanting it to be lived sincerely.

Johnson sums up what "the historian can assert . . . with the highest degree of probability" concerning the historical Jesus. In this response I focus on just one element in that summary but with no intention of slighting, let alone denying, the other ones he mentions.

Here is that element: "Jesus existed as a Jew in the first century . . . [and] was executed by Roman authority in Palestine." Later, speaking of the "character" of Jesus in the four Gospel versions, Johnson notes that, "the Gospels agree on the factual elements identified earlier." And, once again, I focus on that same element. Jesus was "a Jewish male of first-century Palestine who . . . [was] crucified by order of the Roman prefect Pontius Pilate." Josephus and Tacitus agree on that, and Pilate even gets himself named in the Christian creeds. But in order to continue, I bring another scholar into the debate.

In her book *Jesus of Nazareth, King of the Jews* Paula Fredriksen emphasizes one historical detail twice at its start and twice again at its conclusion. On the book's opening pages, she notes the "incontrovertible fact" that, "though Jesus was executed as a political insurrectionist, his followers were not."[1] Again: "Our focus on the anomaly of what we know past doubting to be historically true—that Jesus was executed by Rome as an insurrectionist, but that none of his followers were" (p. 11).

---

[1]Paula Fredriksen, *Jesus of Nazareth, King of the Jews* (New York: Knopf, 1999), p. 9. Further page numbers, noted parenthetically, reference this title.

Then, on the book's closing pages, Fredriksen speaks of "the paradox that has driven this investigation, namely, that when Pilate moved against Jesus, Jesus was the sole one of his movement to die" (p. 240) and later of "the core historical anomaly of the Passion stories: Jesus was crucified, but his followers were not" (p. 255).

I think that is a profoundly important insight that takes the historical data concerning Jesus and Pilate beyond what Johnson gives as a basically secure summary about the historical Jesus. But, that said, I disagree very strongly with Fredriksen's interpretation of *why* Pilate did *what* she has correctly and programmatically summarized as his judicial act. On the one hand, "Jesus was harmless, and Pilate knew it" (p. 241) "because Pilate knew that the message of Jesus' movement posed no threat to Roman power" (p. 243). Furthermore, "the chief priests know what Pilate knows: Jesus himself is not dangerous. But for the first time, this Passover, the crowds who swarm around him are" (p. 253). On the other, Jesus' "pinpointing the arrival of the Kingdom for *this* particular Passover was the spark that ignited all the rest" (p. 257). Even on its own terms, I find that historically untenable. If that *were* actually the spark—and I do not think it was—Jesus had indeed excited the Passover crowds and was executed not just to quiet them but to punish him.

My own interpretation is that Pilate got it precisely right (as did Antipas with John earlier). With *violent* rebels, Roman officials arrested them and as many of their company as they could find. With nonviolent *rebels*, Roman officials arrested the leader and ignored the company. Recall, to repeat what I said in another response, how "a man called Barabbas was in prison with the rebels who had committed murder during the insurrection" (Mark 15:7). On the level of this most secure historicity, Pilate certifies for all time that Jesus was both a revolutionary—hence a need for public, legal, official crucifixion—but also nonviolent—hence no need to round up his companions. For Jesus, and for many other Jews both before and after him in that dangerous first century, nonviolent resistance rather than violent rebellion was the preferred strategy against Roman imperial control.

Johnson also insists that we can learn a lot about the "character" of

Jesus from the Gospel versions in the New Testament. I agree with that very strongly and think "character" is a better focus than the older "self-consciousness." But, continuing from Pilate's witness to the nonviolent "character" of Jesus, I think we can go beyond saying that Jesus "responds to God's will." He does that, of course, but his reason for *non-violent* resistance as given in Matthew 5:38-48 and Luke 6:27-36 is what we might call the "character" of God. That is a God "who makes his sun rise on the evil and on the good, and sends rain on the righteous and on the unrighteous" (Matthew 5:45) and who "is kind to the ungrateful and the selfish" (Luke 6:35). By so acting, says the historical Jesus, you are "sons" (let us say, "children") of that God, for you "must be as" God is.

At the start of his essay, Johnson notes that: "Within the many rival parties that make up Christianity . . . all agree that the humanity of Jesus somehow functions as the model and measure for Christian discipleship. Getting Jesus right, they agree, matters." It even matters, I would add, for getting Christ right. That process is, for me, a dialectic between reason and revelation, history and faith, and, in that interaction, neither can ever obtain absolute domination. What I sense lacking in Johnson's essay is a joyful trust in that dialectic even though both come from the same God. Instead I sense a far greater distrust of history than of faith. But, for myself, while the New Testament starts with the first coming of a nonviolent historical Jesus, it ends with the second coming of a violent theological Christ. Was that, for them or for us, good history and/or good faith?

RESPONSE TO
LUKE TIMOTHY JOHNSON

James D. G. Dunn

I warm to the way Johnson sets up his essay, by spelling out the difference between a faith reading of the Gospels and a historical reading. Where I begin to become a little uneasy is his characterization of attempts to take account of both dimensions in a historically responsible way—described rather dismissively as "a variety of fuzzy mediating positions," "intellectually fuzzy positions," which either bypass "the most fundamental critical questions regarding the nature of historiography" or deal with them "in careless fashion." Johnson does tend to such sweeping characterizations, and of course he is trying to clear the ground for his own way of tackling the historical problem of accessing the human Jesus. But I could only blink with surprise (and disappointment) when he illustrated his point not only by reference to Adolf Schlatter but also to Tom Wright's *Jesus and the Victory of God* as offering "no reflection on what the term *historical* might mean when applied to Jesus." This despite the fact that *Jesus and the Victory of God* is volume two of a series (Christian Origins and the Question of God), in volume one of which Wright has provided a very full discussion of historiographical issues—as also of the importance and function of stories and narratives. It does not really help his case when Johnson refers so dismissively to one with whose reflections on the very issues Johnson is working around would have provided much grist for his mill. And not only Wright!

I welcome the rigor with which Johnson applies historical method, stressing the need for scholarly integrity in historical inquiry. "Jesus can and should be interrogated historically because he is a historical figure." And his assertion of "the limits of the verifiable evidence" and conclusion that with only a fairly limited yield of historical information concerning Jesus we have reached "the limits of what proper historiographical method allows" shows an impressive historiographical integrity on his own part—though I think his limited yield is more limited than both data and historical method allow.

But Johnson's main thrust comes in his repeated denunciation of a source criticism that dismantles the Gospel narratives in order to salvage certain "authentic" pieces in order to reassemble them into a portrayal supposedly more historical than the Gospel narratives, in order to reconstruct a "historical Jesus." In opposition, over against this he sets up his own narrative approach—"the careful and critical literary engagement with the Gospel narratives as narratives," the Gospels considered in their full literary integrity.

I have two problems with this. One is the dismissal of source criticism (and of every attempt to gain a clearer appreciation of the material on which the Evangelists drew). To characterize such "source criticism" as dismantling the Gospel narrative is highly tendentious—posed thus, of course, to highlight his own approach which respects and stays with the narrative of each Gospel. But any inquiry into a piece of writing which draws on earlier material, any attempt to appreciate how the (narrative) coherence of the writing was achieved, is bound to ask about sources—and not necessarily to reject or "dismantle" the narrative, but to understand how the narrative form was achieved. Elsewhere, following his commendatory comments on David Friedrich Strauss, Johnson himself goes on to stress the importance of identifying "all plausible sources as primary and secondary, as firsthand and secondhand." That concern is no less valid for the Gospels. The very fact that the Gospels can properly be regarded as biographies *(bioi)* underlines the relevance, not to say necessity, of inquiring what the sources were for these biographies.

My second problem is that in asserting the desirability (or need) to stay at the level of the Gospels themselves Johnson restricts the historical inquiry to a time forty and more years after Jesus' own mission. By barring the door to any earlier enquiry (source criticism) he is content to leave a full generation's gap between the earliest writing Evangelist (Mark) and Jesus. Now I wholeheartedly agree with him that from the four Gospels we can gain a clear perception of the figure who is portrayed in these writings, who indeed inspired these writings, and also a clear perception of the character of his mission—though it seems to me unavoidable that a sharper distinction has to be made between the Synoptic Gospels and John's Gospel than Johnson is willing to allow. John does not present a Jesus for whom "the kingdom of God" was the chief theme of his preaching, who regularly spoke in parables and for whom ministry to the poor and the sinner was paramount. John presents a Jesus whose self-proclamation is central to his narrative in a way and degree quite far removed from the Synoptics. Surely we have to recognize that John was trying to do something much more different from what the Synoptic Evangelists were trying to do than the differences between the Synoptics. Even though they are all "Gospels," passion narratives with lengthy introductions, to pose the historical questions simply at the level of the Gospels as narratives leaves readers with markedly divergent pictures of Jesus' character and proclamation. It is the naive assumption that John's Gospel is a Gospel of just the same historical value as the Synoptics, which causes some to assert that, as a historical fact, Jesus must have spoken of himself in the language of self-conscious deity, and to maintain the simplistic "mad, bad or god" argument as still legitimate and posing the only options.

Of course we can and should ask historical questions at the narrative level of the Evangelists. But to set the narrative world of the Gospels over against the historical value of the sources and material on which the Evangelists were able to draw is completely unhelpful. We should not treat the narrative world of the Gospels in the same way that we treat the narrative world of Jesus' parables. To be sure, we can learn much about the social world of the time from the parables. But from the parables we do not learn about the history of Jesus apart from the fact that he told such parables. I am not content to know about Jesus, to learn of Jesus, as simply a literary character—a fascinating literary character like

Hamlet or Captain Ahab, (or Prince Charming, or Shrek, for that matter). I may learn a good deal about life from such characters, well crafted by the story teller. But narrative criticism should not be confused with historical criticism. The "historical Jesus" who fascinates historians, readers/hearers of the Gospels and Christians generally is the Jesus who missioned in Galilee in the late 20s of the Common Era—what he actually did and taught as a Galilean teacher and prophet. The concern to know about the Jesus behind the Gospel narratives is not to be so easily dismissed as Johnson seems to imply. It is a concern that may well take the Gospel narratives with deepest respect and complete seriousness, but that also wants to inquire why the differences between the Gospel narratives are present and what we are to make in historical terms of the differences between the Synoptics and John in particular. Such a concern can only be satisfied by pressing through the Gospel narratives to the historical actuality to which they bear testimony.

This is why I argue for turning around the regular logic of "historical Jesus" research and Gospel criticism. Most scholars see the differences between the Gospels, including between the Synoptics, as evidence of how quickly and how far the Jesus tradition moved away from Jesus himself, from the impetus that stemmed from his own mission and teaching. In contrast, however, I see the differences between the Synoptics as evidence of the diverse ways in which the Jesus tradition was used and passed on from the first. It is the fallacy of thinking in terms of an "original" tradition, which alone is "authentic," which has misled most of us for long enough, and which, I suspect, pushes Johnson to the more desperate tactic of ignoring the traditioning process that transpired between Jesus and the writing of the Gospels. But if, despite the passage of these years, the character of the mission and of Jesus is still clear and consistent, if we can still see the imprint that Jesus made clearly in the Gospel materials (here I am at one with Johnson), then we can conclude with strong probability that the same was true in the period before the Gospels were written. The conclusion we can draw, entirely legitimately, is that Jesus made the sort of diverse impact to which the Gospels still attest, that the Jesus tradition never had a single "authentic" (or "pure") form, that Jesus was never remembered with a narrow uniformity. And we can appreciate how the Evangelists crafted their particular narratives by drawing on that earlier tradition, not inventing it, but moulding it to portray the same Jesus with their own distinctive emphases and interests.

A similar case can be made for John's Gospel—as the product and expression of a much more extended reflection on the same Jesus tradition—but to argue that case here would take us too far from Johnson's essay.

RESPONSE TO
LUKE TIMOTHY JOHNSON

Darrell L. Bock

It is a pleasure to respond to such a thoughtful essay on the limits of historical Jesus study. There is much I agree with in this presentation. For example, I agree that Jesus is known by faith and in an empirically unverifiable way, just as our soul is something we sense we possess but cannot prove is there. I certainly agree that the best way to get to know Jesus is through this lens of faith and through the communities he has engendered that allow one to share in the experience of him. This living Jesus is just as real and historical as anything humans can prove through corroborative means, as hard as that is to believe for many whose lives operate at a more material, naturalistic level.

When Johnson turns his attention to a critique of those who accept the Jesus of faith but who nonetheless try to provide a historical grounding for their belief, I sense that he has misunderstood the motives of at least some of those who do so. A theological conservative enters into a discussion of the historical Jesus less to confirm their theological convictions and more to demonstrate a belief that God acts in history. Because God has acted in history, it is possible to see traces of that *activity* and discuss their import even for one who does not possess a full set of theological commitments. Honestly inquiring people might ask, Is there evidence for Jesus outside of sources who have already sided with him? History teaches us, despite the loud objections of some, that the answer is, yes, and a case can be made for Jesus' existence without you having to embrace all I believe about Jesus. To a degree the same is true about what we can argue about Jesus from the biblical materials. One can assemble a case that points to his impact across history, especially in the first century, on historical grounds. Sometimes the way to considering theology can come through history, provided we do not think that you can prove theology by history. In trying to work this way, it is crucial that we appreciate what history can and cannot do for us. Thus an awareness of the limits of what is offered in the historical Jesus, as Johnson gives us here, is a valuable reminder as we enter this discussion.

Yet another emphasis that I would recalibrate is the claim that history cannot render a verdict on Jesus' theological claims anymore than it can on Augustus's, nor can it make a judgment about Jesus' miraculous work anymore than it can about Apollonius of Tyana. Here I wish simply to note that what history can do is trace the impact of such belief and raise the question of why so many have come to embrace the belief that Jesus was more than a mere mortal. History may be limited to that which "falls within time and space as potentially verifiable," as Johnson says, but it can trace those times when the reactions and impact of Jesus on others make you ask why many reacted to him by altering their previous understanding of religious faith. History can ask why so many risked their lives for claims that they believed uniquely applied to him. History can suggest Jesus' unusual activity (to borrow an idea from Josephus) had a character unlike other tales of the miraculous by pointing to Jesus' direct use of authority that most other accounts lack, since he generally does not use prayers, incantations or any intermediary device to generate the healings, unlike other ancient characters who heal.

My point here is one of nuance. History cannot prove such claims, but it can examine what is distinctive about the way they are made or presented. History cannot verify the resurrection, but it can verify that the earliest believers embraced such a belief in contrast to all of their previous expectations about what a resurrection involved. Something caused a shift from a Jewish hope in the raising of all people at the end of history to the bringing back to life of an individual in the midst of it. What caused this new belief? Was it an event? History can show how other explanations beyond a resurrection fail to explain adequately the rise of such belief. But there is more to this argument than merely affirming the resurrection. For example, several events tied to Jesus' earthly ministry are told in a manner in which, even though the authors believed in resurrection, do not reflect that perspective working anachronistically. What church would create an account about Jesus that embarrasses their founding leaders, depicting them as slow to embrace what Jesus told them about the faith's central teaching? And yet that is exactly what the accounts of the resurrection predictions and Jesus' coming suffering do. This helps to point to the authenticity of this kind of material. In other words, history may not be able to prove a resurrection, but it can be used to make a case that the door to its possibility cannot be shut. With this caveat in place, most of what Johnson says about what history shows about Jesus, as well as about the limits of history, I also affirm.

Turning to source criticism and its use in Jesus studies, I share Johnson's observation about how source criticism should be used, especially in appealing to reconstructed sources. Many critics have far too much confidence in their ability to reconstruct a source (or multiple sources) whose existence is hypothesized. This is especially the case when any hypothesized source is further broken down into a series of identifiable layers, as is the case with Q. The source might have existed, but to argue that we can identify the origin and nature of its layers goes far beyond what we can show. Much energy has been spent trying to get back to a pristine and supposedly superior original. This effort asks too much of a tradition rooted in an itinerant minister's teachings in a predominantly oral culture. It also often ignores the fact that such a traveling ministry would have taught on the same themes multiple times, complicating the resulting oral tradition.

Another area where I might want to retain a slightly different emphasis while making the same observation comes in how Johnson discusses the teaching of the Synoptics (especially Mark) versus John's Gospel. Under this topic, I also include the many differences between the Gospels in general. I have argued in detail elsewhere (in my *Jesus According to Scripture*) that the scale of difference many see here may well be exaggerated. Such differences, however, where they exist, are crucial to note and need to be appreciated in studying the Gospels, generally more so than most conservative scholars usually do. The portraits' diversity is obvious, but this need not make it historically problematic or contradictory. Complex characters often generate distinct, but related perceptions. For example, themes in Mark and John of who Jesus is do overlap, suggesting more connection than one might suppose. First, rearranging material along topical lines or in other kinds of groupings is not less historical just because it is not chronological. Second, to choose to highlight how an understanding of Jesus developed or was gradually realized (Mark) versus emphasizing what Jesus was ultimately showing about himself all along (John) may be more a matter of theological and literary emphasis than historical inaccuracy. We need to appreciate that actions have implications, and a series of actions can build to an intended conclusion that one can see on reflection, and yet was there all the time.

The rest of Johnson's essay points to the value of a literary reading. This is something I also value about how the Gospels can and should be read. These diverse portraits of Jesus allow us to examine through the advantage of a triangulation of perspectives a person's depth that resonates far more than if we simply had one story or multiple stories from only one basic perspective. It is like having multiple camera angles on a sporting event and being able to review by instant replay. The more angles you have, the more you can appreciate what happened. My sense is that Johnson plays these accounts a little more against each other than I am inclined to do. I do not see Mark's unintelligent and faithless disciples as so distinct from Matthew's weak but intelligent disciples, because in both accounts these disciples are wise enough to hang in there with Jesus despite Jesus' opponents giving them plausible reason and pressure to consider moving on. Mark is simply more frank about the flaws while Matthew perhaps hesitates to take away from the disciples' courage to stay with Jesus. Both of us are doing what historians regularly do here, that is, attempting to connect the dots of what fragments history leaves behind for us.

On another topic, I agree with the kind of convergence Johnson sees as present in the Gospels in regard to Jesus. Jesus was obedient to God, engaged in self-disposing love and called for a discipleship defined by the example of Jesus' character. I want to add that this call to discipleship went beyond a mere call to imitation. It was ultimately rooted in what Jesus presented about himself as the figure at the hub of the presence of the kingdom of God. The disciples could give up everything for discipleship because they were allying themselves not just with the God of promise from Israel, but with the one through whom and around whom these long-promised blessings were realized. There is more here than Jesus' being obedient to God's will; he is the bearer of promise and the presence of divine rule, something Johnson's appeal to Jesus as ransom and bread get at but could have been said more explicitly. Whether as Son of Man or Messiah in the Synoptics or as the Way and Word in John, Jesus pointed to God beyond his example by revealing God and God's way in ways that pointed to himself as possessing a unique, indispensable role in the program.

Johnson does well to state the advantages of the literary approach. This approach is publicly accessible to all, possesses richer results than the reductionistic historical Jesus approaches and reflects the fact that the Gospels give us the best access to history with respect to Jesus. This literary way discloses that the Jesus of the Gospels we engage is the historical Jesus in terms of his impact. Nevertheless, for those who are not yet able to appreciate what such a reading of the Gospels can do, a careful, sensitive historical reading of Jesus (in contrast to reductionistic or deconstructive readings) can invite people to consider a new question, opening up new vistas. Might there be more to Jesus than meets the naturalistic eye? A combination of careful historical and literary reading points to a positive reply. A carefully balanced both/and approach takes one farther than Johnson's either-or choice between the literary and historical approaches.

4

REMEMBERING JESUS

How the Quest of the Historical Jesus Lost Its Way

James D. G. Dunn

Jesus Remembered[1] was the product and climax of some thirty years' engagement with what is almost universally known as "the quest of the historical Jesus." During the course of the research for the book itself I became increasingly dissatisfied with three key methodological presuppositions which have determined the course of the quest, all three of them more or less from its inception. In reaction I found it necessary to engage in the quest from a different starting point, with a different perspective on the source material and with a different objective in analyzing that material. These three protests and proposals are somewhat scattered and easily missed or lost to view in the scope and detail of the volume (900 pages!). In this essay I will attempt to bring them to clearer view, though it will be understood that the relative brevity of the essay permits neither the detail nor the nuance of the larger volume.[2] Nevertheless, the attempt to focus more sharply on the three protests and proposals may help to make the methodological issues clearer and to highlight their importance. Each of

---

[1]James D. G. Dunn, *Jesus Remembered*, vol. 1, *Christianity in the Making* (Grand Rapids: Eerdmans, 2003).

[2]I give a fuller account in *A New Perspective on Jesus: What the Quest for the Historical Jesus Missed* (Grand Rapids: Baker Academic, 2005); the present essay was originally intended for T. Holmén and S. E. Porter, eds., *The Handbook of the Study of the Historical Jesus*, 4 vols. (Leiden: Brill, forthcoming).

my protests is double-barreled. My proposals do not fall into such a neat repeating pattern.

PROTEST ONE

My first protest is directed in the first place against the assumption that "the Christ of faith" is a perversion of "the historical Jesus"; that *faith is something which prevents a clear historical view of Jesus.* The objective of the first phase of the quest was to find the *man* behind the *dogma,* the *historical* Jesus, the *real* Jesus. The assumption was that the real Jesus must have been *different* from the Christ of faith. The real Jesus was obscured by layers of faith and dogma, hidden behind the Christ of the creeds, the God-man, the second person of the Trinity, the Pantocrator, like an original masterpiece obscured by layers of later "improvements" and centuries of pollution. The quest was motivated by the conviction that these layers of dogma could be stripped away to reveal a more human Jesus, a Jesus more believable by "modern man."

The first to pose the antithesis between the historical Jesus and the Christ of faith in these terms was D. F. Strauss[3] in his sharp critique of Schleiermacher's *Life of Jesus.*[4] Schleiermacher's lectures had been based primarily on John's Gospel, particularly the discourses of Jesus in that Gospel, and had been delivered thirty-two years earlier, prior to Strauss's own *Life of Jesus* in which Strauss had seriously questioned the historical value of the Johannine discourses.[5] So Strauss's reaction to the publication of Schleiermacher's lectures was predictable.

> Schleiermacher's Christology is a last attempt to make the churchly Christ acceptable to the modern world. . . . Schleiermacher's Christ is as little a real man as is the Christ of the church.
>
> The illusion . . . that Jesus could have been a man in the full sense and

---

[3]D. F. Strauss, *The Christ of Faith and the Jesus of History,* trans. and ed. Leander E. Keck (Philadelphia: Fortress, 1977). Originally published 1865 (Ger.).

[4]F. D. E. Schleiermacher, *The Life of Jesus,* ed. Jack C. Verheyden, trans. S. Maclean Gilmour (Philadelphia: Fortress, 1975). Originally published 1864 (Ger.).

[5]D. F. Strauss, *The Life of Jesus Critically Examined* (1835-36, 4th ed. 1846; Eng. trans., 1846, Philadelphia: Fortress, 1972), pp. 365-86. The decisive consideration for Strauss was the fact that the style of speech in the Gospel was everywhere the same, whether that of the Baptist, or of Jesus or of the Evangelist himself, pointing to the conclusion that the style, both of speech and thought, was that of the Evangelist (p. 385).

still as a single person stand above the whole of humanity, is the chain which still blocks the harbour of Christian theology against the open sea of rational science. . . .

The ideal of the dogmatic Christ on the one hand and the historical Jesus of Nazareth on the other are separated forever.[6]

Strauss, then, marks the beginning of the devaluation of the historical value of John's Gospel, which has been a principal feature of the quest for well over a century. And the critical determinant was that John's Gospel expressed so clearly the developed *faith* of the early church: John presents the Christ of faith rather than the Jesus of history.

If Strauss insisted that John should be placed on the faith side of the history/faith divide, the later nineteenth-century liberals were equally insistent that Paul should be placed on the same side. According to Adolf Harnack, Jesus had preached a simple gospel centered on the fatherhood of God, the infinite value of the human soul and the importance of love. It was Paul who had turned the religion *of* Jesus into a religion *about* Jesus. It was Paul who had transformed the simple moralizing message of Jesus into a religion requiring redemption by bloody sacrifice.[7] Here again it was faith, the faith already of the first Christians, which had begun to obscure the clearer outlines of the historical Jesus.

The late nineteenth-century liberals were not worried about dating so early the beginning of the process whereby faith had progressively obscured the lineaments of the historical Jesus. For they were confident that in the Synoptic Gospels, in Mark in particular, they still had direct access to the mind (messianic consciousness) and message of Jesus himself. William Wrede punctured that confidence in a rebuttal which largely determined the attitude of critical scholarship to the Synoptic Gospels for the rest of the twentieth century. He argued that the motif of "the messianic secret," so integral to Mark's gospel, was clear evidence of a later, faith perspective on Jesus; for example, the designation of Jesus as "Son of God" by demoniacs already expressed *Christian faith* in Jesus.[8]

---

[6]Strauss, *Christ of Faith*, pp. 4-5, 169.

[7]Adolf von Harnack, *What Is Christianity?* trans. Thomas Bailey Saunders (London: Williams and Norgate, 1901). Originally published in 1900 (Ger.).

[8]William Wrede, *The Messianic Secret*, trans. J. C. Grieg (Cambridge: Clarke, 1971). Originally published in 1901 (Ger.).

In short, then, faith pervaded the New Testament writings and their presentation of Jesus. No single Gospel could be set over against the others as more historical and less theological. This critical perspective thus established a century ago has continued to dominate the way the Gospels are approached and the use made of them in the quest of the historical Jesus. Subsequent to Wrede, Bultmann simply abandoned the quest (at least for the life and personality of Jesus)[9] and focused attention on the kerygmatic Christ. To be sure, Bultmann's disciples insisted that faith too was interested in the historical Jesus but could never quite manage to cut a way around the roadblock of faith. It was not simply that the writers of the New Testament expressed their faith in and through their writings. It was more the case that the Easter message, Easter faith, had so transformed their apprehension of Jesus that everything they said about Jesus expressed that faith. As Günther Bornkamm put it in the classic expression of the so-called second quest of the historical Jesus:

> We possess no single word of Jesus and no single story of Jesus, no matter how incontestably genuine they may be, which do not embody at the same time the confession of the believing congregation, or at least are embedded therein. . . .
>
> In every layer, therefore, and in each individual part, the tradition is witness of the reality of his history and the reality of his resurrection. Our task, then, is to seek the history *in* the Kerygma of the Gospels, and in this history to seek the Kerygma. . . .
>
> Nothing could be more mistaken than to trace the origin of the Gospels and the traditions collected therein to a historical interest apart from faith. . . . Rather these Gospels voice the confession: Jesus the Christ, the unity of the earthly Jesus and the Christ of faith.[10]

If the second questers tried to retrieve the situation, the latest phase of the quest as represented by the Jesus Seminar marks a reversion to the simplifications of the liberal quest, compounded by the radical skepticism of Wrede and Bultmann. For Robert Funk, the leading

---

[9]Rudolf Bultmann, *Jesus and the Word*, trans. Louise Pettibone Smith and Erminie Huntress (New York: Scribner's, 1935), p. 8. Originally published in 1926 (Ger.).

[10]Günther Bornkamm, *Jesus of Nazareth*, trans. Irene and Fraser McLuskey with James A. Robinson (London: Hodder and Stoughton, 1960), pp. 14, 21, 23. Originally published 1956 (Ger.).

spokesman of the Seminar, the task is as it was 150 years ago: to rescue Jesus from Christianity, to free the historical Jesus from the prisons in which faith has incarcerated him.[11] The method is straightforward: whatever resonates with early Christian faith can be discarded.[12] The desired result is a Jesus amenable to questers' values and prejudices.[13]

In short, then, throughout the history of the quest of the historical Jesus, leading participants have all accepted as a methodological given the twofold proposition: that Christian (post-Easter) faith pervades all our chief sources for the life and mission of Jesus and that this faith prevents the present-day quester from seeing Jesus as he was, or even as he was seen by his disciples pre-Easter. It is against this twofold proposition that I direct my first protest.

PROPOSAL ONE

In direct contrast to this deeply rooted suspicion of faith as a barrier to and perversion of any historical perspective on Jesus, my proposal is that *the quest should start from the recognition that Jesus evoked faith from the outset of his mission* and that *this faith is the surest indication of the historical reality and effect of his mission.*

One thing we can be sure about: that Jesus made an *impact* in and through his mission. There were people who became his disciples; this we can be sure of, since otherwise no one would have remembered this Jesus or have wanted to do so, and he would have quickly disappeared in the soon gathering mists of history. The fact that Jesus made disciples is generally recognized. What has not been given sufficient recognition or weight, however, is the effect of this impact. These disciples encountered Jesus as a life-transforming experience: they followed him; they left their families; they gave up their livelihoods. Why? Because they had believed Jesus and what he said and taught. Because they believed in Jesus. They entrusted their lives and futures to him. Such a response cannot be denied the characterization "faith." Their disciple-

---

[11]R. W. Funk, *Honest to Jesus* (San Francisco: HarperSanFrancisco, 1996), p. 300.

[12]Robert W. Funk and Roy W. Hoover, eds., *The Five Gospels: The Search for the Authentic Words of Jesus* (New York: Macmillan, 1993); see, e.g., the references to the Jesus Seminar in the author index of *Jesus Remembered*, p. 959.

[13]More extensive criticism in *Jesus Remembered*, pp. 58-65.

ship was a faith commitment, already before Easter. Of course it was not yet Easter faith. And Easter faith transformed the pre-Easter faith. But the faith of discipleship was still faith.

The point is obvious. The earliest faith of the first Christians is not a hindrance or barrier to our perceiving the reality of what Jesus did and said and the effect he had. On the contrary, the impact thus made by Jesus is itself the evidence needed by those who want to appreciate the character and effectiveness of Jesus' mission. But what of the challenge posed by Bornkamm? Has that evidence been diluted or overlaid by the subsequent post-Easter faith? To some extent the answer must be "yes." But the second part of my first proposal is that *the original impact of Jesus' mission on his first disciples is, nevertheless, still clearly evident in the tradition preserved by the Synoptic Gospels.*

Here I draw particularly on a neglected article by Heinz Schürmann to the effect that the beginnings of the sayings tradition in the Gospels must lie in the pre-Easter circle of disciples, and thus, as Schürmann added, with Jesus himself.[14] The claim can easily be documented. Consider only the Sermon on the Mount (Mt 5–7) or the parallel material in the Lukan Sermon on the Plain (Lk 6:17-49): the beatitudes, the call to love the enemy and not retaliate, the demand to give to those who beg from you, the warning against judging others, about the speck in someone else's eye and the log in one's own, the tree known by its fruits, the parable of the wise man and foolish man. Which of these shows traces of post-Easter embellishment or perspective? Arguably one or two, but not the bulk of them. Of course, within the present Gospels they are retold within a gospel context, that is, as part of a story climaxing in Jesus' death and resurrection (Bornkamm's chief point). My point, however, is that their form and content show no signs of being originated or shaped by post-Easter faith. Who, for example, in a post-Easter context would have deemed it sufficient to challenge disciples to build their lives on Jesus' teaching (Mt 7:24-27 // Lk 6:47-49) rather than on Jesus Christ himself (as in 1 Cor 3:11)? In other words, here we

---

[14]Heinz Schürmann, "Die vorösterlichen Anfänge der Logientradition: Versuch eines formgeschichtlichen Zugangs zum Leben Jesu," in *Der historische Jesus und der kerygmatische Christus,* ed. H. Ristow and K. Matthiae (Berlin: Evangelische, 1961), pp. 342-70.

have *material that has been given its still enduring content and shape prior to the rise of Easter faith.*

The difference between the two perspectives, the one against which I protest and the one I propose, is well illustrated by their different responses to the hypothetical Q document. Two features of this document are generally agreed among Q specialists. One is that the traditions generally assigned to this document have a marked Galilean character, as indicated by the story of the centurion's servant (Mt 8:5-13 // Lk 7:1-10) and the woes on Chorazin and Bethsaida (Mt 11:21-24 // Lk 10:13-15), and illustrated by the characteristically agrarian setting of many of the traditions, assuming the daily reality of debt, day laborers, absentee landlords and the like. The other is the lack of a passion narrative, such a prominent motif in all four canonical Gospels. From one perspective the explanation of these features is obvious. Assuming that the character of the Q document tells more about its own provenance and the faith of its compilers than about Jesus, the features point to communities/churches in Galilee that did not know the passion narrative or were even opposed to a gospel which climaxed in the crucifixion of Jesus, as in Mark.[15] From my perspective the more obvious explanation for these features is that *the Q material first emerged in Galilee and was given its lasting shape there prior to Jesus' death in Jerusalem.* That is to say, it expresses the impact made by Jesus during his Galilean mission and before the shadow of the cross began to fall heavily on either his mission or the memory of his teaching.

The third part of my first proposal is the straightforward corollary that *we can discern Jesus from the impression he left on/in the Jesus tradition.* Here I wish to take up in my own terms the protest made against the nineteenth-century quest by Martin Kähler. His protest is embodied in the title of his famous essay, *Der sogenannte historische Jesus und der geschichtliche, biblische Christus.*[16] Kähler's point was that "the historical Jesus" was a creation of the questers. The Gospels themselves do not

---

[15]See particularly J. Kloppenborg Verbin, *Excavating Q: The History and Setting of the Sayings Gospel* (Minneapolis: Fortress, 2000), chaps. 4 and 5.

[16]Martin Kähler, *The So-Called Historical Jesus and the Historic Biblical Christ,* trans. and ed. Carl E. Braaten (Philadelphia: Fortress, 1964). Originally published 1892 (Ger.).

give enough information to write the sort of Life of Jesus to which the nineteenth-century questers aspired. Lacking that information, they had to fill in the gaps from another source, a fifth Gospel—themselves, their own values and aspirations. Hence the *"so-called* historical Jesus." In Kähler's view the Gospels give access only to the *geschichtliche Christus,* the "historic Christ," that is, Jesus recognized in and by his historical significance.

It is at this point that I part company with Kähler, since by the "historic Christ" he meant the preached Christ, that is, Christ seen in his post-Easter significance, the crucified and risen Christ seen through the eyes of post-Easter faith. But his protest can be reformulated to express the outcome of my first proposal. That is to say, if we take seriously the undeniable fact that Jesus made an impact on his first disciples, and that that impact is still clearly recognizable in the content and form of the traditions by which Jesus' teaching and practice were remembered, then two things follow.

One is Kähler's point that *we cannot realistically expect to find a Jesus different from the Jesus of the Jesus tradition.* Welcome as it would be for a historian, we simply do not have any other substantive sources for Jesus' mission.[17] We have no firsthand testimony from Caiaphas or from Pilate. We do not know how Jesus impacted others. What we *do* know is how he impacted his *disciples.* If we want to strip away all faith from the traditions as part of our critical analysis of these traditions, we condemn ourselves to impotence and failure; for nothing will be left. If we want to find a Jesus who did not inspire faith, or who inspired it differently, we chase a will-o'-the-wisp. But if we take seriously the evidence of the faith-creating impact of Jesus it becomes a means to our even now being able to discern the effect of Jesus' mission and during his mission.

The other is that *by means of and through this impact we can discern the one who made the impact.* As one can discern the shape of the seal from the mark it leaves on the paper, so we can discern the shape of Jesus' mission from the impression he left on his first disciples: Not the "historical Jesus," as though he was some objective artifact that we could

---

[17]Further details and discussion in chap. 7 of my *Jesus Remembered.*

prise from the traditions and from whom we could then brush off the dirt (faith) of the intervening ages, but the *historic Jesus*, the one who left the impact still evident in the Gospels, the one who transformed fishermen and tax collectors into disciples. For historians who want to understand better the ways in which, and the reasons why, Christianity emerged, what more could be desired as an outcome for "the quest of the historical Jesus"?[18]

PROTEST TWO

My second protest is against a twofold assumption that has been more pervasively determinative of the findings of the quest than is usually appreciated. The first assumption is that *the only way to understand both the relation of the traditions in the Synoptic Gospels and the earliest transmission of the Jesus tradition is in literary terms*. My protest is against the assumption that the processing of the tradition of Jesus' teaching and activities from its first hearers to the written Gospels has to be conceived almost entirely, or even exclusively, as a process of copying and editing earlier written documents.

This should be plain to anyone who is familiar with the history of the quest. Inextricably interwoven with that history is the progress of Gospel criticism. The two have gone hand in hand, often to the disadvantage of both. An obvious first step in the quest was to ascertain, What were the sources for the information about Jesus provided by the Gospels? Source criticism was conceived for the most part, and in effect almost exclusively, in terms of written documents. The relations between the Synoptic Gospels, which obviously overlap to a considerable extent in the material they use, were most readily conceived in terms of Evangelists' using each other's Gospels or a common written source now lost. A synopsis demonstrated that one Evangelist must have been dependent on another, by copying or abbreviating, or expanding, or otherwise editing his source. The dominant solution to the Synoptic

---

[18]My exchanges with Bob Morgan on faith and history may help carry forward the discussion here: Robert Morgan, "James Dunn's *Jesus Remembered*," *Expository Times* 116 (2004-2005): 1-6, and "Christian Faith and Historical Jesus Research: A Reply to James Dunn," *Expository Times* 116 (2004-2005): 217-23; with my own responses—"On Faith and History, and Living Tradition," *Expository Times* 116 (2004-2005): 13-16 and 286-87.

Problem was and still is the "two *document* hypothesis"—Mark as the earliest Gospel, Matthew and Luke drawing on Mark and on a sayings source (Q).[19] B. H. Streeter's authoritative treatment of the Synoptic Problem cautioned against studying the Synoptic Problem "merely as a problem of literary criticism," but in the event resolved the question of Matthew's and Luke's additional material in terms of two further writings (M and L)—hence the "four-*document* hypothesis."[20]

The main alternatives offered to the dominant two-document hypothesis have been those of William Farmer[21] and Michael Goulder.[22] Both continue to exemplify a modern mindset which can conceptualize the history of the Jesus tradition only in terms of copying or editing an earlier written source. And the reemergence of interest in the Q source in the last twenty years has likewise operated entirely from the working hypothesis that Q was a document written in Greek. The most influential analysis of Q, by John Kloppenborg, has even found it possible to stratify the hypothetical Q document into three layers or editions, Q^1, Q^2 and Q^3.[23] In short, the challenge of tracing the tradition history of the Gospel materials, and thus of finding the earliest or most original information for any historical account of Jesus' mission, has been conceived purely as a problem of literary dependency and resolved in the same terms.

The second assumption which I wish to protest against is the assumption that *oral tradition functioned like written tradition;* or that *it is no longer possible to say anything about the oral phase of the Gospel tradition;* or that *only the written tradition is reliable.* It is not entirely true that the literary paradigm for analyzing the Jesus tradition has completely dominated the analysis of the history of that tradition. Voices were raised

---

[19]See, e.g., Werner G. Kümmel, *The New Testament: The History of the Investigation of Its Problems,* trans. S. Maclean Gilmour and Howard C. Kee (Nashville: Abingdon, 1972), pp. 146-51; Kloppenborg Verbin, *Excavating Q,* 295-309.

[20]B. H. Streeter, *The Four Gospels: A Study of Origins* (London: Macmillan, 1924), chap. 9, quotation from 229.

[21]William Farmer, *The Synoptic Problem* (New York: Macmillan, 1964).

[22]Michael Goulder, *Luke: A New Paradigm,* 2 vols., Journal for the Study of the New Testament Supplement Series 20 (Sheffield: Sheffield Academic Press, 1989) in his attempt to dispense with Q (particularly vol. 1 chap. 2).

[23]John Kloppenborg, *The Formation of Q* (Philadelphia: Fortress, 1987). For critique see my *Jesus Remembered,* pp. 147-60.

early on in favor of recognizing an oral period for the tradition, even oral sources for the Gospels. And form criticism emerged in the 1920s as an attempt to penetrate behind the written sources into the oral period.[24] The trouble was that the most influential exponent of form criticism, Rudolf Bultmann, assumed that oral and written tradition were transmitted in the same way. He conceived the whole tradition about Jesus as "composed of a series of layers."[25] The conception was of each layer being constructed on the basis of the preceding layer—a conception no different in effect from that of successive editions of a document. But is such a way of conceptualizing oral tradition and transmission realistic? Bultmann apparently never saw the need to ask such a question.

Others have assumed that oral tradition and transmission would have been so fluid, and anyway is now lost behind the relative fixity of the written traditions of the Gospels, that it is no longer possible to reconstruct any tradition in its oral phase and not worth the trouble to try.[26] Since it is actually technically possible to explain *every* divergence in the Synoptic tradition in terms of *literary* editing, then what need have we of any further hypothesis? Others take the modern standpoint that oral material is unreliable and only written material is reliable. Consequently it becomes important for them to argue that the writing down of Jesus' teaching began very early, even already during his mission.[27] Matthew, the tax collector, is the most obvious candidate for the role of a literary disciple (one who could read and write), who, conceivably, could have taken notes during Jesus' preaching and teaching sessions. What has obviously not been sufficiently appreciated is the fact that in the ancient world the prejudice was reversed: written material was not trusted, because it could be so easily lost, or destroyed, or corrupted in the copying; it was much more preferable to have the teaching or story firmly lodged in one's own

---

[24]E.g., Rudolf Bultmann (with Karl Kundsin), *Form Criticism*, trans. Frederick C. Grant (New York: Harper/Torchbook, 1962), p. 1. Originally published 1934 (Ger.).

[25]Bultmann, *Jesus and the Word*, pp. 12-13.

[26]See particularly Barry W. Henaut, *Oral Tradition and the Gospels: The Problem of Mark 4*, Journal for the Study of the New Testament Supplement Series 82 (Sheffield: JSOT Press, 1993).

[27]See particularly Alan Millard, *Reading and Writing in the Time of Jesus*, Biblical Seminar 69 (Sheffield: Sheffield Academic Press, 2000), pp. 223-29; also E. Earl Ellis, *The Making of the New Testament Documents* (Leiden: Brill, 1999), pp. 24, 32, 352.

mind, retaining the living voice of the teacher.[28]

The consequences of these assumptions are extensive and of a seriousness too rarely recognized. For if there was an "oral period" at the beginning of the history of the Jesus tradition, lasting, say, for about twenty years, and if it is not possible to penetrate into that period with confidence, and if oral tradition is inherently unstable and unreliable, then the quest of the historical Jesus is confronted with *a yawning and unbridgeable gulf* between the tradition as we still have it and the Jesus to whom it bears witness. Here and there we may find some sayings or a motif which reaches out some way over the gulf, but the questers who rely on them to inch back toward "the historical Jesus" are likely to suffer a severe attack of critical vertigo, and the chances of establishing a firm link on the other side of the gulf become ever more tenuous the further they try to reach back.

This is the burden of my second protest against the traditional assumptions which have governed the quest of the historical Jesus. The literary mindset of the nineteenth, twentieth and twenty-first centuries has conditioned the very way in which we conceptualize the processes by which the Jesus tradition first emerged and was initially transmitted. We think in a box of literary dependency, of copying and editing. And we are the more confident of the results of our analysis of that tradition because they are so containable within the box. But the box is one constructed by the fifteenth-century invention of printing, and it prevents us from seeing outside of its containment. We shut out the reality of what an oral society must have been like, and have failed to think through the character of the traditioning process in an oral society. We think that the results of reconceptualizing the processes of oral transmission would be destructive of our grasp of the tradition's "authenticity" because of orality's inherent instability. And the outcome is that we cut ourselves off from the Jesus we want to rediscover and hear again afresh in his own terms.

---

[28]E.g., Paul Barnett, *The Birth of Christianity: The First Twenty Years* (Grand Rapids: Eerdmans, 2005) assumes that unless the earliest Jesus tradition was in *writing*, it is lost to us; in total antithesis to my thesis, Barnett regards a study "based on the culture of orality" as effectively closing off "any pathway to the actual teaching of Jesus" (p. 136).

PROPOSAL TWO

In direct contrast to the blinkeredness of the literary paradigm, I affirm, first, *the necessity of taking the oral phase of the history of the Jesus tradition with all seriousness*. And second, in direct response to any resignation before the difficulty of gaining real access to the tradition in its oral phase, I maintain that it *is* in fact *possible to envisage the oral phase of the Jesus tradition*.

First, it is necessary that we *do* make an attempt to envisage the way an oral society functions, not least in regard to the traditions it regards as important. For first-century Palestine certainly was an oral rather than a literary culture. Those who have inquired most closely into the subject tell us that literacy in Palestine at the time of Jesus would probably have been less than 10 percent.[29] And even if we can argue that a Jewish society would have prized the skills of reading and writing more highly than others, the increase in percentage may not have been very great. The reason why we read so much about "scribes" in Palestine, as well as more widely in the ancient world, is because literary skills were the prerogatives of a relatively small group of professionals. We have to assume, therefore, that the great majority of Jesus' first disciples would have been functionally illiterate.[30] And even allowing for the possibility that one or two of Jesus' immediate disciples were able to read and write (Matthew) and may even have kept notes of Jesus' teaching, it remains *overwhelmingly probable that the earliest transmission of the Jesus tradition was by word of mouth.*

Second, the extensive study of oral communities and of how oral

---

[29]Recent estimates are of less than 10 percent literacy in the Roman Empire under the principate, falling to perhaps as low as 3 percent literacy in Roman Palestine; see particularly William V. Harris, *Ancient Literacy* (Cambridge, Mass.: Harvard University Press, 1989); M. Bar-Ilan, "Illiteracy in the Land of Israel in the First Centuries CE," in *Essays in the Social Scientific Study of Judaism and Jewish Society*, ed. S. Fishbane and S. Schoenfeld (Hoboken, N.J.: Ktav, 1992), pp. 46-61; Catherine Hezser, *Jewish Literacy in Roman Palestine* (Tübingen: Mohr Siebeck, 2001). Birger Gerhardsson refuses to accept that "the Israel of NT times can be characterized as an oral society" ("The Secret of the Transmission of the Unwritten Jesus Tradition," *NTS* 51 [2005]: 1-18 [here pp. 14, 17]); but a society where the Torah was known almost entirely by being *heard* and taught, and where the initial accounts of Jesus were passed on almost exclusively by word of mouth is not yet to be described as a "literate society."

[30]Kloppenborg Verbin properly reminds us that "'literacy' itself admits of various levels: signature literacy; the ability to read simple contracts, invoices and receipts; full reading literacy; the ability to take dictation; and scribal literacy—the ability to compose" (*Excavating Q*, p. 167).

tradition functions has been greatly advanced over the latter decades of the twentieth century. Classic treatments of Yugoslavian epics, of folklore and of oral tradition for example in Africa,[31] have given us a clearer idea of what it must have meant to live in a community where information, knowledge and wisdom were all or mostly retained within an oral framework of memory and tradition in and on behalf of the community. I found Kenneth Bailey's accounts of his more than thirty years experience of the oral culture of Middle East village life particularly insightful.[32] From this material I deduce five important characteristics of oral tradition and oral transmission.[33]

1. *Oral performance is different from reading a text.* The reader can pause in the reading for reflection, can turn back to check something, can look forward to anticipate the outcome. The reader can take the book away and read it again. The editor can take the literary manuscript and make changes to the text and so on. Nothing of this is possible for the hearer of an oral tradition being retold. The hearing is an event, not a thing; the individual hearer cannot press a pause button or put the performance into reverse. It is evanescent, past and gone, and cannot be taken away for later perusal, or returned to for checking. It is not a written text which can be revised or edited. This very basic fact at once compels us to adopt a very different attitude toward the Jesus tradition in its preliterary state. What was happening to the tradition in that important phase of its history? Was every performance different in content and character from its predecessors? Did changes occur then which significantly altered or randomly transformed the tradition prior to its being written down? At the very

---

[31]Particularly Albert B. Lord, *The Singer of Tales* (Cambridge, Mass.: Harvard University Press, 1978); John Miles Foley, *Immanent Art: From Structure to Meaning in Traditional Oral Epic* (Bloomington: Indiana University Press, 1991); Jan Vansina, *Oral Tradition as History* (Madison: University of Wisconsin Press, 1985); Isidora Okpewho, *African Oral Literature: Backgrounds, Character and Continuity* (Bloomington: Indiana University Press, 1992); Alan Dundes, *Holy Writ as Oral Lit: The Bible as Folklore* (Lanham, Md.: Rowman and Littlefield, 1999).

[32]Kenneth E. Bailey, "Informal Controlled Oral Tradition and the Synoptic Gospels," *Asia Journal of Theology* 5 (1991): 34-54; also "Middle Eastern Oral Tradition and the Synoptic Gospels," *Expository Times* 106 (1995): 363-67.

[33]I draw here on my "Altering the Default Setting: Re-Envisaging the Early Transmission of the Jesus Tradition," *NTS* 49 (2003): 139-75 (here 150-55), reprinted in *A New Perspective on Jesus*, pp. 79-125 (here pp. 93-99).

least, recognition of the oral phase of the traditioning process should cause us to look twice at explanations of differences between the Synoptic traditions which rely exclusively on a literary model.

2. We can assume a *communal dimension* for oral tradition. Contemporary literary criticism inclines us to think of an individual author writing with a view to being read by an individual reader—hence such terms as "implied reader" and "reader response." We can think without effort of the sole reader at a desk or curled up on a sofa having a one-to-one encounter with the text. But oral tradition is characteristically community tradition. This was recognized by the pioneers of form criticism in the 1920s but its significance was lost to sight by those locked into the literary mindset. Here Bailey's anecdotal accounts are helpful, as he envisages village communities gathering of an evening to share news and to recall and celebrate tradition that was important to them—what he calls the *haflat samar*. So present day attempts to envisage the earliest disciple groups need to remember that there would have been no newspapers, no radio or television or cinema screen to provide a focal point for the gathering, and in most cases no scrolls of Torah or prophet to be read or consulted, but only the shared memories of what Jesus had said and done, and shared experiences of their discipleship. Furthermore, as the community's tradition, it was not the property of any individual to modify or develop at will. Where the tradition was important to the community, to its identity, there would be a natural concern to maintain the community-determining character of the tradition through all its varied performances.[34]

3. At the same time it is also important to note that an oral community designates or recognizes *particular individuals* to bear the main responsibility (on behalf of the community) to retain and recite the community tradition as appropriate on occasions when the community came together. In the absence of dictionaries or encyclopedias, the bard or apostle or elder or teacher would serve as the community's resource,

---

[34]Although I title my study of Jesus *Jesus Remembered*, my interest here and in that volume is in the way the *tradition* of Jesus emerged, not in theories of "collective or social memory." For interaction with Bengt Holmberg and Samuel Byrskog on the latter subject I may refer to my response to their critiques of *Jesus Remembered* in "On History, Memory and Eyewitnesses," *JSNT* 26 (2004): 473-87.

the storage cistern for the community's reserves of story and wisdom built up and handed down over the years.[35] Luke almost certainly has this sort of thing in mind when he refers to "the apostles' teaching" in Acts 2:42. And the prominence of teachers (e.g. Acts 13:1; Rom 12:7; 1 Cor 12:28-29; Gal 6:6; Jas 3:1) and of tradition (e.g., Phil 4:9; Col 2:6-8; 1 Thess 4:1; 2 Thess 3:6) in the earliest communities points clearly in the same direction. For the "tradition" would be the particular responsibility of the "teachers," and since it was the Jesus tradition which really marked out the assemblies of the first disciples, a large part of that responsibility must have included the rehearsal and performance of the Jesus tradition at such assemblies.[36]

4. In the performance of oral tradition we find *a characteristic combination of stability and diversity, of fixity and flexibility*. In the words of E. A. Havelock, "Variability and stability, conservatism and creativity, evanescence and unpredictability all mark the pattern of oral transmission"—the "oral principle of 'variation within the same.'"[37] There is the same story, or the story of the same event; it is the same teaching, in substance at least; but the telling of the story, or the repeating of the teaching may be very diverse, the diversity determined by such factors as the circumstances of the occasion, or by the desire of the teacher to bring out a particular emphasis or point. A modern parallel is the punch-line joke—itself as near as we may be able to come to modern experience of oral tradition. The buildup to the punch line can be wholly diverse, but if the joke is to "work," the punch line has to be "word perfect" and delivered with due attention to the timing. And this

---

[35]E.g., Eric A. Havelock, *The Muse Learns to Write: Reflections on Orality and Literacy from Antiquity to the Present* (New Haven, Conn.: Yale University Press, 1986) speaks of an oral "encyclopedia" of social habit and custom-law and convention (pp. 57-58).

[36]Richard Bauckham, *Jesus and the Eyewitnesses: The Gospels as Eyewitness Testimony* (Grand Rapids: Eerdmans, 2006), building particularly on Samuel Byrskog, *Story as History—History as Story*, WUNT 123 (Tübingen: Mohr Siebeck, 2000), gives particular weight to the (apostolic) eyewitnesses and criticizes me for maintaining the tradition of anonymous tradents in anonyomous communities (particularly chap. 12). My point, however, was that the nature of the oral traditioning process, as evidenced by the Synoptic tradition, was such that the passing on of the tradition, by whomever (first disciple, visiting apostle, local teacher), has clearly retained the same character and substance.

[37]Werner H. Kelber, *The Oral and the Written Gospel* (Philadelphia: Fortress, 1983), pp. 33, 54; quoting Eric A. Havelock, *Preface to Plato* (Cambridge, Mass.: Harvard University Press, 1963), pp. 92, 147, 184, *passim*.

is what we find repeatedly in the Synoptic tradition of Jesus' mission: the same story, but told differently, and often with inconsequential difference of detail; the same teaching, but often in different wording and set in different contexts. It is this feature of the Synoptic tradition which has always intrigued me about the Jesus tradition, and I have found no better explanation for it than in terms of performance variation, "variation within the same."[38]

5. A final important characteristic of orally performed tradition is that there is *no original version*, equivalent to an original edition of a written text. That there was an *originating* event in the mission of Jesus or a particular teaching which he gave I have no doubt, at least in most cases. But the witnesses would have seen and heard differently; the event or words would have impacted them differently. And their reporting or sharing of that impact would have been different. So there probably would not have been a single original version of any specific tradition; original/originating *event* is not to be confused with original *report* of the event. And if Jesus had given the same teaching or parable more than once, and in different terms (one thinks, for example, of the parable of the talents/pounds—Mt 25:14-30 // Lk 19:11-27), then there may never have been a single original/originating form of words. The immediate corollary has extensive repercussions. For it at once indicates that the search for an original version, as though that alone were "authentic" or "historical," is misguided. Likewise diverse forms of particular traditions are in principle not a problem, they do not constitute a "contradiction," they are not proof that the tradition has (been) developed away from "the true." On the contrary, they probably represent well the ways in which the Jesus tradition was performed in disciple groups and churches, and *from the first*.

What I envisage, then, for the beginning of the Jesus tradition, is that those whose lives were transformed by the impact of Jesus' mission, who became disciples, including those who did not literally follow Jesus, would have shared their experiences when they came together, talking among themselves. In such gatherings the impact made by what

---

[38]Examples in my "Altering the Default Setting," pp. 160-69/106-18, and throughout *Jesus Remembered*.

Jesus did and said would have been put into words, and the oral tradition of these doings and teachings would thus begin to take shape— essentially the shape which it still has in its enduring form. As already noted above, the enduring forms of so much of Jesus' teaching still bear the stamp of his Galilean mission, prior to the climax in Jerusalem. That stamp must have been given to it in such disciple gatherings, no doubt with the chief disciples (the Twelve) having a prominent say in the basic shaping of the tradition. And no doubt the performance tradition after Jesus' departure would have become more varied. But if I am right, the tradition was varied from the first, and the variations which have been preserved in the now-written texts seem again and again to be no different in kind from the variations which we can safely hypothesize as characteristic of the performance tradition from the first.

In other words, it *is* possible to penetrate back into the oral period of the Jesus tradition. For the bridge being pushed over the gulf does not come only from one side. The impact made by Jesus on the disciples, and expressed more or less from the beginning in oral tradition, means that the bridge can in effect be constructed from the other side as well. So long as we do not allow ourselves to be enticed and misled by the will-o'-the-wisp of an "original version," and are content with recognizing a clear but diverse impression made by Jesus still evident in the tradition as we now have it, then we can be much more confident than before of gaining a clear sight of the one who made that impression.

PROTEST THREE

My third protest is against the working assumption that *the quest must look for a Jesus who was distinctive or different from his environment.* Not only would "the historical Jesus," it was assumed, be different from "the Christ of faith," but he must also and nevertheless have stood out from his fellows. Now, I do not wish to play down the distinctiveness of Jesus. That Jesus made a distinctive impact is my own first proposal, an impact attested in the content and character of the Jesus tradition itself. But the assumption to which I object here is that only if Jesus can be *distinguished from his context* is he worthy of our attention (he cannot surely have been just another Jewish teacher); only if his message was different from that of other teachers can we be sure we have the authentic voice of Jesus (and not just the accumulated wisdom of Jewish sages)!

This assumption has in part been a sad corollary to Christianity's long and disgraceful history of anti-Semitism. Until recently, Christian biblical scholarship simply reflected that anti-Jewish tendency, by consistently downplaying or denigrating the continuity between Jesus and his native Judaism. As Susannah Heschel observes, liberal theologians painted "as negative a picture as possible of first-century Judaism" in order "to elevate Jesus as a unique religious figure who stood in sharp opposition to his Jewish surroundings."[39] A classic example is Ernest Renan, who wrote: "Fundamentally there was nothing Jewish about Jesus"; after visiting Jerusalem, Jesus "appears no more as a Jewish reformer, but as a destroyer of Judaism. . . . Jesus was no longer a Jew."[40] And Albrecht Ritschl drew a line in the sand, which was not decisively questioned for most of the twentieth century, when he pronounced that Jesus' "renunciation of Judaism and its law . . . became a sharp dividing line between his teachings and those of the Jews."[41] The neoliberal quest of the last two decades has not been so brash in its anti-Judaism. But a guiding presumption that Jesus was not, could not have been influenced by Jewish apocalyptic thought, and a tendency to align him more with Hellenistic Cynic critique of establishment ethos and religiosity, produced not a greatly different result—a Jesus more recognizable by (and acceptable to) those concerned to find a nonparticularist philosophy and lifestyle.[42]

My own much-used example of the dismaying trend to distance Jesus from his Jewish context is the word *Spätjudentum;* this was a common way of referring to the Judaism of Jesus' time well into the second half of the twentieth century, and it still occurs in some Ger-

---

[39]Susannah Heschel, *Abraham Geiger and the Jewish Jesus* (Chicago: University of Chicago Press, 1998), here pp. 9, 21. See also H. Moxnes, "Jesus the Jew: Dilemmas of Interpretation," in *Fair Play: Diversity and Conflicts in Early Christianity*, ed. I. Dunderberg et al., H. Räisänen FS (Leiden: Brill, 2002), pp. 83-103.

[40]Heschel, *Abraham Geiger,* pp. 156-57.

[41]Heschel, *Abraham Geiger,* pp. 123.

[42]Notably Burton L. Mack, *A Myth of Innocence: Mark and Christian Origins* (Philadelphia: Fortress, 1988), and John Dominic Crossan, *The Historical Jesus: The Life of a Mediterranean Jewish Peasant* (San Francisco: HarperSanFrancisco, 1991).

man textbooks. Why should late Second Temple Judaism be described as "late Judaism"? It is not simply that the term is ridiculous, in view of Judaism's continuing history; if first-century Judaism is "*late* Judaism," what on earth do we call twentieth- or twenty-first-century Judaism?! But the issue is much more serious than a verbal faux pas. For the term actually encapsulates Christianity's historic denigration of Judaism. It expresses the theological view that Judaism's function was solely to prepare for the coming of Christ, of Christianity. As soon as Christ came, Judaism's role was complete. As soon as Christianity was established, Judaism was finished. Hence *late* Judaism, for from that perspective first-century Judaism was the *last* Judaism! The protest at this point is long overdue.

A second working assumption follows. If first-century Judaism was so marked by false religiosity, legalism and hypocrisy, if it was merely preparatory for the climactic revelation which came through Jesus, then the Jesus whom the quest should be looking for would be different from that; he would stand out against his environment. Hence the concern of the quest, as renewed in the 1950s, to find a *distinctive* Jesus. This working assumption came to particular expression in *the criterion of dissimilarity*.[43] To be recognized as a saying which derived from Jesus, the saying had to show itself dissimilar from first-century Judaism; the logic being that a saying which expressed concerns typical of Judaism might have been derived from Judaism; the assumption being that to be recognizable at all, Jesus had to be distinctive. In consequence the quest majored on finding particular sayings which could not be attributed either to Judaism or to the later church(es), and which therefore stood out as different, or which would have been too embarrassing for Jew or Christian to attribute to Jesus had he himself not uttered it.[44]

Hence the typical concern of the second questers to find some saying which would meet this criterion and which could serve as the sure base on which to build a convincing reconstruction of the historical Jesus.

---

[43]Classically defined by Norman Perrin, *Rediscovering the Teaching of Jesus* (London: SCM Press, 1967), p. 39.

[44]The criterion of embarrassment has been given some prominence by John P. Meier, *The Marginal Jew: Rethinking the Historical Jesus*, vol. 1, *The Roots of the Problem and the Person* (New York: Doubleday, 1991), pp. 168-71.

Since the kingdom of God and Son of Man motifs are so well embedded in the Jesus tradition, a typical objective in the second half of the twentieth century was to find which saying was most secure, and to build out from that. Good examples from the post-Bultmannian generation are the assumption of H. E. Tödt and Ferdinand Hahn that Luke 12:8-9 is the most secure of the Son of Man sayings,[45] Werner Kümmel's argument that Mark 9:1 clearly indicates Jesus' expectation that the coming of the kingdom was imminent[46] and Heinz Schürmann's conclusion that the Lord's Prayer for the kingdom to come (Mt 6:10 // Lk 11:2) is the surest way into Jesus' understanding of the kingdom.[47] But the whole attempt was wrong-headed in that a single saying or motif could never provide a sufficiently substantial base on which to build a substantive reconstruction of Jesus' message. It was like building an inverted pyramid, with a resultant and unavoidable tendency for the construction to topple over at the first probing of the base. Or to change the metaphor, the claims and counterclaims regarding different sayings were always liable to lead the quest into a quagmire from which it would be difficult to extricate itself.[48]

PROPOSAL THREE

Once again in direct contrast, my proposal is that the quest of the historical Jesus should come at the task from a different angle.

In the first place *we should look first of all for the Jewish Jesus rather than the non-Jewish Jesus*. This does not mean that we should make the opposite assumption that Jesus' mission was wholly in conformity

---

[45]Heinz E. Tödt, *The Son of Man in the Synoptic Tradition*, trans. Dorothea M. Barton (London: SCM Press, 1965), pp. 42, 55-60 (originally published 1963 [Ger.]); Ferdinand Hahn, *Christologische Hoheitstitel: Ihre Geschichte im frühen Christentum* (Göttingen: Vandenhoeck and Ruprecht, 1963, ⁵1995), pp. 24-26, 32-42, 457-58. Anton Vögtle, *Die "Gretchenfrage" des Menschensohnproblems*, Quaestiones Disputatae 152 (Freiburg: Herder, 1994) continued to regard Lk 12:8-9 as the key to unlocking the problem of "the Son of Man."

[46]Werner G. Kümmel, "Eschatological Expectation in the Proclamation of Jesus," in *The Future of our Religious Past*, ed. James M. Robinson, Rudolf Bultmann, trans. Charles E. Carlston and Robert P. Scharlemann (London: SCM Press, 1971), pp. 29-48 (here pp. 39-41).

[47]Heinz Schürmann, *Gottes Reich—Jesu Geschick. Jesu ureigener Tod im Licht seiner Basileia-Verkündigung* (Freiburg: Herder, 1983), pp. 135, 144.

[48]I echo a comment to the same effect of E. P. Sanders, *Jesus and Judaism* (London: SCM Press, 1985), p. 131.

with the Judaism of his day. Controversies with at least some Pharisees are a prominent theme in the Jesus tradition, and Jesus was crucified with at least the acquiescence of the Jewish authorities. But
against that we must recall that Jesus was brought up as a pious Jew in
Galilee, reciting the Shema, observing the Sabbath, attending the
synagogue, respecting the Torah. The a priori that Jesus belonged
within Judaism is a more secure starting point for any quester than
the assumption that he must have differed from Judaism. On this
point I am wholly at one with what I regard as the main thrust of the
so-called third quest of the historical Jesus, as illustrated, for example,
by the work of E. P. Sanders, James Charlesworth and N. T. Wright.[49]
The old question, Was Jesus the last Jew or the first Christian? speaks
not only of the traditional Christian denigration of Judaism ("the *last*
Jew") but also forces the question into an unnatural polarization
which is neither historical nor helpful in the quest. The points of
continuity are as important as the points of discontinuity, and their
importance for Christian self-understanding as well as for Jewish/
Christian relations should not be ignored.

   In the second place, we would be much wiser to seek out the *characteristic* Jesus rather than the distinctive Jesus.[50] The logic here is
straightforward: any material within the Gospels which is characteristic through and across the Gospels is likely to reflect characteristic
features of Jesus' own mission. It is, of course, quite possible that
particular elements within the Jesus tradition, or particular stylistic
features, reflect the way the tradition was performed and retold by
some highly influential apostle or teacher. But motifs, emphases and
stylistic features which run throughout the tradition in the various
branches which have come down to us or which we can still discern
are most obviously to be attributed to a single originating or shaping
force. And the only real candidate for that role is Jesus himself. Here
my proposal obviously ties back into the first two, since what we are

---

[49]Sanders, *Jesus and Judaism;* J. H. Charlesworth, *Jesus within Judaism: New Light from Exciting
   Archaeological Discoveries* (New York: Doubleday, 1988); N. T. Wright, *Jesus and the Victory of
   God* (Minneapolis: Fortress, 1996).
[50]I here follow the advice of Leander E. Keck, *A Future for the Historical Jesus* (Nashville: Abingdon, 1971), p. 33.

obviously talking about is the characteristic impact made by Jesus on those who initially formulated and began to pass on the tradition of Jesus' mission.

It is not at all difficult to nominate various features of the characteristic Jesus as reflected in the characteristic motifs of the Jesus tradition.

- Characteristic forms, best exemplified by parables and aphoristic sayings, most probably reflect Jesus' own style.

Whatever else he did, Jesus was a parabolist, a teacher of wisdom. It would be flying in the face of all historical probability to doubt that Jesus spoke in parables or in *meshalim*. Focus on these features of the Jesus tradition has been particularly prominent in recent years, but I have no doubt that Birger Gerhardsson and David Aune[51] are better guides on these features than the more prominent members of the Jesus Seminar.[52]

- Characteristic (and distinctive) idioms, such as "Amen" and "Son of Man," most likely reflect Jesus' own speech mannerisms.

There is no reason whatsoever to doubt that the distinctive use of "Amen" to introduce his own teaching rather than to affirm assent with someone else's words recalls a distinctive feature of Jesus' own teaching.[53] Likewise the phrase "the Son of Man" is so distinctive of Jesus' speech that it beggars belief to argue, as some have, that the whole idiom was retrojected into the Jesus tradition—and that, ex hypothesi, by a community which otherwise shows no evident interest in the term![54] That Jesus himself also drew on Daniel 7:13-14 is not so self-evident, but still makes best sense of the overall data.[55]

---

[51]See, e.g., the essays by David E. Aune, "Oral Tradition and the Aphorisms of Jesus," and Birger Gerhardsson, "Illuminating the Kingdom: Narrative Meshalim in the Synoptic Gospels," in *Jesus and the Oral Gospel Tradition*, ed. H. Wansbrough, JSNTA 64 (Sheffield: JSOT Press, 1991), pp. 211-65 and pp. 266-309; also idem, *The Reliability of the Gospel Tradition* (Peabody, Mass.: Hendrickson, 2001). On Jesus' parables see now Klyne R. Snodgrass, *Stories with Intent: A Comprehensive Guide to the Parables of Jesus* (Grand Rapids: Eerdmans, 2008).

[52]See above nn. 11-13, 42.

[53]In *Jesus Remembered*, pp. 700-701, I refer especially to Joachim Jeremias, *The Prayers of Jesus* (London: SCM Press, 1967), pp. 112-15, including his note that Jesus' use of "Amen" was "without analogy in the whole of Jewish literature and in the rest of the New Testament" (p. 112).

[54]See *Jesus Remembered*, sec. 16.3-5, particularly pp. 737-39.

[55]Ibid., pp. 747-54, 760.

- The most characteristic feature of the Jesus tradition's record of Jesus' preaching, "the kingdom of God," almost certainly reflects one of the most characteristic emphases of Jesus' own preaching.

The attempt to play off one emphasis in the kingdom of God tradition against the other, the kingdom as already present and the kingdom as yet to come, flies in the face of the deep-rootedness of *both* emphases in the Jesus tradition,[56] and tells us more about modern impatience with emphases which we find hard to reconcile than proper respect for characteristic features of the Jesus tradition.

- Equally characteristic of Jesus' ministry was his success as an exorcist.

As with the other characteristic features of Jesus' mission, his reputation as a successful exorcist is beyond dispute. Exorcisms are the largest single category of Jesus' healing ministry in the Synoptic Gospels; his fame as an exorcist and "doer of extraordinary deeds" is attested within both Christian and non-Christian sources (e.g. Mk 1:32-34, 39; 3:10-11; Josephus *Jewish Antiquities* 18.63); as a successful exorcist his name was widely regarded as one to conjure with by other exorcists (e.g. Mk 9:38; Origen *Contra Celsum* 1.25; *Papyri graecae magicae* 4.1233, 3020); and, not least, Jesus himself was recalled as referring to his exorcistic ministry and drawing out its significance (Mk 3:22-29; Mt 12:22-30 // Lk 11:14-15, 17-23).[57]

- Nor should we ignore the fact that Jesus' mission was characteristically Galilean in location as reflected in the details of his parables and ethical teaching.

Although John's Gospel suggests more contact with Jerusalem than the Synoptics allow, the latters' focus on Galilee assuredly indicates that Galilee was the predominant locus for his mission, rather than that there were Galilean communities which preserved the memory of Jesus independently of Jerusalem.[58] Both aspects are confirmed by the fact

---

[56]See ibid., chap. 12, sec. 12.4-6.
[57]Fuller detail in ibid., pp. 670-71.
[58]The most recent attempt to reconstruct a history of Christianity's beginnings which sets the Acts of the Apostles to one side, by Ron Cameron and Merrill P. Miller, eds., *Redescribing*

that the early Christian leadership appears to have been exclusively Galilean rather than Judean.

Of course, recognition that a characteristic theme in the Synoptic tradition is best seen as reflecting a characteristic theme of Jesus' mission does not mean that every element in that theme is an unelaborated memory of Jesus' teaching and activity. A characteristic motif is likely to have been extended in the retellings of the tradition, precisely because it was characteristic. The historical value of a *characteristic feature* of the Jesus tradition will not depend on the historicity of *particular* sayings or narratives. At the same time, the fact that a particular saying or action attributed to Jesus belongs to a characteristic feature of the tradition of Jesus' mission increases the probability that the particular item does record something that Jesus said or did. That is to say, the burden of proof shifts against those who insist on approaching every element of the Jesus tradition with a systematic skepticism. Nor, contrariwise, does my proposal imply that we can be wholly confident of the detail of what Jesus said or did in any specific teaching or event. Bearing in mind my earlier proposals, it is important to remember that what we see of Jesus, we can see only through the eyes of diverse witnesses, and that what we hear of Jesus we can hear only with the ears of assemblies who listened to such retellings and recitals of the Jesus tradition.

Nevertheless, the point of my proposal is that *the characteristic emphases and motifs of the Jesus tradition give us a broad, clear and compelling picture of the characteristic Jesus.*[59] A Galilean Jesus who called Israel to repentance and disciples to faith, one through whose ministry the blessings of God's final reign were experienced, one who was heard as speaking for God and with the authority of God, and one who antagonized the priestly authorities and was crucified by the Romans. I could go on, but hopefully enough has already been said to indicate how extensive is the portrayal of Jesus which results, a portrayal which sits

---

Christian Origins (Atlanta: SBL Press, 2004), has proved to be a failure.

[59]C. H. Dodd, *The Founder of Christianity* (London: Collins, 1971) expresses my point well: "The first three gospels offer a body of sayings on the whole so consistent, so coherent, and withal so distinctive in manner, style and content, that no reasonable critic should doubt, whatever reservations he may have about individual sayings, that we find here reflected the thought of a single, unique teacher" (pp. 21-22).

firmly within the diversity of first-century Judaism, which has clear
outlines and emphases, and which goes a long way to explaining how
the impact of Jesus and his mission set in motion a movement whose
impetus has never waned.

In conclusion, not least of value in approaching the Jesus tradition in
the ways I have advocated is that we thereby gain much more of a sense
of that tradition as *living tradition*. The memory of what Jesus said and
did as formulated in the Jesus tradition was not regarded as a kind of
sacred relic, to be shut up in some reliquary or encased in Perspex to be
venerated and carried in procession before reverent assemblies. It was
their lifeblood, their living breath. It enabled them to reexperience the
remembered Jesus, to hear him afresh and to witness for themselves
what he had said and done. It was living because they lived by it and it
enabled them to live lives of discipleship.

The classic examples, which exemplify the difference between the
old way of questing for Jesus and the way advocated above, are the
Lord's Prayer and the words of the Last Supper. Typical of the traditional quest is to treat these as written texts, to assume that they were
known only as written texts, to separate away as much as possible of the
faith which preserved these texts, to inquire after their (written) sources
and the redaction which has brought them to their present shape and to
look for the distinctive features of each by setting it over against the
typical features of Jewish prayer and Passover tradition. But to assume
that Matthew or Luke only knew the text because they had access to a
written text (Q or Mark), and had not known the words until they read
them in written form, simply attests a blinkeredness of historical imagination on the part of those who cannot extricate themselves from the
literary mindset. It is much more plausible that these words were known
because they were used regularly within the gatherings of Jesus' disciples
from earliest days, more or less from the first as part of the embryonic
liturgy by which the first churches called to memory and reenacted two
of the most important elements of the heritage passed down from Jesus.
Rather than to be regarded as cadavers suitable only for clinical dissec-
tion, the differing traditions and the developing traditions, as attested
not least in the manuscript tradition of these texts, should have been

seen as evidence of traditions much used and much beloved, whose development still bears witness to the symbiotic relation between the living tradition and the living church. The fact that precisely these texts, the Lord's Prayer and the words of institution of the Last Supper, the Eucharist, continue to develop, with differing forms familiar in the various liturgies of Christian worship now current, and still with their origins in the Jesus tradition clearly recalled, simply confirms that the tradition can retain its living character without losing its roots down through many generations.

This suggests in turn that those who still experience the Jesus tradition as living tradition may well be best placed to appreciate the initial stages of the traditioning process, that it is the ear of faith which is likely to hear the Gospels most effectively, and that the living quality of the Jesus tradition is most likely to be experienced by those who in effect sit with these early assemblies in sharing their memories of Jesus and in seeking to live by them.

RESPONSE TO JAMES D. G. DUNN

Robert M. Price

I do not feel obliged to accept Professor Dunn's chronology as a starting point in my own "historical Jesus" quest. As he views it, the whole business began with the itinerant Jesus for whom many were moved to abandon home and livelihood, forming what we should call a cult, obeying his dicta as best they could and passing them on, and cherishing his every word and deed as a source of guidance and edification. This picture is by no means unreasonable. But let us recognize that such a scenario by no means guarantees that most, or even many, of such traditions ("reports") really originated with the Master. It is doubtful whether any of the vast ocean of Islamic hadith goes back to the Prophet Muhammad. The reason for this is simple: the more a saying's or a practice's authority can be enhanced by ascription to the Great Man, the more new ones will be so ascribed. It is absolutely obvious to every Gospel critic of every stripe that the Nag Hammadi treatises purporting to contain fulsome teachings of Jesus are completely spurious. It will just not do to remind us in general terms that a great teacher's teaching would have been remembered, since it is equally likely that new teaching may be falsely ascribed to him. Consider also the case of the Buddha.

FROM FAITH TO FAITH

Professor Dunn rightly points out that those who devote themselves to a guru's teaching (have faith in it) will naturally spread those teachings/ that faith. This hardly requires distortion. But that is not the end of the matter. I may in the process embellish what I believe I heard because, like the reader of any text, I become the cocreator of it as I uncon-sciously fill in gaps of understanding simply *by* (as I believe) *under-standing*. I do not imagine that it is some dogmatic agenda that leads Plato scholars to divide his Socratic Dialogues into three periods dur-ing which he comes less and less to report his master's sayings until fi-nally he seems to be using Socrates as a mouthpiece for his own views. Plato would have understood "his" doctrines as merely the unpacking of what was implicit in Socrates's teachings or even in his unanswered questions. He would no doubt have cringed at the thought that he was appropriating his master's name to authorize his own ideas, just as Shankara would have repudiated any suggestion that he was doing aught but explaining what the *Vedanta Sutras* said. Accordingly, various hearers of Jesus may well be imagined as unwittingly embellishing their Lord's teachings as they meant to do nothing but pass them along. I cannot be too severe with the man in *Monty Python's Life of Brian (of Nazareth)* who thought he had heard Jesus say, "Blessed are the cheese makers," nor of his neighbor who glossed the saying to include "any manufacturers of dairy products."[1]

But then it turns out that Dr. Dunn does countenance a large-scale transformation of the faith of Jesus' followers in light of Easter. He just denies that the Christians remixed and rewrote the pre-Easter materi-als in light of their faith in the resurrection. He notes how a great deal of the Q material seems innocent of any resurrection as conditioning the righteous teaching of the pre-Easter Jesus. This he deems the result of the fact that Q comes from the pre-Easter period, that (as Edgar J. Goodspeed,[2] E. Earle Ellis[3] and others have suggested) they were al-ready writing it down. Schmithals holds the similar view that Q was pre-Messianic and non-Messianic; it stemmed from Galilean followers of Jesus who heard only later that Jesus was dead and risen—and didn't believe it.[4] But this didn't mean they weren't still great fans of their

---

[1]Graham Chapman, John Cleese, Terry Gilliam, Eric Idle, Terry Jones, Michael Palin, *Monty Python's The Life of Brian (of Nazareth)* (New York: Ace Books, 1979), p. 14.
[2]Edgar J. Goodspeed, *Matthew, Apostle and Evangelist: A Study on the Authorship of the First Gospel* (Philadelphia: John C. Winston, 1959), pp. 116-17.
[3]Personal conversations, 1975, though I am sure he has said it in print since then.
[4]Walter Schmithals, "The Parabolic Teachings in the Synoptic Traditions," trans. Darrell J.

Lord. Matthew's/Luke's incorporation of Q into Mark's kerygmatic narrative, Schmithals reasons, was an attempt to invite the Q-Christians to join the Jerusalem-based risen Jesus sect. In a sense, Schmithals's point may be seen as reinforcing Dunn's: the Q sayings are so little colored by any resurrection preaching that the two may have seemed antithetical.

HERMETICALLY SEALED

Here we see an island representing a larger, subsurface continent of an issue whose peaks peep out elsewhere as well. For instance, already Schweitzer[5] and Dibelius,[6] while characterizing Jesus as a preacher of apocalyptic eschatology, freely admitted that little if any of his moral or pious teaching (with a few obvious exceptions) was predicated on the short time span before the end. Within Judaism, note how Jacob Neusner characterized the Mishnah as noneschatological, embodying a worldview practically exclusive of Messianism. Hyam Maccoby took him to task over this, contending that Mishnaic law was simply topic specific.[7] It no more ruled out eschatology than it did stories of the Genesis Patriarchs, the latter coming in for treatment in the Midrashim instead. But no Rabbinical Jews rejected any category in favor of any other. They just considered them one at a time. Again, the question is whether one may simply have preserved a sect's teaching in neatly circumscribed categories. I certainly don't know. But Professor Dunn seems to suppose that the Evangelists did that: they did not let post-Easter revelations contaminate or recolor pre-Easter materials. One might say that, for Dunn, the Gospel writers and/or tradents kept the pre-Easter Jesus alongside the post-Easter Jesus as an Old Testament alongside a New Testament. This is just the way Bultmann saw it when he insisted that the preaching of Jesus was merely a presupposition for New Testament theology and actually formed no part of New Testament theology.[8]

Doughty, *Journal of Higher Criticism* 4, no. 2 (Fall 1997): 3-32.

[5]Albert Schweitzer, *The Kingdom of God in Primitive Christianity*, trans. L. A. Garrard (New York: Seabury Press, 1968), pp. 100-101.

[6]Martin Dibelius, *The Sermon on the Mount* (New York: Scribner's, 1940), pp. 51-52.

[7]Hyam Maccoby, "Jacob Neusner's Mishnah" *Midstream* 30, no. 5 (1984): 24-32.

[8]Rudolf Bultmann, *Theology of the New Testament*, trans. Kendrick Grobel (New York: Scribner's, 1951, 1955), 1:3.

But there are others who, as concerned as they are to maximize Old-to-New Testament continuity, seek to minimize any discontinuity between the pre- and post-Easter Jesus. Joachim Jeremias displays this tendency in his writings on the Sermon on the Mount.[9] Jeremias realized it would be quite a problem if Jesus (as Hans Windisch,[10] for example, held) in the Sermon material was stipulating behavioral requirements for entry into salvation. That would be salvation by works, and the Lutheran Jeremias could not have that. So he proposed that the Sermon material (spoken on one or many occasions) was predicated on what was not actually explicit in the Gospels: the proclamation of salvation by grace through faith, or, in Jesus' idiom, the free offer of God's kingdom to those willing to accept it unpretentiously, like children with open, empty hands. I find the approach exegetically implausible.

On the other side of the divide we find the very poster boy for the liberal Jesus quest: Adolf von Harnack. He famously measured the distance between the parable of the prodigal son and the Pauline preaching of the atonement. If Jesus had known the conditions of salvation would have altered so drastically in a matter of a few weeks, would he have wasted his breath on a parable teaching people that simple repentance was sufficient for salvation? Hardly. But even Harnack's contrast serves to underline Dunn's point, does it not? And then the question is how we are to explain the differences between various presentations of faith in Jesus. Dunn adopts a sequential approach, or so it appears to me. It is like the traditional Christian approach to the Old Testament, effectively abrogated by the New Testament. Similarly, later verses of the Qur'an are said to abrogate earlier ones with which they may conflict.

By contrast, Schmithals (and to a greater extent, Burton L. Mack) perceives a pluralism as far back as we can go. Mack deconstructs the traditional myth of a linear progression of a single master-teacher Jesus Christ leading to his passion and resurrection, what Mack calls the Big

---

[9]Joachim Jeremias, *The Sermon on the Mount*, trans. Norman Perrin, Facet Books Biblical Series 2 (Philadelphia: Fortress, 1963), p. 23.

[10]Hans Windisch, *The Meaning of the Sermon on the Mount: A Contribution to the Historical Understanding of the Gospels and to the Problem of their True Exegesis*, trans. S. MacLean Gilmour (Philadelphia: Westminster Press, 1951).

Bang, following which different Christians interpreted their (or their apostles') experiences of the risen Jesus in different ways and in conceptualities drawn from Philonic Judaism, Gnosticism and mystery religions. The resultant Jesuses are quite different (one a Jewish king, one the eternal Logos, one a magical healer, one a Cynic, one a feminist, one a community organizer, etc.). The familiar canonical "Jesus Christ" turns out to be the fruit, not the root, of early Christianity, a composite, not a fountainhead. One may try to play connect the dots with the various proto-Jesuses, positing which elements were "original," which were originally unrelated and were fictively grafted on, which actually stemmed from which other. The result may be valid in the eye of the beholder more than anywhere else.

To me, the key weakness in Professor Dunn's timeline is his placing of Epistle Christianity after Gospel Christianity. The Christianity of the Epistles is surely post-Easter or, better, presupposes a heavenly, divine Christ, but to me it does not seem in broad outline to presuppose the Jesus story of the Gospels. Here I represent the viewpoint of the Christ-Myth theory, the hypothesis that the Gospel Jesus, Jesus of Nazareth, represents a subsequent historicization of a mythic deity, much as the Samson of the book of Judges is a literary incarnation of the Hebrew sun-god myth. It is a universal pattern for raw myth, starring heavenly gods and planetary bodies, to develop into legends starring humanized demigods and finally legendary heroes. On this schema, the Epistles know nothing of a Jesus who was a miracle worker or healer, even a teacher, because these elements were not yet available: they had not been invented. Even the few Corinthian "words of the Lord" (*not* "words of Jesus") seem, especially in light of 1 Corinthians 14:37, to make the best sense as prophetic oracles coined by Christian prophets.

If only there were an entire absence of moral maxims and commands from the Epistles! Then we could invoke the familiar genre argument (see just above) according to which certain materials are systematically excluded from certain genres (maybe). But there is plenty in the way of epistolary paraenesis. Professor Dunn understands the numerous parallels between Gospel sayings and epistolary exhortations, maxims and the like to denote unattributed sayings of Jesus. But I just cannot accept this: who would try to clinch an argument or give force to an admonition by bringing the teaching of Jesus to bear—and then not put his name on it? It defeats the purpose. I see no way around this.

ORALLY—OH REALLY?

Like many recent scholars, Professor Dunn wants us to take seriously the impact on Gospel criticism of orality studies such as pioneered by Albert Lord and Milman Parry (or the impact someone thinks they *ought* to have). On the assumption that the Gospels are the deposit of oral transmission in early Christian circles, we are told, we ought not to interpret them by the point-for-point comparisons of parallel texts: our Gospels' variations stem instead from the range of innovation allowed by the conventions of the oral storytellers. But this is a futile attempt to return to pre-Schleiermacher theories of the Gospels as independent repositories of oral traditions. If we see them this way, we can return to the old Sunday School apologetic of one auto accident reported, albeit at something of a distance, by four independent eyewitnesses. But it fails for the same reason that the same approach (not yet gussied up by appeals to what saga singers sing in Serbian Starbucks) failed a century ago: the Gospels make too much sense when considered as *inter*dependent literary documents. Apologists would like nothing more than to be able to wish away as so many accidents the patterns of redactional alterations, with their historical and theological implications, traced out by Conzelmann,[11] Marxsen,[12] Perrin,[13] Bornkamm, Barth and Held.[14] But, again, it makes too much sense. When some (e.g., A. J.

---

[11]Hans Conzelmann, *The Theology of St. Luke*, trans. Geoffrey Buswell (New York: Harper & Row, 1961).

[12]Willi Marxsen, *Mark the Evangelist: Studies on the Redaction History of the Gospel*, trans. James Boyce, Donald Juel, William Poehlmann, with Roy A. Harrisville (New York: Abingdon, 1969).

[13]Norman Perrin, *What Is Redaction Criticism?* Guides to Biblical Scholarship (Philadelphia: Fortress, 1969); idem, *The Resurrection according to Matthew, Mark, and Luke* (Philadelphia: Fortress, 1977).

[14]Günther Bornkamm, Gerhard Barth and Heinz Joachim Held, *Tradition and Interpretation in Matthew*, trans. Percy Scott, New Testament Library (Philadelphia: Westminster Press, 1963).

Mattill Jr. [15]) manage to mount a significant challenge to Conzelmann on Luke, for example, it is only because they do an even better job of redaction criticism. One cannot simply wish away the results, which show we are dealing with literary, written texts. It even becomes a question, as Schmithals asks, of whether the whole notion of an initial period of oral tradition may have been an ad hoc attempt to connect these documents with their hero who was set in an earlier period.[16] I see Dr. Dunn as starting on the other foot: choosing to pursue the orality model consistently, without seeing he has reduced it *ad absurdum*.

---

[15]A. J. Mattill Jr., *Luke and the Last Things: A Perspective for the Understanding of Lukan Thought* (Dillsboro: Western North Carolina Press, 1979); Eric Franklin, *Christ the Lord: A Study in the Purpose and Theology of Luke-Acts* (Philadelphia: Westminster Press, 1975).

[16]Walter Schmithals, *The Theology of the First Christians*, trans. O. C. Dean Jr. (Louisville, Ky.: Westminster John Knox, 1997), pp. 40-43.

RESPONSE TO JAMES D. G. DUNN

John Dominic Crossan

The first protest in Dunn's essay is "against the assumption that 'the Christ of faith' is a *perversion* of 'the historical Jesus'" (my italics), and that protest receives his counterproposal that "the quest should start from the recognition that Jesus evoked faith from the outset of his mission and that this faith is the surest indication of the historical reality and effect of his mission."

On the one hand, I agree completely with that proposal. Jesus' proclamation of the kingdom of God was ab initio a faith challenge, and, although Jesus emphasized God over himself, I cannot see any objection to his hearers including him in their faith response. The Proclaimer incarnates the Proclaimed. How, as Yeats asked in another context, can one tell the Dancer from the Dance?

Two Footnotes

One is that I myself prefer the label *reconstruction* to *quest*. The other is that for Jesus the kingdom of God was a question of presence and not just of imminence, and of a bilateral human-divine collaboration and not just a unilateral divine intervention.

On the other hand, those who—in past and present—oppose "the Jesus of history" to "the Christ of faith" usually mean something much more precise. It is not just "faith" in general that is stripped from Jesus but some specific theology, denomination or church that opponents have in mind.

A personal example: "the reconstruction of the Jesus of history" from my scholarly research *is* the incarnate image of God from my Christian faith. But I find the Jesus of history who proclaimed love of enemies based on the character of God (now in the Q Gospel at Matthew 5:43-45 // Luke 6:27-36) to be already *perverted* by the Christ of faith who will return as a transcendental killer in the book of Revelation.

A violent Christ of faith is, indeed, a fundamental *perversion* of the Jesus of history. The external proof of that comes from Pilate, who understood that Jesus was resisting Roman imperial control nonviolently. Hence his double decision to execute him officially, legally and publicly but not to bother rounding up his companions. That is how Rome handled nonviolent revolutionaries.

Notice, for contrast, how "Barabbas was in prison *with the rebels* who had committed murder during the insurrection" in the parable of Mark 15:7. Notice also in another parable from John 18:36 how the core confrontation between the kingdom of God and the empire of Rome is between nonviolence and violence. Jesus' double negation that "my kingdom is not from this world" and "my kingdom is not from here" means—in between—that "my followers" will not "be fighting" even to protect or free me.

Yes, of course, the Jesus of history demanded ab initio a response of faith in the presence of God's nonviolent kingdom. But I would add that there have always been interpretations of the Christ of faith which should have been rejected as perversions of the Jesus of history. For another example that goes even beyond the book of Revelation—think about the apocalyptic participation of Christians as children in the Narnia books or Christians as soldiers in the Left Behind series.

Dunn's second protest is against the assumption that "*the only way to understand both the relation of the traditions in the Synoptic Gospels and the earliest transmission of the Jesus tradition is in literary terms.*" I make, once again, a basic distinction.

WRITTEN TRADITION

With regard to our present Synoptic Gospels, I am fully convinced that, as Dunn says *disapprovingly*, "the dominant solution to the Synoptic Problem was and still is the 'two document hypothesis'" of Mark and Q as written sources used independently by Matthew and

Luke. I think that was and still is right and no truculent language about "a blinkeredness of historical imagination on the part of those who cannot extricate themselves from the literary mindset" deters me from that conclusion. Two hundred years of research got at least that one right.

On the one hand, when Matthew or Luke was copying (yes, copying—be it directly by eye on a text or indirectly by ear from a reader) Mark or Q, they still operated very much within *oral sensibility* and therefore even when they intended to accept a section fully and without any reservation, they would allow themselves far more freedom in formulation, alteration and variation than we would accept today within our *scribal sensibility*. But oral tradition operating without any document is not the same as oral sensibility operating within a document. And neither is performative variation the same as hermeneutical variation or polemical variation.

The claim by Dunn "the variations which have been preserved in the now-written texts seem again and again to be no different in kind from the variations which we can safely hypothesize as characteristic of the performance tradition from the first" is not an adequate summary. We can indeed discern *performative variations* as Matthew or Luke uses Mark within oral sensibility, which are not different in kind from such variations within general oral tradition. But we can also discern—especially cumulatively—disagreements in theology that create divergent versions by deliberative omission or intentional commission.

On the other hand, therefore, neither oral tradition nor oral sensibility is operative in examples such as the following triad—chosen almost at random. Mark 6:2 calls Jesus "the carpenter," but Matthew 13:55 calls him "the carpenter's son" and Luke omits any parallel. Or again, with the same process, Mark 10:35 has "James and John, the sons of Zebedee" make an unseemly request, and Matthew 20:20 has it come from "the mother of the sons of Zebedee" while Luke, once again, omits the whole incident. Finally, Mark 15:8 has the "crowd" before Pilate, but Matthew—yes, copying from that Markan source—escalates from "crowd" in his parallel 27:15 to "crowds" in his 27:20 and to "all the people" in his infamous 27:25. ("His blood be upon us and upon our children.") That is not the benign *performative variation* of orality but the deliberate *polemical variation* of a confrontational theology.

ORAL TRADITION

Dunn proposes "the necessity of taking the oral phase of the history of the Jesus tradition with all seriousness" and that "it *is* in fact *possible to envisage the oral phase of the Jesus tradition.*" I agree—but that can only be done when we accept the documentary relationship between our present Gospel versions and do not confuse oral sensibility within that relationship with oral tradition outside it. By the way, as a delicate protest of my own, I said all of that from *In Fragments* (1983) through *The Birth of Christianity* (1998). One should not reinvent the wheel without at least acknowledging that it has been done before.

In that latter book, but following and dependent on Stephen J. Patterson's study on "Wisdom in Q and Thomas" in the Gammie memorial volume of 1993, I was able to discern a large complex of materials (thirty-seven units) used independently by those two Gospels. Judging by the similar but heavily redacted content combined with total lack of sequential similarity, I judged those materials to be oral tradition and the biggest chunk I could discern.[1]

That presumes, of course, that the Q Gospel exists as a written document used by both Matthew and Luke, and also that the *Gospel of Thomas* is independent from the Synoptics. If those conclusions are correct, we have a very large complex of oral tradition still very much observable behind and before any written document. Yes, indeed, oral tradition must be taken seriously, and, yes, it can be envisaged, but not by confusing performative oral tradition outside the written Gospels with performative oral sensibility within them and certainly not by confusing either of those processes with theologically motivated adversarial or confrontational variations within the genetic transmission of our present Gospel versions.

---

[1]Stephen J. Patterson, "Wisdom in Q and Thomas," in *In Search of Wisdom: Essays in Memory of John G. Gammie*, ed Leo G. Perdue, Bernard Brandon Scott and William Johnston Wiseman (Louisville: Westminster John Knox, 1993), pp. 187-222.

The third and final protest by Dunn results in this proposal: "we should look first of all for the Jewish Jesus rather than the non-Jewish Jesus." Of course, but one footnote. If you think even a single non-Jew ever heard Jesus, the only way such a person could have understood his Jewish eschatology would have been to think of him within Greco-Roman Cynic eschatology. I still see no reason to withdraw that judgment unless you think non-Jews never heard Jesus. But to construe that judgment as denying that Jesus was Jewish is just plain indecent.

It is not enough, however, to insist that Jesus was Jewish. So, for example, was Josephus—or, for that matter, Caiaphas. Of course, Jesus lived, died and, indeed, rose as a Jew. He was a homeland Jew within eschatological Judaism within Roman imperialism. What he did—and for which he died—was to turn that eschatological Judaism nonviolently against that Roman imperialism. Reconstructions of the historical Jesus that leave out *either* eschatological Judaism *or* Roman imperialism in the Jewish homeland or Jesus' nonviolent resistance from the former against the latter are all equally inadequate. Dunn says that "we have no firsthand testimony from Caiaphas or from Pilate. We do not know how Jesus impacted others." I think that is quite wrong. We have very clear evidence of his impact on Pilate. It is called crucifixion.

Finally, Dunn concludes with this: "Those who still experience the Jesus tradition as living tradition may well be best placed to appreciate the initial stages of the traditioning process, that is the ear of faith which is likely to hear the Gospels most effectively, and that the living quality of the Jesus tradition is most likely to be experienced by those who in effect sit with these early assemblies in sharing their memories of Jesus and in seeking to live by them."

I tend to reverse the order of those final actions. It is those who lived by them who "remembered" them best. And, once again, a delicate protest. I myself said that some time ago like this: "I ask whether *remembering his sayings* or *imitating his life* is the primary mode of continuity from the historical Jesus to those who walked around with him and remained around after him. The *Didache* . . . used as a criterion of authenticity the ways *(tropoi)* rather than the words *(logoi)* of the Lord.

Continuity was in mimetics rather than in mnemonics, in imitating life rather than in remembering words."[2]

In confirmation, I cite a more authoritative source than either of us. Jesus upbraided those followers who confessed his name but did not imitate—or better, participate in—his way of life, his nonviolent resistance to the normalcy of civilization's violent injustice. And, presumably, those who proclaimed that "Lord, Lord" from the Q Gospel in Matthew 7:21 // Luke 6:46 were not deficient in memory but in commitment.

---

[2]John Dominic Crossan, *The Birth of Christianity* (San Francisco: HarperSanFrancisco, 1998), p. 404.

RESPONSE TO JAMES D. G. DUNN

Luke Timothy Johnson

Professor Dunn's essay provides a helpful epilogue to his monograph *Jesus Remembered* by reflecting on the methodological principles he rejected and embraced in writing that large work. He distances his own approach from three premises governing contemporary historical Jesus research and offers what he considers to be a sounder and more commonsense approach.

There are a number of Dunn's affirmations that I find easy to approve. I certainly agree in principle that elements in the Gospels in all likelihood go back to Jesus because of the impression he made on those who followed him. I agree that the communication of the memory of Jesus in the church through oral transmission is of great importance—that the composition of Gospels was not merely a literary but also an oral process. I agree particularly with his two examples: the shape of the Lord's Prayer and the Lord's Supper alike suggest the plausibility of their transmission through worship. I agree wholeheartedly that the historian should look to what is broadly characteristic of Jesus rather than to the demonstration of the authenticity of individual fragments of tradition. Dunn's point here, I think, is close to what I suggested concerning points of convergence among the sources.

The closer I look at Dunn's proposals, however, the more I find cause for disagreement than agreement, or perhaps better, reasons for extremely strong qualifications. The problem, I find, is that while Dunn's proposals make perfectly good sense in themselves, they do not really address the critical problems facing those seeking to use the Gospels as sources for the historical Jesus.

Take, for example, his first protest, against distinguishing the Jesus of history from the Christ of faith. While acknowledging that the Gospels are composed totally from the perspective of belief in the resurrection and exaltation of Jesus as Lord, he objects to the absolute way in which this faith perspective has been applied (and is applied, readers know, in my essay as well!) by historical questers. He insists that there was a kind of faith (commitment) to Jesus during his lifetime, that Jesus made a deep impression on his followers and that the Gospel traditions bear evidence of this "historic" Christ.

At the logical level, it is difficult entirely to disagree with Dunn's position. To do so would require the position that the church simply made up everything reported about Jesus in the Gospels from its faith perspective. Such is plainly not the case: there is a genuine "memory of Jesus" that is transmitted from eyewitnesses to "ministers of the word" (Lk 1:2). But it is difficult to move from such a truism to genuine historical discrimination.

We can ask, for example, about the character of the disciples' pre-Easter faith. We can recognize that Peter's confession of Jesus as Messiah indicates such a commitment. Yet the very Gospels that report the confession move quickly to show the inadequacy of that "faith," first by correcting Peter's confession in light of Jesus' passion and resurrection, and second, by showing how the disciples abandoned Jesus when the moment of his self-predicted destiny arrived.

Indeed, the variations in the wording of Peter's confession in each of the four Gospels reveal the degree to which the Evangelists, building on the resurrection perspective, shaped Peter's declaration itself. Mark has Peter say, "You are the Messiah" (Mk 8:29), whereas Luke has him declare, "You are the Messiah of God" (Lk 9:20). John has Peter declare, "We have come to believe and are convinced that you are the Holy One of God" (Jn 6:69). In Matthew, finally, Peter says, "You are the Messiah, the Son of the Living God," in response to which Jesus bestows on him the keys of the kingdom of heaven (Mt 16:16-19). Precisely such variations, I would argue, make more impressive the point of convergence of all four accounts, namely, that during Jesus' ministry, Peter expressed faith in him as God's anointed. Yet these interpretive variations also prevent the historian from determining precisely what Peter said, much less what he might have meant by saying it.

My position is that the Gospels *both* contain real memories of Jesus *and* the shaping of them from the resurrection perspective, *as well as* the shaping of the memory through the prism of Scripture. Such energy in interpretation suggests there is really something to remember; but such levels of interpretation make the historian wary of overconfidence in describing the basis of the memory in detail.

Dunn's efforts to find material free from such interpretive shaping leads him, paradoxically, to affirming something like the principle of dissimilarity, and to the highly unlikely claim that *"the Q material first emerged in Galilee and was given its lasting shape there prior to Jesus' death in Jerusalem"* (his emphasis). Now Dunn knows full well that the material designated *Q* by scholars is not a distinct literary production but rather the result of critical analysis of certain Synoptic material; he knows further that the "lasting shape" of Q is not definitively determinable through such analysis. But when he proposes that the itinerant followers of Jesus packaged a collection of his sayings within the course of a tumultuous yearlong ministry that led to riot and death in Jerusalem, he claims more than is historically plausible. His desire to balance the scales tilts them disastrously in another direction.

Dunn also issues a protest against the dominance of written compositions as the medium for remembering Jesus and asserts the need to take the oral tradition seriously. As I state in my opening remarks, I fully agree with the significance of the oral tradition as the medium for the memory of Jesus within communities. But Dunn's complaint that such oral tradition has been ignored by scholars is off base. He acknowledges that the development of form criticism was a response to a sense of skepticism concerning the written Gospels as sources for the historical Jesus, and that, especially with Martin Dibelius, considerable attention was paid by form critics to the social and ecclesial settings within which oral transmission took place. Dunn's real objection, I think, is that form critics also assumed the postresurrection perspective among those who transmitted the Jesus traditions, while he wants to recover traces of pre-Easter oral tradition deriving from Jesus' first followers.

Dunn's positive assertion is a more sophisticated version of the appeal made years ago by Riesenfeld and Gerharddson—also in protest against form criticism. While the Scandinavian scholars made the analogy to practices of oral memorization among the rabbis, Dunn's work invokes a more folkloric and relaxed process of oral memory. The response to each position, however, is the same: whatever oral processes may have preceded the composition of the Gospels, only the written texts are now available to us. Virtually all the patterns of similarity and dissimilarity we find in the Gospels, moreover, can be accounted for more often and more naturally by the process of literary transmission and redaction than through variations in oral performance.

It is striking that Dunn offers only one concrete example of how oral tradition has an explanatory value, namely the parable of the talents/pounds in Matthew 25:14-30 and Luke 19:11-27. He suggests that the variations here may be due to Jesus' giving the same teaching at different times and in slightly different forms, so that there may never have been a single original version. I offer three short comments. First, this appeal to "different times, different wording" is a staple of apologetic criticism found already in Augustine's *Harmony of the Gospels* (with respect to the Sermon on the Mount/Plain) and used frequently for this parable. Second, while it is hypothetically possible and probable that Jesus repeated himself, such an appeal does not adequately account for the specific patterns of similarity and dissimilarity found in Synoptic passages. Third, with respect to this particular parable, it is clear that Luke's version is not simply an oral variation, but has been carefully crafted and placed in its precise narrative context by the Evangelist himself as a means of interpreting the story of Jesus that the Evangelist is telling.

In his final protest, Dunn joins a long line of critics who, embarrassed by the long, crypto-Marcionite history of pitting a liberating "Christian" Jesus against a lawbound and stifling "Judaism," seek redress by emphasizing the "Jewishness" of Jesus. While the elimination of theological tendentiousness from historical inquiry is always important, and in this case critical, I am not sure how much such a new emphasis actually accomplishes, beyond relieving inherited guilt. I have space for only three comments.

First, searching for a Jewish Jesus is not a historiographical principle or criterion but a predetermined goal. Second, the goal leaves unexamined the truly difficult question, namely, what constitutes "Jewish" in first century Palestine. The available evidence points to an irreducible variety of Jewish life and literature in the Second Temple period. The field of historical Jesus research is littered with efforts to render a "Jewish" Jesus through isolating one aspect of this variegated Jewish life and measuring Jesus against it: we are familiar with Jesus the Zealot, Jesus the Pharisee, Jesus the Essene, Jesus the Chasid.

Third, even those seeking a Jewish Jesus are forced to locate him historically by the ways in which he stands out among other varieties of Jewish expression. If Jesus can be reduced to just another Zealot or just another Pharisee, after all, he would not be historically visible at all. Some application of "dissimilarity" is inevitable: other rabbis told parables, but there are ways in which Jesus' parables can be distinguished from those of the rabbis; other Chasids had wonders associated with them, but none had the reputation for working so many healings and exorcisms over such a short span of time. To distinguish Jesus among other Jews, to be sure, is something else altogether than making Jesus something other than a Jew, and on this point, I fully agree with Dunn.

RESPONSE TO JAMES D. G. DUNN

Darrell L. Bock

James Dunn is certainly one of the most influential scholars writing on historical Jesus issues today. One of the merits of his thorough *Remembering Jesus* volume is that it is a treatment that gives an up-to-date look at the array of issues one must grapple with in pursuing this topic. His essay is a nice distillation of his labor in terms of method, although it is less so in specific content. In typical fashion, Dunn has both praise and critique for efforts to unearth the historical Jesus. His essay's outline is clear, so I will use it as the basis for my response.

PROTEST 1

In contrast to many of those engaged in seeking the historical Jesus, Dunn claims the Christ of faith is not a perversion of the historical Jesus. This echoes the complaint made by Luke Timothy Johnson that reductionistic or deconstructive historical Jesus efforts are not really so helpful. I agree with this protest and seek to make this point in my own essay in this book by working through the event details to indicate that they cohere culturally. In terms of the Gospels' presentation of Jesus' ministry, they show a much tighter connection between the historical Jesus and the Christ of faith than many historical Jesus presentations suggest. The presence of faith need not prevent a clear view of Jesus. This protest represents a direct challenge to the first quest, which stripped away much of what made Jesus unique. This uniqueness caused people to be drawn to him as a singular figure. I also agree with Dunn that we should not accuse Paul of doing something that did not originate from Jesus.

PROPOSAL 1

Dunn argues that people should see that Jesus inspired faith in many from the very beginning of his mission, an indication of the historical reality of his ministry. In many ways, this very correct observation is the strongest critique of Price's Jesus myth option. Something *and* someone got this new movement rolling, taking it in directions distinct from the Judaism out of which it emerged. The impact and effect Jesus had on people must have been that starting point. Moreover, Dunn contends that this overall influence, however overlaid with post-Easter faith, still gives us access to the original impact because its themes are still evident in the tradition. I also agree here. The detailed discussion I might have with Dunn involves how much post-Easter reflection we have in the tradition at any given point. The example from the Sermon on the Mount and the sayings traditions as rooted in Jesus is a good one. These traditions reach back to Jesus and give very little evidence of post-Easter influence. I have chosen in my essay to highlight events (rather than the sayings Dunn highlights). This inclusion of events adds yet another dimension of meaning in order to understand Jesus. In fact, sometimes events make the sayings more comprehensible and do so without adding elements that call for a post-Easter reading, since they fit a Jewish milieu.

Another key point comes in the discussion about Q. Dunn argues that this teaching material was collected and given lasting shape prior to Jesus' death. This is another way of saying what I have long sensed about Q (or a source like it), namely that this material was intended not as a narrative about Jesus like the Gospels, but as an anthology of Jesus' teaching to pass on. So the material can be grouped into set topics as T. W. Manson showed long ago (John the Baptist and Jesus [six units], Jesus and his disciples [six units], Jesus and his opponents [seven units], the future [twelve units] and random sayings that do not fall into the previously mentioned categories [six units]).[1] To treat Q as a comprehensive look at Jesus is to misunderstand the purpose behind this source.

---

[1]For a chart on Q material of the passages named, see Darrell L. Bock, *Studying the Historical Jesus: A Guide to Sources and Methods* (Grand Rapids: Baker Academic, 2002), pp. 174-75.

In regard to Kähler, Dunn is correct to affirm his view that we have to deal with these "faith" documents because they represent the best sources we have about Jesus. We do get the "historic" Jesus. The point made is much like the one Johnson made in his presentation.

PROTEST 2

Dunn argues against a key assumption often used in the historical pursuit of Jesus. He critiques a strictly literary dependence model of understanding the Gospels' development. In my view, this critique is on target. Orality was far more prevalent in that culture. The moving away from a strictly literary model, which is a historically proper move for a first-century setting, is a kind of Pandora's box for being able to nail things down in terms of sources and sequence. The issue is, as Dunn notes, that the presence of orality and variation flexibility, as an element of that orality, works as a kind of wild card, destroying our ability to be completely confident of cause and effect relationships between the sources. As neat as the Two (or, better, Four) Document (Mark, Q, unique Matthew, unique Luke as our four written Gospel sources) and Griesbach (Matthew, Luke, then Mark, as the Gospel order) hypotheses are, they do not reflect the messiness of a tradition that surely had oral dimensions associated with it. Second Temple Jewish culture in the Levant, as well as much of Greco-Roman culture, was oral when it came to passing on the description of events and relaying the actions of significant people. Dunn is also right that the presence of an oral model does not mean that only written tradition is reliable. These oral cultures had ways and means of passing on materials in a way that captured the attention and memory of real events rooted in history. This orality was neither as layered as Bultmann claimed nor as fluid (read: free to go anywhere) as others have argued. Dunn rightly observes that the gap these twenty years of orality provide produces a break in the chain of transmission that does not allow us to navigate back to a pristine original tradition. On the other hand, I want to note a key flaw in the underlying assumption that argues for a pursuit of only this "original" model. It is that Jesus may have presented given themes multiple times over his travels during his years of ministry, which means it is misleading to think that there is only one pristine way to describe an event or present his teaching on themes. This is why the earliest version is not necessarily a hermetically sealed version taking us back to the real Jesus.

PROPOSAL 2

So Dunn contends that we must take seriously the oral phase of the time. Again, I agree. The renewed study of this area of orality is an important recent advance, and much research into how this works still needs to be done. Oral performance is distinct from reading. In many contexts it is communal, overseen by selected individuals. It involves both fixity and flexibility, rooted in an originating event, not an original version of the account. All of these points Dunn makes are well taken. I simply observe that the kind of model in mind between fixity and flexibility does show up in our actual sources. In the variations found within our written sources, we can see that the core or gist of a story is amazingly consistent in such examples, even as other details differ in spots. Also, the role of these tradition supervisors needs to be better appreciated. For example, Luke notes that when Judas was replaced, the requirement for his replacement was a long and direct experience with Jesus in the group (Acts 1:21-22). It is no accident that Justin Martyr in referring to the Gospels in the mid-second century often called them memoirs of the apostles, as a way of describing what they were (*First Apology* 66-67; *Dialogue with Trypho* 103).

PROTEST 3

Dunn rejects making the criterion of dissimilarity central to constructing a portrait of the historical Jesus. This criterion only presents a Jesus who is distinct from his environment. However, the best Jesus is not only the distinctive Jesus. I concur here as well. Far more useful are the other criteria, such as multiple attestation, embarrassment and a variation on dissimilarity, where passages that present Jesus as a bridge between Judaism and what emerged in the church have a high claim to authenticity.

PROPOSAL 3

So Dunn proposes, as have many before him (like Schweitzer and Caird), that the starting point is to look for the Jewish Jesus. This is precisely why in my essay we spend so much time highlighting Jewish background to make sense of what was described as taking place. This is also why the model of Crossan fails, because it does not do enough with Jesus' Jewishness nor the Jewish controversies Jesus engaged in with the various sects of Judaism, especially the Pharisees. The call to look for the characteristic Jesus is also appropriate. Here multiple attestation, along with coherence, can help us get there, although we also must reserve the right to respect singularly attested teaching, especially if it connects to what already coheres. This was why I proceed as I do in my essay by looking to certain centrally attested events. Were more space available, much the same could and would have been done with key themes in Jesus' teaching. Dunn is right to point to characteristic forms and idioms, including in all likelihood the Son of Man, his emphasis on the kingdom of God, Jesus as an exorcist and the focus of the tradition on the Galilean ministry. All of these take us down paths that lead to the historical Jesus. My only wish is that Dunn's essay would have filled out this portrait a little more. As my essay suggests, I think there is more detail available here than the brief survey we were given. More debatable might be just how much goes back to Jesus in a particular way. Often times we must recall that we are hearing the "voice" of Jesus in the tradition rather than his exact words, a distinction I have recognized and defended elsewhere.[2] Even with this seemingly less detailed orientation, a credible portrait of Jesus is possible, as Dunn outlines and I have elaborated with more detail. Indeed, Jesus both was and is remembered in the traditions that flowed, like a vivid memory of Jesus' most important work, into our Gospels. Such traditions were regularly used, as Dunn notes with the Lord's Prayer and the Last Supper. They also were well remembered.

Dunn has given us an essay rich in methodological observation. I do wish he had given us more of what he thinks actually emerges about Jesus that is solidly rooted in such a perspective. For that, I suppose, he would urge us to read his *Jesus Remembered*.

---

[2]Michael J. Wilkins and J. P. Moreland, "The Words of Jesus in the Gospels: Live, Jive, or Memorex?" in *Jesus Under Fire: Modern Scholarship Reinvents the Historical Jesus* (Grand Rapids: Zondervan, 1995), pp. 74–99.

THE HISTORICAL JESUS

An Evangelical View

Darrell L. Bock

PRELIMINARY REMARKS ON THE VALUE, LIMITS AND ROOTS OF HISTORICAL JESUS STUDY

Can the lion and the lamb lie together? For many people, the idea of an evangelical engaging in a historical Jesus discussion is an oxymoron. For many critics, the evangelical view of Scripture is said to skew evangelicals' discussion of Jesus issues. For many evangelicals, especially lay evangelicals, the skepticism surrounding much of historical Jesus work is to be shunned as a rejection of the Bible as the Word of God. So can there be evangelical approaches to the historical Jesus?

I believe the answer is yes. To get there, however, one must appreciate the nature of what historical Jesus work seeks to achieve as well as the limitations under which such a historically oriented study operates when it seeks to cross thousands of years to do its work. In addition, there is a difference between what one might believe in part by faith and in part because of trajectories one might see in historical work and what one can demonstrate is likely rooted in the accounts tied to Jesus. Historical Jesus study has developed over time and has had many different emphases and shifts in method. The goal is to pursue what it can show to be most likely about Jesus through the variety of sources and objects *(realia)* we currently possess. It does so with a limitation of total available sources, as well as with the boundaries of time that impede our ability to understand first-century culture, which we have to try to reconstruct in its pluralistic complexity of both Greco-Roman and Jewish elements. This means the results of such study are very provisional in nature. New finds could greatly change "established facts," just as the discovery of the Dead Sea Scrolls brought a new and significant impetus to the understanding of Jesus in a Jewish context. This development came along after Albert Schweitzer pleaded for us to understand Jesus in such a milieu almost a half century earlier, when he was sounding a death knell for the dogmatic first quest. What he lacked, the Scrolls helped to supply, giving fresh routes by which to appreciate Jesus and his world.

Historical Jesus study began as a project of the Enlightenment to strip Jesus of the doctrinal layers allegedly said to be tied to him by the early church, so that only a historical Jesus should remain. The history of historical Jesus study has shown the process is a little like trying to divide an atom or separate out cleanly a strand of DNA. It is a difficult exercise, that is, full of judgments. Some say there have been three quests, while others suggest that once the quest started down this road in the eighteenth century, it never let up. Numerous Jesus portraits have resulted. Some say this diversity negates the exercise and shows its inability to cope with the data. But recent historical Jesus study has for the most part started in a Jewish context to understand Jesus, a starting place that makes sense in light of Jesus' roots and our still accumulating knowledge of Second Temple Judaism.[1] This approach beats the other options of earlier quests. The first quest was flawed, arguing that dogmatics can have no place in studying Jesus (as if Jesus did not engage in theology). The second quest struggled, arguing that Hellenistic layers could be discovered and surgically and cleanly removed from the Gospel portraits about Jesus, only to have the Dead Sea Scrolls raise the possibility that some of those Hellenistic roots could also be quite Jewish. The strength of the so-called third quest, whether or not it really is a

---

[1]This starting point has been crisply defended recently by James Charlesworth in his book *The Historical Jesus: An Essential Guide* (Nashville: Abingdon, 2008).

third quest, is its starting point in the very milieu in which Jesus lived and spoke. This has opened up fresh ways to appreciate what Jesus claimed and how he likely went about it, at least during most of his public ministry.[2]

So there is value in seeing what can be shown historically to be likely in understanding Jesus and his relationship to his Second Temple Jewish context, as long as one keeps in mind that the Jesus of Scripture is a Jesus remembered. Jesus is remembered by those who associated themselves with him or those who walked with him. Some of these people may well be responsible for the roots of tradition we have about Jesus. If Acts 1:21-22 is a guide, then part of the point in being an apostle is having a direct experience of Jesus, being "an eyewitness and minister of the word" (Lk 1:2) responsible for the oral traditions tied to Jesus.

That this kind of nonautobiographical portrait of someone can be accurate and/or valuable is easy to establish. We often think that the only testimony worth having about a person is his or her autobiography. However, this is mistaken. Granted, first-person material is nice to possess. To have it certainly helps in understanding an aspect of what drives a person. However in the case of Jesus, all we have is what others have said about him and what others have reported that he said. To be in such a position does not mean that we have lost access to Jesus. Just think of how history is enhanced when colleagues of a great figure write about their impressions of that figure through his or her words and deeds. The story of Jesus is very much a story of his impact on others. Without that, his life and work matters little. So in this case, such multiple angles on a personality are of great significance in dealing with a leader's impact and motivations. This is what the Gospels give us, and such a multiperspectival impression can be as historical as the autobiographical words of the individual.

I make this point about impact because a prominent Jewish scholar once asked me how we can know anything about Jesus because he left

---

[2]Some studies, such as those by Ben Meyer, are careful to distinguish what Jesus did publicly and what he taught his disciples privately, a key distinction to keep in view when discussing how Jesus went about disclosing his intentions.

us no writing of his own. (We were discussing my claim that Jesus is to be appreciated within a context of messiahship that can make sense in a Second Temple Jewish context, a fact I will argue in this essay.) He had issued his challenge at an informal dinner with his program's graduate students, who ironically numbered about twelve, in honor of my visit. I responded by saying, "Let us assume that you died and left no writing. Do you think I could ask your students about what you taught and how, so that I might get a multidimensional read on who you were and what you taught? Could I discover something of value about the historical professor?" I think this is true and this is what I believe I can show the Gospels give us.

One of the ways we can come to this conclusion is through careful historical study, using the rules historical Jesus scholars use, while understanding that the bar is being raised to a level of significant demonstration. The limits of time traversed, the task of trying to reconstruct culture and the difficulty that historical method has with singular, uncorroborated testimony means the results regarding many particulars are likely to come up short of demonstration. The method and its standards mean that a full portrait is lacking that might well emerge if singular testimony could be more easily integrated into the method.[3] In an approach where so much rests on some type of corroboration, much potential evidence has been lost or at least hangs in a kind of suspended animation by not meeting the historical researchers' standards.

Thus the results of historical Jesus study, using the criteria of authenticity (multiple attestation, dissimilarity in one of its variety of forms, coherence, Aramaic substratum, embarrassment, cultural appropriateness and/or historical plausibility), are likely to be varied and will only give us, at best, access to the gist of Jesus, relying as it does on the impact that he simultaneously made on several at once. It is unlikely

---

[3]Singular testimony is one of the reasons the Gospel of John is so little used in such study. Well more than 80 percent of John's material is unique to his Gospel. Most scholars use it sparingly in such work, even though there is a growing sense that this material is also significant in what it contributes at key spots. However, given the difficulty of knowing how to show it can meet the standards set, I will appeal to it very rarely in this study. Its inclusion would open up many additional lines of study.

to give us a full and completely rounded off understanding. Historical Jesus studies can give us a start and can open doors for discussion between people of distinct approaches to Jesus. For these reasons, the discussion is worth having and pursuing, even if its results will always be limited in scope.

THAT JESUS EXISTED

It is sometimes questioned whether Jesus existed at all. In fact, there is wide ranging evidence that he did. Josephus, in his *Jewish Antiquities* 18.63-64, discusses Jesus in a context dealing with Pilate's oversight of the region. Although it is clear that the text as it exists today has been embellished by Christian copyists of Josephus at certain points, key parts of the passage are seen as authentic by most scholars, noting the reputation of Jesus as a performer of unusual works ("he was a doer of wonderful works"), discussing the opposition to Jesus by Jewish leaders, which led to his crucifixion ("when Pilate, at the suggestion of the principal men amongst us, had condemned him to the cross"), and observing that his death did not stop the emerging of a new faith ("the tribe of Christians, so named from him, are not extinct at this day"). A later reference to James as the brother of the so-called Christ assumes that the Christ figure had already been discussed (*Jewish Antiquities* 20.200: "he [Festus] assembled the Sanhedrin of judges, and brought before them the brother of Jesus, who was called Christ, whose name was James, and some others"). Other early second-century Roman texts from Tacitus[4] and Suetonius[5] analyze the bare elements along similar lines. Thus both Jewish and Roman sources from within a century of Jesus' time testify to his existence. Later Jewish sources also assume Jesus' existence (*b. Sanh* 43a, 107b). There is no evidence that those who opposed the movement attributed to him denied his existence.

---

[4]*Annals* 15, 44: "They [Christians] got their name from Christ, who was executed by sentence of the procurator Pontius Pilate in the reign of Tiberius. That checked the pernicious superstition for a short time, but it broke out afresh—not only in Judea, where the plague first arose, but in Rome itself, where all horrible and shameful things in the world collect and find a home."

[5]*Life of Claudias* 25, 4: "He [Claudias] expelled the Jews from Rome, on account of the riots in which they were constantly indulging, at the instigation of Chrestus." Most interpreters regard the reference to Chrestus as a misspelled reference to Christ.

AN EVANGELICAL TAKE ON JESUS
A LOOK AT KEY THEMES THAT SHOW THE GIST OF JESUS' MISSION

In such a summary essay, it is impossible to cover all of the elements that make up a case for the historical Jesus in detail. So I opt to present key themes, events and sayings that help us to zero in on what Jesus was about. It is key here that Jesus emerged in a complex cultural context that had Jewish and Greco-Roman elements, often fused together in ways that are hard to separate. Jesus himself came out of a practicing Jewish context and launched what at least was a Jewish reform movement, a call to national and religious renewal along the lines articulated by many of the prophets. The real debate about Jesus stems from whether he saw himself as more than a prophet, namely, as the central figure around the arrival of God's promise and kingdom, even to the point of making its arrival and sustenance possible.

Because Jesus did not leave any of his own writings, a question becomes how can we know his intentions? In sum, the answer is that his intentions may be best seen in his actions, many of which were symbolic and had a context within Jewish expectation. These events appear in the faithful transmission of his teaching, within a culture rooted in memory that was a part of Judaism. These events, especially the multiply attested ones or ones that meet the other authenticity criteria, give us adequate access to the key points of his actions and their impact. So we turn to his life's central themes and the events that we believe are sufficiently likely to give us the historical contours of Jesus' activity.

Association with John the Baptist. It is important to start here because this association places Jesus in a setting where John issued a call for the nation to repent. The tradition about Jesus being baptized by John comes to us multiply attested. The Markan tradition, John and even some sources outside the Gospels allude to it.[6] Discussion over the exact significance of this event and what it shows depends on how much of the scene, including the words from heaven, are taken to be a reflection of the original experience.[7] However, that Jesus participated

---

[6]Some suggest Q had it. *The Gospel of the Ebionites* is said to have contained a reference (Epiphanius *Against Heresies* 30.13.7-8).

[7]If the words *from heaven* reflect the experience of Jesus passed on to his disciples, then there is

in such a baptism is very likely, given that the picture is of Jesus submitting to John in baptism. Such an admission is a potentially embarrassing point that makes it unlikely that a community that gave Jesus a uniquely exalted status created this scene (meeting the criterion of embarrassment). In fact even within the Gospel tradition, we see some nervousness here, as the unique exchange between John and Jesus shows in Matthew 3:14-15.

What is important to the historical Jesus discussion is that the historically quite probable association of Jesus with this baptism indicates an identification Jesus had with John's mission.[8] Jesus shared John's call to the nation for renewal and identified with it. The significance of this is that Jesus was not merely a moral teacher of ethical wisdom, a second category virtually every treatment of the historical Jesus accepts at some level.[9] The events that involve Jesus' ministry more directly indicate these added dimensions.

The character of Jesus' ministry: Reaching out to the fringe. Another key multiattested element of Jesus' ministry is his reaching out to those on the fringe of society. His association with people regarded as the fringe of society, as unclean or as likely reprobates was something that created both reaction against him and interest in him (e.g., tax collectors: Mark: Mk 2:15-16 // Mt 9:10-11 // Lk 5:30; Q: Mt 11:19 // Lk 7:34; M: Mt 21:31; L: Lk 15:1; lepers: Mark: Mk 1:40 // Mt 8:2; 10:8; Mk 14:3 // Mt 26:6; Q: Mt 11:4-5 // Lk 7:22-23: L: Lk 17:10-17; the poor: Q:

---

an identification of Jesus as Servant-Son in a kind of commissioning. Jesus is seen as Messiah from the allusion to Ps 2, something the early tradition of apostolic preaching about Jesus also affirms (Acts 10:37-38). He also is identified with the Servant through an allusion to Is 42. However, I am not making a point of this here. My point is that the consistency of the tradition at various levels on the start of Jesus' public appearance shows a point of religious agreement between John and Jesus on the need to call the nation back to covenantal faithfulness.

[8]For a careful defense of the sociological situation for John the Baptist, see Robert L. Webb, *John the Baptizer and Prophet: A Sociohistorical Study* (Sheffield: Sheffield Academic Press, 1991), and his "Jesus' Baptism: Its Historicity and Implications," *Bulletin of Biblical Research* 10, no. 2 (2000): 261-309.

[9]Some historical Jesus studies want to limit Jesus to being a teacher of wisdom only. The most well-known recent effort in this regard is the Jesus Seminar of the 1990s. All eschatological features to his ministry are products of the later community. Even the famous Q source is divided by some into Q^1 and Q^2 (others positing even additional recensions of Q) to reflect this view. I find this unlikely. The eschatological Jesus is too multiattested in the tradition's sources *and* forms to be excluded from being rooted in Jesus. This case becomes even more established by the other events I shall contend are demonstrably historical.

Mt 5:3 // Lk 6:20; Mt 11:4-5 // Lk 7:22-23; Mark: Mk 10:21 // Mt 19:21; Mk 12:41-42 // Lk 21:2-3; L: Lk 4:16-19; 14:13-14, 21; 16:19-31; 19:1-10). This, in addition to the table fellowship he extended to such people along with his urging those he taught to reach out in a similar manner, showed that the mission he had was open to people normally excluded from such consideration. Jesus engaged with people in ways that led to the criticism of his associations (Q: Mt 11:19 // Lk 7:34; L: Lk 15:1). This was a way of indicating that he intended his message for a wide range of people because Jesus came to seek and save lost sinners (Mark: Mk 2:17 // Mt 9:13 // Lk 5:32; L: Lk 5:8; 15:1-32; Lk 19:10). There is a contrast here with the kind of elaborate piety some Jewish groups expected. One thinks of the long initiation process required at Qumran as an example. The elaborate discussions of sin, piety and purity were a part of movements within Judaism that emerged even more fully after the temple destruction in works like the Mishnah. Before that period, works like *Jubilees* also reflect a concern to be the righteous in ways that could lead to a type of separation from other elements within Israel. Jesus' approach stands in contrast to such approaches to holiness.

The call of Jesus' ministry: Total commitment. One of the features of Jesus' teaching, at least as it is seen in the Synoptics, is that he spends much time discussing what he announces (the kingdom of God) and what he brings (the forgiveness and the mercy of God) without making himself an *explicit* object of hope. This feature of his teaching is tricky because his actions and other activities do give an indication that he is very much at the center of what is coming. In fact in many ways, the kingdom and its benefits arrive with his presence and activity. Such an open door of opportunity from God comes with a call, one to totally embrace and receive what God is bringing through him. So Jesus taught about a discipleship that demanded all. It meant primary allegiance to God, even over one's family. A series of texts express this idea (Mark: Mk 8:34–9:1; Mt 16:24-28 // Lk 9:23-27; Q: Mt 8:19-22 // Lk 9:57-60; Mt 10:37-38 like Lk 14:25-26; L: Lk 9:61-62). The uniqueness of how Jesus says and does this is another element lending an air of dissimilarity to his teaching. In the tradition, Jesus is the one teacher who people follow, and he does the inviting rather than the students coming to him.[10] In the tradition, outside of Scripture, his teaching is the only "teaching" that counts. We do not see teachers arising alongside Jesus to give their take on the arriving kingdom in the Gospels. His word alone is important. The commitment he calls for in entering into the way he is leading and his consistent insistence that his teaching is to be heeded shows the importance of what Jesus was bringing and announcing. This emphasis on his teaching alone is perhaps best indicated by his familiar refrain, "the one who has ears, let him hear," and its variations (Mt 11:15; 13:9, 15-16, 43; Mk 4:9, 23; 8:18; Lk 8:8; 14:35; Markan, M and L traditions are included here).

The subject of Jesus' ministry: The kingdom of God and the promised age of God. One of our contributors to this volume has called the kingdom of God one of the least disputed facts about Jesus.[11] Although not a common phrase in the Hebrew Scripture, the idea that God rules is a frequent concept within it and Second Temple Judaism.[12] However, this concept, as Jesus used it, is not about the inherent sovereignty God has as Creator. Rather it treats the idea of his promised redeeming rule expressed afresh in the world in the arrival of a newly dawning age of shalom.[13] This kingdom vindicates the righteous and brings ultimate justice. This is the kingdom come near (Mark: Mk 1:14-15) or the kingdom come upon one (Q: Mt 12:27-28 // Lk 11:19-20). This was a presence that kings and prophets had longed to see (Q: Mt 13:17 // Lk 10:24) and involved acts that pointed to the arrival of something God has begun to do anew (Q: Mt 11:2-6 // Lk 7:18-23, with its allusions to the salvation acts Isaiah noted; something Qumran also affirms in 4Q521, yet at Qumran it is in expectation only, not realization, as with Jesus).

---

[10]Samuel Byrskog, *Jesus the Only Teacher* (Stockholm: Almqvist and Wiksell International, 1994); Martin Hengel, *The Charismatic Leader and His Followers* (Edinburgh: T & T Clark, 1981).

[11]James D. G. Dunn, *Jesus Remembered*, Christianity in the Making 1 (Grand Rapids: Eerdmans, 2003), p. 383.

[12]Charlesworth, *The Historical Jesus*, p. 56.

[13]Jesus' presentation of the kingdom was multifaceted. Each occurrence of the expression needs to be evaluated. At its core it looks to the vindication of God's people in a rule of God that brings ultimate peace. Its coming is both present and now in inauguration and yet to come in consummation. It involves both God's presence and a realm to be ruled. Its calling leads to a life of dedication to the Father and service. For details see Darrell L. Bock, *Jesus According to Scripture* (Grand Rapids: Baker Academic, 2002), pp. 565-93.

This kingdom, as many parables note, starts out small and ends up large. This was not the common Jewish expectation of the promised kingdom, even in its various forms. That kingdom expectation was of a powerful, all-encompassing presence and of great victory (*Psalms of Solomon* 17–18 is perhaps the most well-known example). This kingdom would grow from a seemingly tiny start, barely noticeable until it encompasses all (Mark: Mk 4:2-9 // Mt 13:3-9 // Lk 4:4-8; Mark: Mk 4:30-32 // Mt 13:31-32 // Lk 13:18-19; M: Mt 13:24-30; Q: Mt 13:33 // Lk 13:20-21).[14]

Now this kingdom did have a consummative phase that was much more like the common expectation. Here the righteous would be vindicated, judgment would come, and shalom would be established and rule, as Satan was defeated in ways Judaism also anticipated (*Testament of Moses* 10:1-2; Q: Mt 11:21-24 // Lk 10:12-15; Q: Mt 8:11-12 // Lk 13:28-29; Q: Mt 5:3-6, 11-12 // Lk 6:20-23; Mark: Mk 13 // Mt 24 // Lk 21; L: Lk: 16:19-31; L: Lk 16:1-8; M: Mt 18:23-25; M: 13:24-30; shalom pictured as a banquet: Q: Mt 22:2-10 // Lk 14:16-24; M: Mt 25:1-13; L: Lk 12:37; 15:24; 22:30).

This message is received, accepted, embraced or experienced. This is what the miracles picture: a gift sought and received in the recognition that Jesus provides it. Although the Twelve are commissioned to do such works in Jesus' name, the Gospels never tell a detailed story of these representatives performing any healings.[15] Jesus drives these actions. Casting out demons by the finger or Spirit of God means the kingdom has come in its initial expression (Q: Mt 12:27-28 // Lk 11:19-20). The healing of the paralytic shows the authority to forgive sin (Mark: Mk 2:1-10 // Mt 9:1-8 // Lk 5:17-26). Here the initiative of those seeking Jesus is affirmed, as with Zacchaeus later (L: Lk 19:1-10).

Everything said about Jesus up to now points to a figure who preached and enacted a special time's arrival and the realization of acts of delivering promise. What came with Jesus was the focus of his message. This has caused some to call Jesus primarily a prophetic figure. Prophetic he was, but his actions pointed to someone more unique than

---

[14]Even Thomas has elements of these themes: *Gospel of Thomas* 9, 20, 21, 57, 96.
[15]Summaries do appear, but only as a result of Jesus' commissioning them.

the title *prophet* suggests. The category of prophet as a comprehensive summary of Jesus and his career understates who he was and what his actions denoted. Who Jesus showed himself to be was as crucial to appreciating his mission as what he brought because the one who brings kingdom promise has a unique place in God's program. I now turn to this idea.

The focus of the Age: Jesus, the one to come and the declared Anointed-Sent One who will suffer. I will treat the authenticity of specific key events below. One of the most important of these will be Peter's declaration at Caesarea Philippi. In it, there appears a fundamental contrast between the popular perception of Jesus as a prophet of one kind or another and the picture of him as the central figure of promise, the Messiah (= Christ). This theme appears with a variety of titles, including the "one to come" (Q: Mt 11:12-14 // Lk 7:18-20; John: Jn 6:14) and one greater than a prophet (Jonah; Q: Mt 12:41 // Lk 11:32) or king (Solomon; Q: Mt 12:42 // Lk 11:31). Jesus presents himself as one who acts like a prophet and yet also brings the deliverance promised (L: Lk 4:16-30, which is an expanded version of a Markan traditional text: Mk 6:1-6 // Mt 13:54-58). When this deliverance is associated with the coming of the eschaton, then Jesus' role can be called messianic, even if he did not use the title in public all that often.

This disclosure of his role in public was concealed, in part, because of the difficulty it could have raised in confusing Jesus with a political revolutionary. However at points, it did come out, such as at the atriumphal entry and in the temple cleansing, two other events considered in detail below and rooted in the tradition we received through Mark.[16] John's Gospel also points to this proximity between the coming prophet and king when he says in 6:14-15, "Now when the people saw the miraculous sign that Jesus performed, they began to say to one another, 'This is certainly *the Prophet who is to come into the world.*' Then Jesus, because he knew they were going to come and seize him by force to make him king, withdrew again up the mountainside alone." Such hesitation is also seen after Peter's declaration when Jesus calls them to

---

[16]By *atriumphal entry*, I mean that unlike other dignitaries who were received by key officials, Jesus' entry into Jerusalem was met with hesitation by them.

silence (Mark: Mk 8:30 // Mt 16:20 // Lk 9:21), something he also does with the heavenly declaration to the three at the transfiguration (M: Mk 9:9 // Mt 17:9 with variation Lk 9:36).

The hesitation to go forward in public has been a source of controversy, made famous by Wrede's claim that the "messianic secret" is something Mark created to make a messianic ministry out of something that was not messianic under Jesus.[17] It is hard to understand why the early church would do so if the impetus did not come from Jesus. It is even harder to understand how the title *Christ* became so quickly and deeply attached to Jesus' name in the early church if he had not taught in a way to suggest he was the Messiah and especially if he had refused to take on the term in private or public discussion. In fact in a little-known historical detail, Wrede renounced his own view of the secret before he died in a private letter to Adolf von Harnack.[18]

Part of the reason for Jesus' care in using the term *Messiah* was that it could be used to incite people to revolt politically against Rome, as the Bar Kochba revolt of the next century shows. However, another reason was that Jesus saw his messianic activity as more complex than most of the varieties of messianic Jewish expectation of the Second Temple Period.[19] Jesus embraced the view that this key figure would suffer as well as bring victory. This dimension of his calling is introduced in a manner that would have been very unlikely for the church to have created only after Easter. The Gospels introduce this theme when Jesus calls Peter, the lead disciple, "Satan." This rebuke appears when the disciple denies that suffering is a part of Jesus' calling. The scene

---

[17]William Wrede, *The Messianic Secret* (London: James Clarke, 1971).

[18]Martin Hengel, *Studies in Early Christology* (Edinburgh: T & T Clark, 1995), pp. 7-15, and with more detail in his and Anna Maria Schwemer's *Jesus und das Judentum* (Tübingen: Mohr Siebeck, 2007), pp. 507-10; also H. Rollmann and W. Zager, "Unveröffentliche Briefe William Wredes zur Problematisierung des messianischen Selbtverständnis Jesu," *Zeitschrift für neure Theologiegeschichte* 8 (2001): 274-322, esp. 317; Andrew Chester, *Messiah and Exaltation*, WUNT 207 (Tübingen: Mohr Siebeck, 2007), pp. 309.

[19]It is discussed but much less than certain whether Qumran had a suffering role for any eschatological figure. Other than this, Jesus' emphasis here is unique in a Jewish context. On this variety, see John J. Collins, *The Scepter and the Star: The Messiahs of the Dead Sea Scrolls and Other Ancient Literature,* Anchor Bible Reference Library (New York: Doubleday, 1995), and Jacob Neusner, W. S. Green and E. Frerichs, eds., *Judaisms and Their Messiahs* (Cambridge: Cambridge University Press, 1987).

points to authenticity based on what is called the criterion of embarrassment. Would the church create an event where it compares its lead apostle to the paragon of evil? Thus this uniquely highlighted theme of the suffering of the one to come points to a key feature of Jesus' depiction of himself. Here is where the multiply attested Suffering Son of Man sayings fit (Q: Mt 12:40 // Lk 11:30 [but with a variation of emphasis]; Mark: Mk 9:9, 12 // Mt 17:12, Mark: Mk 9:30 // Mt 17:22 // Lk 9:44; Mark: Mk 10:33 // Mt 20:18 // Lk 18:31-32; M: Mt 26:1-2; Mark: Mk 14:21 // Mt 26:24 // Lk 22:20; Mark: Mk 14:41 // Mt 26:45; Mark: Mk 8:31 // Lk 9:22; L: Lk 24:7 [alluding back to the predictions]). This theme included the idea that Jesus came to give his life as a ransom for many (Mark: Mk 10:45 // Mt 20:28). It is a task that he will reinforce at the Last Supper through the bread and cup, another key event I shall develop later.

So Jesus preached a coming deliverance and claimed to help bring it to pass. This vindication did not come in raw power but also in service, including mercy, acceptance and sacrifice. The ostensive absence of power in Jesus' ministry was one of the features that must have perplexed many who tried to consider his claims. The criterion of embarrassment shows itself again here in a passage where John the Baptist asks if Jesus is the coming one. The query generated a reply that did not respond directly, but that implicitly spoke of what Jesus did as pointing to the time. By simple deduction one could determine the figure Jesus saw himself to be (Q: Mt 11:2-6 // Lk 7:18-23).

Jesus was doing three things when he treaded so carefully there. First, he was being careful not to be misunderstood and have his effort hijacked into a raw political movement. Jesus was doing things that were socially radical and even revolutionary, but his point was not to challenge Rome at a strictly political level but to appeal to Israel to be a distinct kind of people before God in a way that did not seek the use of coercive political power. His mission called for a transformed society through transformed characters and communities, an effort not to be undertaken by the edge of a sword but through a life of commitment, service and love. Second, he sought to be clear in all he did that he was more than one of the Jewish prophets. However, third, he was also undertaking an effort to reshape and recast the portrait of messiah as Jewish people embraced it in its various forms at that time. This was why at times he seemed to reject the title or at least deemphasize its popular association with him. Even the disciples needed to appreciate its reshaping before they could speak of Jesus openly in this way. For the most part, then, Jesus reserved the public disclosure of this role until he was ready to fully press the case in Jerusalem.

The provision for the Age: A life reflective of divine provision, forgiveness of sin and the Spirit. So what is the goal of kingdom life? Its desired product is a life of virtue that lives in service and honor to God. This is best depicted in what is certainly one of the most famous parts of Jesus' life, the Sermon on the Mount (Mt 5–7). Whether this was a singular address or a compilation of Jesus' teaching about following him, the remarks were a call to a life of exceptional qualities and attributes. This life of character was to reflect responses that went beyond how sinners in the world live. It extended forgiveness without conditions, sought to meet needs and evaluated sin not on the basis of external standards but in light of a sincerity of heart where a yes was yes, anger was not harbored, enemies were prayed over, people were not seen as objects of lust. Such attributes were said to reflect God's character, genuinely reflecting an individual's being a descendant of God.

The prayer Jesus is said to teach the disciples in both of its forms (Mt 6: 9-13; Lk 11:2-4) urged them corporately to acknowledge God in his uniqueness yet with the intimacy of a caring Father. It also encouraged them to appreciate God as the provider of life's basic needs and as the one who places us in a position to forgive because we have been forgiven. He even protects from temptation because the petition to not be led into temptation was a call to be protected by God and go where he leads. In a world that often operated in honor and shame garnered by one's own independent standing in support of the political state, Jesus called his disciples to give ultimate honor to the one who created life and the one who sustains it, trusting God to be their protection and provision.

Jesus' ministry of meeting needs, even those of people who had little to give back, showed the value of every human being. These actions pictured God's desire to reach out to help those who recognized their need for help. The Jesus tradition is full of accounts where people sought out Jesus because they recognized that he was able to provide things not normally made available. These signs of God's rule and the inauguration of a fresh time of deliverance were themselves to be a model for the disciples' service because he sent out messengers whose activity mirrored his own in every respect save one: the power the disciples exercised was a derived authority they received through Jesus.

Now I recognize that one of the most controversial parts of Jesus' work today was his miraculous activity. However, our ancient sources are consistent in not challenging that Jesus performed unusual works. What was debated by Jesus' opponents was the source of those acts. The Jewish retort that Jesus' power was either a reflection of magic, sorcery or of satanic power is not a denial that these activities took place but an effort to place their origin in a sphere outside God's benevolent activity.[20] Josephus, certainly no Christian, more neutrally and simply said what Jesus did was unusual *(paradoxan)*. What is often missed in modern debates over whether such works took place is the message through example that God cared and that those who walked in Jesus' way should seek to give themselves to the kind of service (not necessarily miraculous) where word and deed says God reaches out and cares.

Jesus' attitude appears to have been that sin, endemic to the human condition, was not to be a barrier to reorienting one to God's ways. So in key spots he spoke of forgiveness (Mark: Mk 2:1-12 // Mt 9:1-8 // Lk 5:17-26; L: Lk 7:36-50) or of regaining the lost (noted above). To heal the sick was the call of the Great Physician, but the prerequisite was the need of a person to sense that they were sick and in need of a physician

---

[20]This theme runs through the centuries, whether it be in the Beelzebul controversy of the Gospel tradition, the debates Justin Martyr had with Trypho or in the Talmudic tradition even centuries removed from Jesus. On this consistent line of response, see Graham Stanton, "Jesus of Nazareth: A Magician and a False Prophet Who Deceived God's People," in *Jesus of Nazareth Lord and Christ: Essays on the Historical Jesus and New Testament Christology*, ed. Joel B. Green and Max Turner (Grand Rapids: Eerdmans, 1994), pp. 164-80. For a careful treatment of Jesus' miracles in a Second Temple Jewish context, see Eric Eve, *Jewish Context of Jesus' Miracles*, Journal for the Study of the New Testament Supplement Series 231 (Sheffield: Sheffield Academic Press, 2002). Eve highlights how Jesus' miracles have a direct authority emphasis to them that most Jewish parallels involving miracles lack.

who could remedy the human condition (Mark: Mk 2:17 // Mt 9:12 // Lk 5:31; pictured in the multiply attested ministry acts of Jesus to those who were sick; L: Lk 5:1-11). Jesus did not spend much time elaborating on how this worked; he simply went around showing it was taking place. When he did speak, it was his own work that cleared the way. Nothing says this as eloquently as the Last Supper, an institution rooted in wording that is part of a two-stranded tradition with Mark and Matthew supplying one form of wording and Luke and Paul giving a variant version. All these versions agree that Jesus saw in his death a kind of delivering Passover that also seems to have had atoning or substitutionary power, in that it inaugurated a fresh covenant through a death undertaken for many. So forgiveness and mercy were core values of the kingdom. Even Jesus' parables showed this theme (M: Mt 18:21-35; L: Lk 15:1-31). The call to be merciful as the Father is merciful and the prayer to forgive as one has been forgiven reside here as well.

But how was one to achieve this shift in values? It was here that another theme became important. The fresh covenant that Jesus inaugurated in the new era had an expectation that God would create a new heart (Jer 31:31-33; Ezek 36:25). Again multiattested tradition shows Jesus teaching in such terms. Although this theme is not prevalent in Markan material, it does appear with John the Baptist's declaration that Jesus would baptize in the Spirit (Mk 1:8 // Mt 3:11). Luke even makes the response an explanation of how one could recognize that Jesus had brought the Spirit (Lk 3:15-17), making explicit what the other Gospels imply. The promise of the Spirit would enable disciples to stand strong in the midst of persecution (Mk 13:11 // Mt 10:20 // Lk 12:12) and be witnesses (L: Lk 24:49). This theme was the burden of Jesus' remarks in John's portrayal of the upper room discourse and the promise of the advocate to come (Jn 14–16). The picture appeared to foresee a cleansing that was able to fill a now clean vessel with God's effective presence, a precursor to the early church's image that the new community was a sacred locale of God's presence, a temple no longer confined to one locale. This was an illustration not unlike the parabolic picture where the kingdom starts out small but grows into a comprehensive presence (parables of mustard seed and leaven). The association of word, seed and Spirit is at work here (the Jewish *Memra* and divine wisdom).

I have spent some time touching rather quickly on key themes. But does this story cohere in the key events tied to Jesus? One of the notorious problems in Jesus studies is trying to determine a sequence of events in Jesus' ministry. The various locations of similar teaching betray a couple of important factors here. Jesus engaged in an itinerant ministry. He surely taught such themes as he moved from place to place. Tradition, especially oral tradition, might recall the fact of what he emphasized less than the locale because of such repetition. That Jesus taught these things is what it records. Thus this absence of particularization in terms of the events' locales is not as much of a problem as it is often made out to be. Some of the variation in our tradition in terms of timing may not be, as is often suggested, that the tradition of events comes in one size or frame only, but because these traditions reflect the product of a ministry on the move. So all I claim in this overview of Jesus' teaching is that these are some of the keynotes of his kingdom message.

However, our final section looks at key events and searches for coherence. It considers the question about what produced Jesus' death. This final survey does not suffer from this timing problem. The events I turn to now are parts of the final stage of Jesus' ministry. They produce a compact sequence that also yields a coherent thematic line. Placed in its cultural context, these events point us in the direction of why Jesus was put to death and what was seen to be at stake. The sequence shows that two opinions about Jesus collided: either he was the central figure of God's program, whom God would vindicate and exalt, or else such a claim was so theologically exaggerated that it must be judged to be blasphemy. In this climactic confrontation the issue was the nature and extent of Jesus' authority. It not only coheres with what already has been said, it also coheres with the result that Jesus ended up crucified as a result of a combination of pressure from the Jewish leadership and a judgment made by the one who had the authority to put people to death in Judea, Pontius Pilate—a historical conclusion that Josephus also presents. When Christians came to argue that God had vindicated Jesus and emptied the tomb into which the crucified one had been placed, the debate over Jesus, both of history and faith, extended into the message of the early church and the church of the centuries, painting along lines the historical Jesus had already drawn.

The Decisive Conflict to Vindicate the Claim—Key Events of the Passion Week and a Precursor

Peter's declaration of Jesus as the Christ. This scene involves one of the few Synoptic texts where Jesus probed for an indication of who he was from his disciples. A few features of this event point to the use of tradition and authenticity. The specification of a locale, and one outside the realm of Israel, are details that do not fit Mark in that he rarely specified location. Neither does this detail fit the Markan emphasis on the character of Jesus' mission being to Israel. A created event might well have been expected to speak to Israel more directly. Caesarea Philippi was a region full of the Roman gods' spiritual influence, having been a spot of polytheistic worship for centuries by Jesus' time. Peter's statement about Jesus was not one only about Israel. However, a statement created by the later church surely would not have been as ambiguous as this text is. So this speaks against the event as created. In addition the following scene has Jesus rebuke Peter as Satan, forming a contrast with this event that assumes Peter's remark. Jesus' rebuke was almost certainly not invented because this would have been an embarrassing story to create about a lead apostle (the criterion of embarrassment). It indicated clearly that whatever Peter did understand, he still lacked important elements of the portrait. This kind of rebuke was even more unlikely as a church creation. Jesus' hesitation to be strictly a powerful political and militaristic king also coheres with other texts (Jn 6:13-14).

Did Jesus accept this declaration? The answer is both yes and no. The affirmation centers on the fact that Peter appreciated that Jesus was more than the prophet whom the populace held Jesus to be. For Peter, Jesus was not merely a messenger of God, but the Promised One at the center of God's kingdom program. This was affirmed by Jesus, but the idea Peter had also needed shaping, which led to an aspect of denial and the call to be silent. Jesus needed to reconfigure Peter's expectations, adding notes of suffering and explaining that vindication would only follow it. The church surely understood the thrust of Jesus' response as positive because, without it, there never would have been the common association of Jesus as the Christ, even to the point of making it a central way to refer to him.

The point is significant because it sets a trajectory to what Jesus was doing. He was the key figure of the new era, the hub of God's program of deliverance. He was not one prophet among many, but the antici-pated anointed one. However, there were aspects of this portrait that needed to be appreciated before Jesus himself could be preached. This explains Jesus' call for silence and his increased instruction about suf-fering that immediately followed. Jesus saw himself as a messianic fig-ure, but only when carefully defined in a way that incorporated his service into that role.

The atriumphal entry into Jerusalem. The key doubts about this event's historicity center on the fact that Jesus was not stopped on his entry as a regal pretender. Surely if he entered the city in such a bold manner he would have been stopped immediately. So some contend this event did not happen as it is portrayed. However, this view of the scene might be imagining too much. Jesus was one among many pil-grims approaching Jerusalem, whose population was said to triple dur-ing such pilgrim feasts, possibly reaching up to 100,000 from tens of thousands. Pilgrims entering the town would have been in a celebratory mood, probably singing among other activities. They might well have chimed in, but in Matthew 21:11 they did so only seeing Jesus as a prophet, a reputation he had established popularly, but one short of what the actions represented. Some others may well have joined the disciples in calling out in praise of the entering Son of David (Mt 21:9). The kingdom hope Jesus might well have generated popularly may have led to some responding in this manner, but how many actually appreci-ated all that he had been doing here is not clear. The Lukan text might be of help here in attributing the laying of palms to disciples, a group placed modestly at just over a hundred in Acts. An action like this by an isolated few, during such a commotion, would not necessarily attract a great deal of attention except from those keeping an eye on Jesus, namely, the religious leadership that did question the practice in Luke 19:39-40. Even if they had wanted to act, to seize Jesus immediately in this setting would have risked really setting off an uproar.

A second feature that raises issues is the explicitness of Jesus' act. Is this not out of character for his ministry? The answer to that question is certainly yes, but the contrast is the point. Jesus now approached the capital to press the issue of his identity. He entered the city with actions that evoked kingship like Solomon's entry (1 Kings 1:33-37) and the hope of a coming king like that in Zechariah 9:9. Yet unlike the arrival of other dignitaries, the city did come to meet Jesus. Certainly the civic leaders did not. There were no speeches for him as there were for other dignitaries who entered ancient cities with pomp. It was a claim to kingship made in very modest terms. This entry lacked the sense of awe and wonder that most dignitaries received, even though those who appreciated Jesus called out in praise. This is why the entry has been called atriumphal.[21]

This event is one of the few told in all four Gospels, underscoring its importance. The variation in the accounts shows that more than one source is likely in view. This story was unlikely to have been created in an early church that seemed to be careful about antagonizing Rome. Why would they create it if it could be denied? Its presence throughout the material suggests it was there because it did occur. Its presence also suggests that Jesus entered the city intent on being reckoned with and assessed. His disciples knew why he was coming and said so. His opponents, if Luke can be accepted, challenged his claim, something their later action confirms. Jesus' action here set the stage for the decisive confrontation.

The temple incident. Virtually everyone looking at this event sees it as important to understanding Jesus. There are few who doubt its authenticity. It is multiattested in at least two distinct versions (Mark: Mk 11:15-19 // Mt 21:12-17 // Lk 19:45-48; John: Jn 2:13-22).[22] It is one of the few

---

[21]Brent Kinman, *Jesus' Entry into Jerusalem: In the Context of Lukan Theology and the Politics of His Day* (Leiden: Brill, 1995). The work is summarized and updated in "Jesus' Royal Entry into Jerusalem," *Bulletin for Biblical Research* 15, no. 2 (2005): 223-60. This is part of a collection of essays to appear from the Institute for Biblical Research Jesus Group in 2009. These essays take key events tied to Jesus and assess their meaning in context, walking through the scholarly debate in more detail than we can afford here. This work is as yet untitled and will be edited by Robert Webb and Darrell L. Bock.

[22]One issue is the chronological difference in these accounts in John as opposed to the Synoptics. A few see two distinct cleansings, but those who opt for one cleansing usually see John

events to appear in all four Gospels. It is seen as a catalyst for Jesus' arrest in the Synoptics, a view that makes cultural sense. Moreover it is not clear why this event would have been created had it not taken place. What would have been gained by creating such an event? The early church sought to be careful about being seen as seditious, and yet this event plays right into that danger. Thus that it took place best explains its presence.

The reason for seeing the act as important is obvious. For Jews, the temple represented the most sacred locale in the world. It was home to the only temple of the faith, and they saw it as the place of the divine presence. So holy was the innermost area that a human, namely, the high priest, visited it only once a year to bring the offering of atonement. As such, the locale was particularly sensitive, and a Roman fortress, the Antonia, located on its northwest corner, kept an eye on it for trouble. However, it was the priests who were permitted to control the area, as they stationed themselves around the temple, especially at the Huldah gates where most people entered the temple area proper. This configuration allowed a potentially quick reaction should events get very dangerous or chaotic. The hope was to prevent Romans from having to enter the area.

Herod the Great rebuilt the temple mount and expanded the area so that it covered about thirty-five acres. Jesus' action likely took place near the Royal Portico at the southern end of the temple mount, where the moneychangers and traders would have been. Temple worship required pure doves and animals. The moneychangers allowed men needing to pay the temple tax to purchase the required Tyrian shekels, which although they had symbols on them offensive to Jews, were of the highest quality and silver content. These were the least offensive coins available at the time.

Now, what has been said about the presence of authority around the temple does raise the one objection about the scene that might militate against its acceptance. If Jesus caused such a disturbance, then why

---

as moving the account forward to preview the different plane on which Jesus speaks about the temple. However, one can make a case given the differences between the Synoptic accounts and the importance placed on it that this would have been one of the more well-known events, which likely circulated in the oral tradition.

wasn't he stopped and arrested there on the scene? The answer may well be found in appreciating the size of the temple, the location of the moneychangers and the nature of Jesus' action. Being on the opposite end of the temple and being confined to a rather tight and busy area, the scene likely failed to gain the attention of the fortress across the way because it occupied a spot where traffic could become congested. There also might have been hesitation in acting quickly against someone who was known to have some popular following; they might have felt it was better to take note and wait for a better time to challenge him rather than inflame what could have become a volatile situation.

Jesus' objection to the moneychangers has been seen in various ways: a protest against the commercialization of the temple, a protest against the temple itself or as a call to spiritual reform beginning at the temple. At the least, Jesus' overturning the tables involved a symbolic prophetic action, a rebuke of the leadership and the way it ran the temple. As such, Jesus challenged what was regarded as official religious authority, which was why the scene following this event had the religious leadership ask where Jesus got the authority to do such things.[23]

The reason for Jesus' action may well be complex. Although Jesus did predict the destruction of Jerusalem, and although at a later time sacrifices were viewed as unnecessary, Jesus was not pronouncing the destruction of Jerusalem or the cessation of sacrifices with *this* incident.[24] The evidence of various sources, especially the Qumran Scrolls, shows that there was a belief by many about corruption in the temple, but those guilty of corruption were almost exclusively seen as the ruling priestly families, not the regular priests who served daily in the temple (1QpHab VII, 7-13; IX, 2-16; XI, 2-15; XII, 1-10; 4QpNah Frag. 3-4, 1.10 [=4Q 169]; CD-A VI, 134-17; 4Q Ps 37 II, 14 and III, 6, 12; 4Q MMT 82-83; also *1 Enoch; Testament of Moses* 5:3–6:1).

---

[23]All of what is said here is true regardless of the more contentious question of whether Jesus sought reform or predicted the destruction of the temple here. For the issue here, see E. P. Sanders, *Jesus and Judaism* (Philadelphia: Fortress Press, 1985), pp. 61-76, who argues for a prediction of destruction, and Craig A. Evans, "Jesus' Action in the Temple: Cleansing or Portent of Destruction," *Catholic Biblical Quarterly* 51 (1989): 237-70, who opts for cleansing.

[24]Part of the evidence suggesting this conclusion is the participation of the new community at the temple after Jesus' death.

The confrontation Jesus had with the leadership may well be an element here, but it is unlikely to be all that is at work. So although such corruption might have been a factor, Jesus' purpose seemed more comprehensive, involving a prophetic protest pointing to an eschatological hope. Jesus looked to the future in saying the house will be a house of prayer for the nations. Like the prophets before him, Jesus took strategic action *in the temple* to reorder how people viewed the temple and its proceedings. Numerous Jewish texts point to the expectation that at the end time the temple worship would be what it should be, and people from many nations would come there to worship (Ezek 40–48; 4Q 174, where the house of David arises and the temple is rebuilt, an act pointing to restoration). Jesus' action was a critique of the current worship and the ruling priests but also expressed his conviction about the temple's sanctity. The action implied an unparalleled authority, one that probably carried messianic overtones because of this event's following his entry and the eschatological nature of these acts. It also pointed to the fulfillment of promises that God (or the Messiah) would set things right in the temple. The juxtaposition of the revived Davidic dynasty and the hope for a restored Jerusalem, expressed in the fourteenth and fifteenth benedictions,[25] reflects such a hope in Judaism, as does language of purging to righteousness in *Psalms of Solomon* 17–18. The temple incident was a symbolic messianic act like the Lord's Supper and the triumphal entry.

The Last Supper. The event of the Last Supper is deeply rooted in the tradition, even existing in two slightly distinct forms, as mentioned earlier. There is little doubt an important meal took place on the night of Jesus' arrest. There is a complicated debate about this meal's timing and nature. Was it a Passover meal? The tradition of the Synoptic Gospels says so (Mk 14:1-2, 12-17), although John leaves another impression (Jn 18:28). Again, what could be said was that the mood of the Passover season was surely a part of the scene, given the meal at the least came on the edge of Passover, making the association a simple transition.[26]

---

[25]The fourteenth and fifteenth benedictions are part of an ancient national Jewish prayer called *Shemoneh Esreh*. It was recited three times a day by all Jews. It was called The Prayer. Although this juxtaposition is post-70, its association of city and David is likely to be earlier.

[26]One thinks of how Christmas overtones impact many events in December in our present day. For a treatment of the issues tied to this scene see Scot McKnight, *Jesus and His Death: Histori-*

This meal with its inauguration and suffering language gives insight into Jesus' actions. His suffering would bring a fresh covenantal reality, with his death being a representative act on behalf of many/you (many: Mt 26:28 // Mk 14:24; you: 1 Cor 11:24 // Lk 22:19 [also in v. 20]). An allusion to Isaiah 53 was possibly intended in the appeal to the "many."[27] There also was an allusion to the new covenant, a move made explicit in the Paul and Luke version (1 Cor 11:25 // Lk 22:20). Jesus saw his death as involving the suffering of an innocent like the Isaianic portrait (Lk 22:37).[28]

The institution of fresh deliverance and covenantal liturgy in the shadow of the Passover represented a significant claim of authority. It was a move Jesus made in a private setting with his disciples. It served to underscore the various acts of authority he had already undertaken as a part of his confrontational trip to Jerusalem. Jesus had already taught that a prophet could not die outside of Jerusalem (L: Lk 13:33; Q: Mt 23:37 // Lk 13:34), a claim that cohered with what was taking place here. This act indicated that Jesus saw himself as the hub of eschatological activity and the one whose act of suffering brings the new era. At the least, this was an act of *the* eschatological prophet, one who functioned as the expected leader-prophet like Moses. However, if Jesus' other acts in this week framed it, including his challenge to understand what Psalm 110:1 meant, then a messianic implication was also intended. Jesus acts as a leader-prophet who delivered in such a way that promises of the eschaton were to be seen as coming with him. This sacrifice opened up a covenant. In addition, in the context of a ministry that had called Israel to turn back to God, a sacrifice dealing with sin to clear the way for turning was also likely to be present. So whether

---

ography, the Historical Jesus and Atonement Theory (Waco, Tex.: Baylor University Press, 2005), pp. 259-73; Martin Hengel and Anna Maria Schwemer, *Jesus und Judentum*, Geschichte des frühen Christentums 1 (Tübingen: Mohr Siebeck, 2007), pp. 582-86. This second study argues for a Passover meal, while McKnight argues for the Passover season. Hengel also speaks of the opening up of a covenant offering in this symbolism.

[27]The word *many* appears five times in this Isaianic text. It is almost a refrain. It should be noted, however, that some are not convinced this is enough to see an allusion here.

[28]A claim that this text interrupts the flow and is a product of the early church must cope with how little is being claimed here. An early-church product would likely have made more of Is 53 than takes place here.

Jesus spoke of the sacrifice being for "you" or for the "many," it was the representative feature that was present in what would be largely synonymous language. The idea of a celebration of this meal to come in the future does invoke the idea of the eschatological or messianic banquet, adding to the likelihood that Jesus saw himself acting as the leader in the ushering in of the new era and not merely as a prophetic figure.

The Jewish examination of Jesus. I have made this event the focus of a full monograph, as well as follow-up studies.[29] It is important to appreciate what this event was. It was not a formal Jewish trial. Efforts to suggest that the leadership broke their own mishnaic rules—assuming raising such a source is not anachronistic—ignore the fact that the Jewish leadership did not have the right to execute someone in Judea. So what we have in this scene reflects a Jewish effort to collect evidence to take to the Roman prefect, who did possess such authority. This goal also explains to us why the meeting took place quickly and at night. There was no desire to hold Jesus for long or to prolong getting a decision. With Pilate in Jerusalem, matters could be handled quickly. So the scene is better described as an examination of Jesus.

Some scholars object that there were no witnesses to this event from among the disciples to give a report on what took place. However, the lines for possible disclosure here are multiple. First, we have the potential for witnesses, like Nicodemus or Joseph of Arimathea. Second, the kind of access a figure like Paul had to the leadership during the period of his opposition to the New Way is also a potential source. Third, there was a decades-long debate between the fledgling Jesus movement and the leadership in Jerusalem in which such key issues would surely have surfaced. Annas II, a descendant of Annas and Caiaphas, was responsible for James's death in the early sixties, showing how long the debate over the new movement lasted (*Jewish Antiquities* 20.200). In the public debate over Jesus, the case against him surely would have been made. So

---

[29]The initial study was *Blasphemy and Exaltation in Judaism and the Final Examination of Jesus* (Tübingen: Mohr Siebeck, 1998). The key subsequent study was "Blasphemy and the Jewish Examination of Jesus," *Bulletin of Biblical Research* 17, no. 1 (2007): 53-114. I have paid additional attention to authenticity issues in this *Bulletin of Biblical Research* piece. A full presentation of this event is forthcoming in a yet-to-be-titled collection of essays on the historical Jesus by several Jesus scholars of the Institute for Biblical Research, due to be published in 2009.

the likelihood that these issues would have become known through the "Jerusalem grapevine" is good.

At the event's core was the exchange between Jesus and the high priest. Jesus was asked to explain who he was. His reply, as recorded in the Synoptic Gospels, invoked Psalm 110:1 in all versions (Mt 26:64; Mk 14:62; Lk 22:69) and Daniel 7:13 in Matthew and Mark. This was the crux of this scene. One could make a strong case for both citations being linked by Jesus originally, given the likelihood that both texts appeared to have mattered to him (for Dan 7:13, see Mark: Mk 13:26 // Mt 24:30; // Lk 21:27; Q: Mt 24:27 // Lk 17:22, 24; for Ps 110:1, see Mt 22:41-45; Mk 12:35-37; Lk 20:41-44).[30]

However, as a matter of historical Jesus debate, all one needed to trigger the offense was that Jesus alluded to one of these two texts. The high priest could have responded with a blasphemy claim had either text been noted.

The appeal to Psalm 110:1 with its reference to being seated at the right hand of God meant that Jesus anticipated divine vindication and expected to be ushered into God's very presence, in some way sharing God's presence and glory, a thought that was controversial to Jews, some of whom entertained the possibility of something similar for a few potential figures,[31] while other Jews thought that such an exaltation was unthinkable.[32] So for the Jewish leadership, a Galilean teacher

---

[30]The way in which Ps 110:1 is posed as a riddle and is stated theoretically not confessionally does not reflect the clarity of an early-church creation and suggests authenticity. Jesus' self-designation as Son of Man, which is as multiattested as any title tied to him points to the likelihood that he reflected on this phrase. The likelihood he did so without considering its scriptural roots is very hard to accept. I actually think it is likely he alluded to both texts. For more detailed argument, see my *Bulletin of Biblical Research* article, cited in note 27.

[31]The *Exagoge of Ezekiel* 68-82 entertains the possibility of Moses seated on the "thrones" of God (note the plural for thrones, an allusion to Dan 7:9!) of God. This text is not eschatological, but is a midrash on Exodus 7:1, which reads literally in the Hebrew, "I will make you god to Pharoah." So in this text, Moses is portrayed in a dream as sharing God's authority when he acts in announcing the plagues. This is not the same as a direct exaltation, but moves in that direction. *First Enoch* and its portrait of the Son of Man sees a second power in heaven who shares final judgment with God in lines developed from Dan 7:9-14. This authority seems to be very much like what Jesus affirmed at the trial. I have an article forthcoming that argues for a date for this section of *1 Enoch* that is contemporary to or just before the time of Jesus' ministry.

[32]Two passages are of note here. One is *3 Enoch* where the angel Metatron escorts Enoch and claims to be "little YHWH" only to be punished for the claim later as having offended the

like Jesus did not qualify for such a claim, not having the credentials of greatness that the other candidates had, that is, *if* they even accepted such a possibility.

If Jesus had only appealed to Daniel 7:13-14, with its image of the Son of Man riding the clouds, then the high priest also would have reacted because such riding of the clouds was something only the deity did in the Hebrew Scriptures. The implication in such a reply was that Jesus would return as the Son of Man to exercise judgment. The implication would have included the idea that one day Jesus would judge his current opponents! So this again would be seen as a claim to share divine prerogatives, as well as a direct challenge to the leadership. If Jesus uttered both sayings, then the point was that one day he would sit in God's presence and exercise such judgment authority.[33]

In any of these three scenarios (Ps 110:1 alone, Dan 7:13-14 alone or both texts together), Jesus' reply claimed an equality with God that the leadership would have judged as slander against God's unique glory. With a Danielic allusion, the challenge to the leadership was more direct, as Jesus—although he is a defendant now—claimed that one day he would be the judge of the leadership. This also could have been seen as blasphemous in light of Exodus 22:28 ("You must not blaspheme God or curse the ruler of your people," NET Bible). A way to contextualize this reply is to think of it as worse than a defendant claiming to be able to live in the temple's Holy of Holies, the earthly symbol of God's presence in heaven. Part of what made the remark so offensive to the leadership was its suggested locale in heaven. Jesus invoked not the symbol of God's presence but his own presence next to the very real glory of God.

uniqueness of God. So this text shows a rejection of the sharing-glory-with-God idea. The second text is a famous exchange involving Rabbi Akiba, who upon positing the possibility of a figure seated by God is challenged by other rabbis with the rebuke "Akiba, how long will you profane the Shekinah?" The writers of these texts would have been offended by a reply like Jesus' whether he appealed to Ps 110:1 or to Dan 7:13.

[33]Although Dan 7:9-14 foreshadows a coming to heaven to receive authority, the sequence in Jesus' reply sees a coming from heaven to exercise this authority. So Jesus is developing Daniel, in all likelihood because of the vindication that he anticipated and expressed through Ps 110:1. I think Luke only cites the Danielic title and Ps 110:1 because in one sense it is the key text that establishes the motif of a presence with God in heaven. Jesus' language here is laid out in a manner that makes it clear he is not reading this text in a metaphorical way that points to his role on earth but to a vindication and position in heaven.

The regarding of Jesus' response as blasphemy was not a charge the leadership could have brought to Rome. However what it permitted them to do was raise the issue of Jesus being disruptive to the *Pax Romana* in Judea. If he had claimed to be a figure who bears independent authority apart from Rome, that claim could have been taken to Pilate and presented as a disruptive presence in the province. To translate that as a claim to be a king independent of Rome was all that was needed to merit Pilate's consideration. So the leaders believed they had good reason to go to Pilate and raise a charge of sedition to which Pilate would have been responsible to act on as Caesar's representative protecting his interests.

Examination by Pilate and crucifixion. For this scene, it is best to work backward. The *titulus* represents a summary of the charge.[34] Crucifixion was the most horrific type of death.[35] The Romans used it as a deterrent, and as such, this kind of death became an opportunity to broadcast to Roman subjects, "Don't do this or you will end up like this." A placard with the charge broadcasted to the public the kinds of crimes that resulted in such an undesired and shameful end. In Jesus' case, the charge was "King of the Jews." This meant that whatever led Pilate to exercise his authority to execute, it was the claim to be a king that registered with the prefect. Jesus' crucifixion is among the most certain of events tied to his life. Crucifixions took place in response to some form of rebellion or sedition against Rome. So Jesus was not crucified merely for being a prophet.

What is curious about this crucifixion was that Jesus possessed no army to threaten Rome, so why did Pilate move against Jesus? Certainly with his legions the Roman prefect did not fear that Jesus would overrun Rome. Jesus gave no indication he desired to possess such rebellious and powerful forces. It is here again that the core portraits of our earliest sources agree. Pilate became convinced that Jesus and his claims had the potential to disrupt the Judean province, one already made volatile by

---

[34]The *titulus* refers to the placard that indicated the charge against one crucified in public.

[35]See Martin Hengel, *Crucifixion in the Ancient World and the Folly of the Message of the Cross* (Philadelphia: Fortress, 1977).

religious fervor and commitments of various sorts.[36] The Jewish leadership, with which he worked, had brought this Galilean teacher to him, portraying him as a threat to Judean stability. They did so with some insistence. The charges we see raised had to do with Jesus inciting the people. The sources consistently argue that the issue was whether Jesus claimed to be a king of the Jews (Mk 15:3 // Mt 27:11, elaborated in Lk 23:2-3). Now Jesus' appointment as king had not come from Rome. Allowing such a claim to persist would have been a poor precedent to permit in a potentially unstable region, especially when Pilate's top priority was to keep the peace and protect Caesar's interests.

The mocking we see associated with Jesus' various examinations was also directed at regal claims (Mk 15:18 // Mt 27:29; Jn 19:3). Again it is unlikely that the early church fabricated these charges or the mocking, given how much trouble it would have raised if it had not really been a part of the original story and also given how unflattering a portrait it gave of the government.

Although some argue that the role of Pilate is difficult to untangle, the sources suggest he was faced with a practical choice. Act against Jesus, who clearly had stirred up the leadership in Jerusalem and seemed quite capable of generating popular excitement and religious fervor, or release him, inciting the anger of those Pilate worked with on religious issues. In addition, to act aggressively against Jesus, who likely had raised the specter of independence from Rome in regal-oriented claims, was a good popular precedent to demonstrate. Our knowledge of how Pilate minted coins (the first to mint coins with Roman symbolism in Judea) and how he acted to confirm Roman authority, even to the point of causing religious offense, shows he was not above making it clear who controlled the region. To be able to do so with the support of the religious authorities made palatable what probably initially seemed a use of excessive force against Jesus.

The situation of the Jewish leadership is also important here. This is an opportunity to have Rome rule concering Jesus. If Jesus had been re-

---

[36]Pilate had seen this firsthand in the Jewish reaction to his effort to place standards in Jerusalem, an act Pilate retreated from when it became clear a bloodbath might result (Josephus *Jewish Antiquities* 18.55-59).

leased after having been examined by Rome, this would have been a
terrible result for the Jewish leadership. Such a potential disaster might
well explain the insistence seen in the text from the leadership. These
elements of the story have a solid claim to being credible. They help us
to understand and confirm Jesus' own actions and the perception of his
claims by others. We need to remind ourselves that this linkage of the
Jewish leadership and Pilate was not something limited to early Christian sources. Josephus also makes this association in his brief discussion
about Jesus (*Jewish Antiquities* 18.63-64). So we have multiple attestations that stretch across ideological lines. Jesus' crime was to claim to be
king of the Jews. For those who did not believe him, this would have
been seen as a threat to the peace and well-being of the region. The
charge coheres nicely with this traced line of emphasis.

One other feature that should be noted here is that the new community quickly came to call Jesus by the name Christ. The question
becomes, Why choose such a name to be the moniker for Jesus (1) if
he denied the connection, (2) if he did not teach about himself in such
a role and (3) if raising such a title could be seen as a challenge that
would cause those in authority to react? It seems far more probable
that people made the association so publicly and prominently because
the connection came from Jesus. This is likely the case even if Jesus
gradually disclosed the idea in the context of his ministry and went
more public toward the conclusion of his ministry. So working back
from the *titulus* is one of the key ways to gain an appreciation for how
people saw Jesus by the end of his ministry. They saw him as a messianic claimant.

Resurrection as vindication after a certain death. In one sense to
come to the resurrection is to move outside of historical Jesus study.
This is for two reasons: (1) Jesus does nothing here—he is portrayed as
the beneficiary of a divine act—and (2) normal historical means can
hardly confirm such a claim. All that one can do is to trace the event's
impact. Nonetheless, the resurrection is significant to cover because it
completed the claim of vindication that Jesus had raised at his Jewish
examination, one that had become a catalyst for theological reflection

in the movement Jesus launched. As such, it has historical value.[37]

Before getting to the resurrection, we must confirm that it was likely Jesus was dead and buried. Do the details we have of such a burial in our sources fit with Jewish custom?[38] In short, they do.

Numerous details of the burial that can be checked fit carefully within the cultural backdrop. The Mishnah (*Sanhedrin* 6:5-6) requires a corpse's burial; even the body of a convicted criminal was to be buried before sundown. The Romans were known to permit such burials. However, the family cannot receive the body, nor can they place the criminal's body in the family's tomb. This explains Joseph of Arimethea's involvement. Buried bodies were washed, wrapped and anointed for seven days after the burial as part of the mourning. So the women go as soon as was permitted, given the Sabbath's having intervened and their knowledge that an initial anointing had taken place. This means that our sources leading into the scene are completely culturally credible, even down to the details of why the women waited to anoint Jesus and the kind of tomb in which Jesus ended up.

Several features of this event that can be evaluated at a historical level suggest that the early church did not invent it.

1. The first witnesses to the empty tomb were women, according to the Gospel sources. In a culture where women did not have the right to be witnesses, would one make up a story to sell a difficult idea (physical resurrection) to a skeptical culture by beginning with people who had no cultural value as witnesses? The detail not only shows the value of women to the movement but also suggests that the women were in the story because they were key to the event's disclosure.[39]

---

[37]I agree with the judgment of Richard Hays, *The Moral Vision of the New Testament* (San Francisco: HarperSanFrancisco, 1996), pp. 165-66, who says, "I part company with many New Testament scholars and theologians who think it inappropriate to describe the resurrections as a historical event." He goes on to speak of something extraordinary taking place that rallied dispirited disciples and that "God did something beyond all power of human imagining by raising Jesus from the dead."

[38]I deal here with claims that Jesus was simply left to rot on the cross in order to further shame him as an executed criminal. This discussion also treats claims or any ideas that Jesus somehow survived his scourging and crucifixion. Everything in all our sources argues that he died. The nature of crucifixion alone is enough to make this certain.

[39]In fact, it is this cultural problem that may well explain why 1 Cor 15:3-9 lacks their mention.

2. It would have been possible within Judaism to create a vindication story of Jesus that would have been less problematic. Judaism held that the resurrection would come at the end of history. So why not create a story (if we are to argue that the story was created), that simply says the resurrection would come at the end and Jesus would lead the judgment? Think how clean an approach this is. It fits Jewish theology. There would be no need to claim an empty tomb. Yet what we have in our sources is a "mutation" of this Jewish expectation. These sources claim Jesus was raised within history, an unprecedented exception to the expectation. The question is why create a mutation. More compelling is that something in the experience of the disciples created that change of view. More than that, these early disciples were willing to die for this belief. Is that likely if someone among the disciples had created the claim?

3. The reaction to the women reflects the criterion of embarrassment. When the women reported their story of the empty tomb, the reaction was not, "Well, of course, it is Jesus!" No, rather these future church leaders saw the women as hysterical. The new community leadership acted much like one might expect modern, skeptical people to react. Is this likely if one creates the account? Why not have them be in simple awe?

4. If the event's creation is a solid explanation for this teaching, then why are there no detailed stories about Jesus appearing to Peter or James, two of the key leaders of the church? If these stories are so easy to create, then why not detailed appearance accounts of two of the most important early leaders, who the sources suggest saw Jesus?[40]

A resurrection pointing to vindication would lead to the conclusion that God had vindicated the historical Jesus, giving credibility to his claims and mission. I have argued that this mission can be corroborated at a historical level. Jesus' ministry centered on a call to Israel to come back to covenant faithfulness to her God and to recognize that a new era, the promised era of deliverance, was coming with Jesus' message and actions. This deliverance was eventually to be extended to the nations. As one who stood at the hub of God's program and as the inau-

---

[40]James's experience is noted in 1 Cor 15:7, while Peter's is noted in Lk 24:34. Both summaries are told with amazing brevity.

gurator of the kingdom, Jesus claimed a role that many Jews would have seen as messianic. However, to that portrait, revealed in a selective and qualified manner, Jesus added the idea that this deliverer would have to suffer to initiate the new era's covenant. Jesus' actions showed him consistently reversing the present evil in the world, acts that could be interpreted as Satan's defeat, and thus the new age's arrival. Because people could not see such claims demonstrated in an empirical way, Jesus linked words and deeds so that what could be seen would make credible what could not be seen. If God was acting through him to do the kinds of things he was doing, then that served to underscore the credibility of Jesus' message and acts. For the new community, the ultimate example of this kind of vindication of Jesus' message came in the resurrection. So they preached that this claimant Jesus was the hub figure of God's program and resided at God's side, sharing in the divine mission and presence. The result of resurrection disclosed the fullness of who Jesus is and was, why Jesus called God his Father and how he had the authority to explain and challenge with regard to God's will on matters such as the Sabbath and other activities tied to Torah. What emerged from the Jesus of history was a figure inextricably linked to the Christ of faith. Our essay has argued that this linkage and conclusion is no accident, even at a historical level. A messianic Jesus who saw himself standing at the hub of God's program and completely vindicated as Son of Man at God's side produced a coherent, corroborated narrative for the early church. Such an account of him stands solidly rooted in what the historical Jesus actually said and did.

RESPONSE TO DARRELL L. BOCK

Robert M. Price

THE JEWISH MILIEU

It is not uncommon to find conservative critics and apologists appealing to Martin Hengel's work[1] to remove the boundary between Judaism and Hellenism in first-century c.e. Judaism when their goal is to secure some Greek item for a Palestinian Jesus, then retreating to the old dichotomy when they feel the need to insulate Jesus (or early Christian views of him) from some element of Hellenism they consider dangerous or unseemly (*theios anēr* Christology, miracle stories as evangelistic propaganda, Gnosticism). My impression is that such switching back and forth is opportunistic, the common goal being to vindicate the historical accuracy of the Gospel traditions (or stories or sayings). There is a prima facie reasonable assumption that the historical Jesus was comfortably ensconced within Second Temple Judaism, so that, when the gospel Jesus sounds Jewish, this is why. But this seems to me quite circular. Isn't this in many ways just the point at issue? I think that what we have here is a postulate of ecumenical correctness. Jews and Christians, trying to get together in some sort of harmonious accord after centuries of hostility, have decided to embrace a portrait of Jesus that will be as inoffensive to Judaism as possible, the party line, I would call it, of *Bible Review*, a united front against minimalists of either Testament. Another advantage for traditionalist scholars is that such a "maximally Jewish Jesus" allows for the most direct and pure

---

[1]Martin Hengel, *Judaism and Hellenism: Studies in Their Encounter in Palestine During the Early Hellenistic Period* (Philadelphia: Fortress, 1981).

transition from the Old Testament to the New without admitting of any adulteration from noncanonical quarters (e.g., mystery religions, etc.). So it will seem, at any rate, until the next time it becomes useful to abolish the Jewish-Hellenistic divide.

Darrell Bock rejoices with many post-Qumran scholars that much Johannine terminology and conceptuality need not be surrendered to Gnosticism or Hermeticism since much of it appears also in the Dead Sea Scrolls. But Bultmann already saw that their presence there only attested precisely the sort of Hellenistic Jewish syncretism he was positing for John's gospel.[2] (See also Kurt Rudolf's location of Jordan baptizing Gnosticism in the same orbit with Qumran baptism, as Mandaean John the Baptist legends have always told us.)[3] Professor Bock points with relish to the Gandhi-like appeal of a historical Jesus to the despised outcasts, sinners and lepers, at least implicitly as an example of the criterion of dissimilarity. This openness to the marginalized does not seem to have been characteristic of Second Temple Judaism, and thus it must have arisen from Jesus' own unique insights. Indeed it might have, but is it not more natural to view this aspect of the Gospel Jesus as a result and a function of the great controversy over whether and how to extend Jewish Jesus-Messianism to "Gentile sinners" (Gal 2:11-21)? I find myself convinced by the argument of Robert Eisenman that wholesale Romanized co-optation of Christianity is the only way to understand a scenario in which an ostensible Jewish messiah opposes the leaders of his own people, minimizes or mocks their sacred institutions and conveniently repudiates anti-Roman violence, even to the point of counseling Jews to turn the other cheek and not chafe at a Roman commandeering one to carry his field pack.[4] A Jewish messiah who actually commands payment of Roman taxes and welcomes quisling toll collectors and Roman centurions!

---

[2]Rudolf Bultmann, *The Johannine Epistles: A Commentary on the Johannine Epistles*, trans. R. Philip O'Hara with Lane C. McGaughy and Robert W. Funk, Hermeneia (Philadelphia: Fortress, 1973), p. 17.8.

[3]Kurt Rudolph, *Gnosis: The Nature and History of Gnosticism*, trans. P. W. Coxon, K. H. Kuhn and R. McL. Wilson (Harper & Row, 1983), pp. 227, 280, 363.

[4]Robert Eisenman, *James the Brother of Jesus: The Key to Unlocking the Secrets of Early Christianity and the Dead Sea Scrolls* (New York: Viking Press, 1996), pp. xx-xxxiii.

Bock is willing to accept the core of Mark 8:27-30's Caesarea Philippi confession (ignoring Gerd Theissen's striking argument that Mark has created the scene on the basis of his own previous scene in Mk 6:14-16).[5] He sees it as Jesus' grand redefinition of the Jewish "messiah" concept as that of a (or the) suffering servant. But that is like redefining "Patton" as "Pacifist." This has always seemed to me an obvious piece of later Christian rationalization, and one never made explicit in the Gospels anyway. In fact it has much in common with what Wrede thought that Mark had done with his "Messianic Secret"[6]—attempting to coordinate and harmonize two major competitive views of the Messiah, in Mark's case two Christian views (Jesus had been the Messiah during his earthly life/ Jesus had been proclaimed Messiah only at his resurrection), in Bock's a Jewish and a Christian view: theocratic king and sacrificial redeemer. Bock expresses skepticism toward Wrede's reconstruction, but he and all conservatives take for granted its very twin. And his skepticism simply ignores Bultmann's reasoning, which I find pretty persuasive. For Dr. Bock, it is hard to see how the title Messiah should have become so closely associated with the name Jesus so early if Jesus himself had not made the link. But Bultmann and others noticed the occurrence in the New Testament (at least Rom 1:3-4; Acts 2:36; 3:19-21) of a species of adoptionism according to which Jesus received the honor of Messiahship only at his resurrection, as the widespread use of Psalm 110, an enthronement psalm, would also imply.[7] Pray tell, asked Bultmann, how such a Christology could ever have come about had Jesus taught his disciples that he was already the Messiah? And, more recently, there is the notorious case of Lubavitcher Rebbe Menachem Mendel Schneerson, a charismatic Hasid who preached the soon-coming Messiah's kingdom without once intimating that he might be the Messiah in question. His disciples widely expected it, but he would neither affirm nor deny it. Then, once he died, his people's faith burst like a cocoon, and

---

[5]Gerd Theissen, *The Miracle Stories of the Early Christian Tradition*, trans, Francis McDonagh, (Philadelphia: Fortress, 1983), pp. 170-71.
[6]William Wrede, *The Messianic Secret*, trans. J. C. G. Greig, Library of Theological Translations (London: James Clarke, 1971; orig. German 1901).
[7]Rudolf Bultmann, *Theology of the New Testament*, trans. Kendrick Grobel (New York: Scribner's, 1951, 1955), 1:26-27.

the messiahship of the Rebbe was afoot. This is almost exactly the scenario envisioned by Bultmann for Jesus. I do not believe his reconstruction can be so easily brushed aside.

UPON THIS ROCK I WILL BUILD MY JESUS

Professor Bock also believes in a list of assertions about Jesus we can take as read. For one, Jesus did indeed exist. I suppose he does not consider worth mentioning the still-lively dispute about whether either of the references to Jesus in Josephus is textually authentic. I am surprised anyone thinks relevant the Suetonius reference to "Chrestus," which surely means to picture Chrestus as an instigator present on the scene in Claudian Rome. I consider the Tacitus reference authentic (though it is odd no pre-Eusebian Christian listing Roman persecutions ever refers to this passage in the *Annals*). But suppose the Josephus and Tacitus passages were original to their contexts. All they attest is that by the time of writing, the Christian preaching heralded a historical Jesus, which no one doubts. The question is whether a Jesus-god had already been historicized, a favor others did Hercules and Osiris, and these texts cannot help us there. And did no Jewish opponent ever deny Jesus' historicity? Why is it not at least a natural, viable reading of Justin's Rabbi Trypho to understand him this way? "You have invented a messiah for yourselves." Everyone takes this to mean, "You Christians have made the wrong man into a messiah," which indeed it might conceivably mean, but that seems to me to bear apologetical stretch marks.

Can we take for an "assured result of criticism" that Jesus received the baptism of John? I do not see what automatically exempts the scene from the same form-critical skepticism that brackets the Matthean Great Commission as secondary. The one invokes Jesus' own example to urge the candidate's immersion, while the other simply has Jesus give the order. But, as Dr. Bock affirms, representing the tradition of scholars, does not Jesus' baptism pass the criterion of embarrassment with dripping colors? If it had not happened, who would have made it up, bequeathing a terrible theological headache to subsequent Christians? Why would Jesus receive ministry from another, presumably a superior? (John's sect never let them forget *that*.) And why would Jesus have reported to confess his sins and receive absolution? Neither was a problem when the tradition got off the ground. At first, association with the renowned Baptist was a feather in one's cap. In 1 Corinthians 1:14-16 (cf. 1 Cor. 16:15-18) certain church leaders are similarly appealing to a pedigree from Pauline baptism. It would have been only later, once strife between the two sects set in, that the association with John became as much a liability for apologetics as an asset. And as for the "remission of sins," even Mark seems to see nothing amiss here, since he does nothing to correct the impression that Jesus does not consider himself "good" (Mk 10:18).

Dr. Bock seems to have no trouble welcoming aboard all the "I came"/"the Son of Man came" sayings and the rest of the Son of Man sayings. I'm afraid that I would have to accept the bouncer Bultmann's judgment again.[8] "Friend, how did you get in here without noticing that all these 'I came' sayings assume a retrospective theological/soteriological summing up of Jesus' incarnation?" They cannot stem from him, midway through that mission. It's postgame stuff. Plus, one must consider Norman Perrin's meticulous deconstruction of the Son of Man sayings as stemming from Christian scribal exegesis of Daniel 7:13 combined with both Psalm 110:1 and Zechariah 12:10.[9] The first was read as referring to the enthronement of the crucified ("pierced") Jesus as of his resurrection (Acts 2:34-35). The second referred to his future coming in judgment, when his heavenly throne should appear in the sky for the final assize, when all would see (Mt 24:30; Mk 14:62; Rev 1:7). Indeed, from these sets of midrashic connections came all the Gospel sayings about the coming of the Son of Man. Not one of the Gospel Son of Man sayings is a genuine utterance of a historical Jesus.

"MY TIME GROWS SHORT," THE SPIRIT SAID. "QUICK!"

Can we be sure Jesus entered Jerusalem on Palm Sunday, riding on a donkey borrowed from Zechariah 9:9? The story looks like it is based

---

[8]Rudolf Bultmann, *History of the Synoptic Tradition*, trans. John Marsh (New York: Harper & Row, 1968), p. 155.
[9]Norman Perrin, *A Modern Pilgrimage in New Testament Christology* (Philadelphia: Fortress, 1974), chap. 2, "Mark 14:62: The End Product of a Christian Pesher Tradition?" pp. 10-22.

on 1 Samuel 9:5-14, where Saul and his companion are likewise looking for donkeys and enter a city. The acclamation of the crowd comes right from Psalm 118, an entrance liturgy for pilgrims arriving at Jerusalem ("he who comes in the name of the Lord"). Even the palm fronds appear to be details from Psalm 118:27. What is left of the story? If Mark's account preserves any historical core, it is one that knows nothing of the royal character of the one greeted, as Mark's crowd says nothing about Jesus as king, but only about the coming Davidic kingdom. Matthew, Luke and John all conspicuously add what was conspicuously absent from Mark: Jesus' identity as a king.

Is it possible that a thoroughly Jewish historical Jesus enacted a rite that entailed the (even symbolic) consumption of human flesh and blood? Here we have something that fits nowhere else but a Dionysus or Osiris cult. And anyone can see that. Blink away the apologetical scales for a moment, and you will see it too. And certainly the compilers of the *Didache*, with a completely different eucharistic rite (chapter 9), never heard of this one. Nor did the various Christian groups who celebrated with bread and water, or bread and salt.

The trial of Jesus? Did Nicodemus share the minutes of the meeting with the Evangelist later? Declaring oneself Messiah was not blasphemy, albeit a costly mistake. But did Jesus say he was? Not according to the equivocal "confessions" of Matthew and Luke: "If you say so!" They derived this from manuscripts of Mark which read as a couple of ours still do. I take the majority reading "I am" as secondary. And the slapping, as well as the whole scene, probably comes from 1 Kings 22:24-27, Jesus taking the punching bag role of Micaiah ben-Imlah.

RESPONSE TO DARRELL L. BOCK

John Dominic Crossan

First, and most important, I agree with Bock that the ancient antago-
nism between "Jesus of history" and "Christ of faith" should be given a
respectful burial. It has well served its original purpose of breaking the
control of theological interpretation over historical reconstruction and
now it is—wherever still present—an impediment to both. The person
that I—as a historian—call "the historical Jesus" is exactly the same
one that I—as a Christian—call the "incarnate Word." But I never,
ever, confuse those twin visions of that same person. And, of course,
"the historical Jesus" that I have reconstructed makes and demands a
response of faith to his proclamation of the presence of God's kingdom.
An historian as historian alone may certainly refuse faith-acceptance of
that claim, but no adequate and honest historian can deny that the historical Jesus made it.

Next, there are several places where I would disagree with Bock on
individual points that he makes. But, for the moment, I will cite only
one which touches on methodology. I restrict myself to one such item
because my primary disappointment with his analysis lies elsewhere.

This concerns his use of "the criterion of embarrassment." It is, in
theory, a valid discriminant. It is absolutely valid, for example, as applied
to the baptism of Jesus by John. It is, as Bock notes, "a potentially embarrassing point that makes it unlikely that a community that gave Jesus a
uniquely exalted status created this scene (meeting the criterion of embarrassment)." That increasing embarrassment may be traced chronologically (and genetically) from Mark, through Mathew and Luke, into
John—which finally erases the baptism of Jesus completely.

But it is also a very dangerous criterion to use in dealing, for example, with Mark. That author contains a repeated and rather ruthless critique of the Twelve. Here are some examples: The Twelve have "hardened hearts" in 6:52 and 8:17, and that is an extremely serious accusation—just compare 4:12 with 8:17-18. Furthermore, among the Twelve, the leading and renamed Triad of Peter, James and John are obtusely indifferent to Jesus' three prophecies of execution and resurrection. First it is Peter in 8:31–9:1, then all of the Twelve in 9:31-37, and finally James and John in 10:33-45. You can see how "embarrassed" Matthew is with that last incident as he rephrases it in Matthew 20:20-28 (blame the mother), and Luke omits it entirely after Luke 18:31-34. Finally, Peter denies Jesus three times in Mark 14:66-72 and, of course, it is Judas, "one of the Twelve," as Mark always reminds us (3:19; 14:10, 43), who betrays Jesus.

However one explains that animosity toward the Twelve in terms of Mark in the early 70s, I would absolutely not use the "criterion of embarrassment" to judge those incidents as historical from Jesus in the late 20s. In my best historical reconstruction, Mark created much of them precisely to "embarrass" the (presumably, later theological heirs of the) Twelve, the Three, and especially Peter. "Would the church create an event where it compares its lead apostle to the paragon of evil?" Bock asks concerning the incident at Caesarea Philippi, where Jesus calls Peter "Satan." No, the church would not, but Mark would—and did. Following him, Matthew 16:23 also cites that Peter-as-Satan accusation but only after inserting the preceding encomium of Peter in Matthew 16:17-19. Luke solves the problem by omitting any parallel to the Peter-as-Satan unit.

Finally, however, the following is my major disagreement. Allow me, for the moment, and *dato non concesso* of course, to accept the overall historical reconstruction presented by Bock in his essay. If Jesus did and said all that Bock proposes, I still cannot understand why anyone heeded him, why he has any followers at all. The historical Jesus moves through Bock's analysis like a transcendental shadow. I could never get from that "historical Jesus" to any "incarnate Christ." It is, as I see it—and in Christian theological language—*ex*carnation not *in*carnation, not in-flesh-ment, not em-bodi-ment at all.

To make my point I must take a long quotation from the middle of Bock's paper. In my judgment it contains both for Jesus in particular and others in general a very serious confusion of terms.

> This disclosure of his [messianic and eschatological] role in public was concealed, in part, because of the difficulty it could have raised in confusing Jesus with a *political revolutionary*. . . .
>
> So Jesus preached a coming deliverance and claimed to help bring it to pass. This vindication did not come in *raw power* but also in service, including mercy, acceptance and sacrifice. The ostensive absence of *power* in the ministry was one of the features that must have perplexed many who tried to consider his claims. . . .
>
> Jesus was. . . being careful not to be misunderstood and have his effort hijacked into a *raw political movement*. Jesus was doing things that were *socially radical and even revolutionary*, but his point was not to challenge Rome at a strictly political level but to appeal to Israel to be a distinct kind of people before God in a way that did not seek the use of *coercive political power*. His mission called for a transformed society through transformed characters and communities, an effort not to be undertaken by the edge of a sword but through a life of commitment, service and love. (italics added)

For me that confusion obscures both the reconstruction of Jesus by history, the confession of Jesus by faith and, on a personal level, my own ability to agree—as I do—with the positive parts of that section.

First, there is that sequence within three successive sentences of first "raw power," then simply "power" and finally "raw political movement." Since Bock does not explain "raw," I am unsure about his meaning. If he means by it a movement only about power for the sake of power, I more or less agree with him. On the one hand, Jesus was about God and God's kingdom on an earth reclaimed for God. But on the other, is that not about power? Or, again, if he is using power as it is so often used in casual discourse to mean force and violence, then we are in complete agreement. But we should never concede that equation. "Power" can be either an act of force and violence *or* an act of proclamation and persuasion.

Next, there is that denial that Jesus was a "political revolutionary" followed by the affirmation that he was "socially radical and even revolutionary." That is a distinction without a difference unless, once again, "political revolutionary" entails violence and "social revolutionary" does not. That seems to be what Bock means as he goes on to say that Jesus wanted "not to challenge Rome at a strictly political level," because he did not seek the use of "coercive political power" or "the edge of a sword."

Finally, to cut through that confusion in terms and concepts and express my own agreement with the core of it as both history and theology, I would rephrase it as follows. Jesus proclaimed and incarnated the nonviolent power of God's kingdom as here and now present on this earth in direct confrontation with Rome's Empire. That confrontation was economic and political, social and religious, radical and revolutionary but also and absolutely nonviolent. Its program was to take back creation for the nonviolent God who "makes his sun rise on the evil and on the good, and sends rain on the righteous and on the unrighteous," according to Matthew 5:45.

The most important New Testament witness to Jesus' vision and mission is Pilate who, from the imperial viewpoint, got it completely correct. He recognized that Jesus was an anti-imperial radical and an anti-Roman revolutionary, and so he decreed an official, legal, public and exemplary crucifixion. But he also knew he was *nonviolent,* and so he made no attempt to round up his followers. That is clear from the magnificent parabolic juxtaposition in Mark 15:7 where, on the one hand, "a man called Barabbas was in prison with the rebels who had committed murder during the insurrection," but, on the other, Pilate never attempted to round up the companions of Jesus. One Son-of-the-Father was a violent revolutionary, the other—and for Mark, the true—Son-of-the-Father was a nonviolent revolutionary.

There is another and equally magnificent parabolic juxtaposition that makes this same point during that same crucifixion narrative, but this time in John. Jesus tells Pilate that "my kingdom is not from this world" and "my kingdom is not from here" (Jn 18:36a, c). If he had only said that, or when it is cited only as that, it is quite ambiguous. It could mean: God's kingdom is not on the earth but only in heaven, is not in the present but only in the future, is not of the body and the exterior life but only of the soul and the interior life. But in between those frames is this sentence: "If my kingdom were from this world, my followers would be fighting to keep me from being handed over to the Jews," or more accurately, handed over by the Jewish high-priestly authorities to you, Pilate (Jn 18:36). What could be clearer? In the last and final analysis, Pilate, God's kingdom opposes your Roman Empire and every other one before or after it. And that, Pilate, is about the awesome power of *nonviolent* religio-political radicalism and politico-religious revolution.

RESPONSE TO DARRELL L. BOCK

Luke Timothy Johnson

Darrell Bock's essay starts off well enough, I think. He argues for the possibility of genuine historical knowledge about Jesus even if it is limited by the nature of the sources. Like Dunn, he finds the quest for a Jewish Jesus to be promising, and (also like Dunn) thinks in terms of the historic Jesus, that is, the Jesus as heard and reported by followers on whom he had an impact. He denies, however, that dependence on such secondhand sources means "that we have lost access to Jesus"; just the opposite: "such a multiperspectival impression can be as historical as the autobiographical words of the individual." Bock states further that the application of the various criteria of authenticity yields only "the gist of Jesus" and cannot "give us a full and completely rounded off understanding." I find much to agree with in these opening comments, and I emphasize them because I find that the last part of Bock's essay decisively shifts ground.

His next pages also are for the most part unexceptionable. He seeks to establish the fact of Jesus' existence from outsider sources, and then to provide the sort of list of historically demonstrable facts about Jesus that I sketched at the start of my essay. He includes Jesus' association with John the Baptist, his reaching out to marginal elements in Jewish society, his call for total commitment and his message concerning God's rule and God's future age. My own list was actually larger. I included the probability that Jesus spoke in parables, interpreted Torah and chose disciples. The difference between Bock's approach and my own can be seen, however, in the title he gives to this list: "a look at key themes [note, not facts or patterns] that show the gist of Jesus' mission."

Whereas I was content to enumerate facts about which a historian can be reasonably confident, and refrained from drawing any conclusion about what those facts—considered individually or as a group—signified, Bock goes in the opposite direction. These themes "help us to zero in on what Jesus was about." Indeed, he considers this list, which I consider as the sum of what the historian responsibly can demonstrate with considerable probability, to be only the door that invites us to a much fuller understanding of Jesus. With Ben Meyer, he claims that Jesus' "intentions may be best seen in his actions." Although he concludes this section modestly, with the assertion that events that meet the test of all the criteria "give us adequate access to the key points of his actions and their impact," it soon becomes evident that Bock regards the Gospels as giving the historian privileged access to Jesus' intentions, and even his very thoughts.

This premise, in fact, dominates the rest of his essay, and, in my view, disqualifies the essay from serious consideration as a historical study. In effect, Bock reads the Gospels as reliable on every point and capable of revealing Jesus' inner thoughts and motivations. He does this, furthermore, without ever again seriously discussing or employing any properly historiographical criterion. If at any point he had entertained the possibility of some passage of the Gospels not yielding real historical knowledge, his essay would have gained in credibility. As it is, Bock's "evangelical" reading appears to be a matter of reading not only history but Jesus' personal psychology straight from the pages of the Gospels, no criticism necessary.

Bock discusses the distinctive theme in Mark's gospel that has been termed "the messianic secret." Rather than deal with it as an aspect of Mark's composition, he takes it as reflecting Jesus' historical usage. More than that, he knows why Jesus instructed people not to reveal his messianic status. In the following citation, I italicize the phrases that I regard as particularly problematic.

> Part of the reason for *Jesus' care in using the term Messiah* was that *it could be used* to incite people politically against Rome, as the Bar Kochba revolt of the next century shows. However, another reason was that *Jesus saw his messianic activity* as more complex than most of the varieties of messianic

Jewish expectation of the Second Temple period. *Jesus embraced the view*
that this key figure would suffer as well as bring victory.

I take each of the italicized phrases in turn. First, not only does Bock
ascribe the Markan theme to Jesus himself, and to his "care in using the
term," but he understands the motivation for this care—Jesus does not
want to incite people politically. Bock supposes, however, that Jesus
himself would be aware of this political consequence of messianic rhetoric—known to us only through Josephus and other historical sources.
In a manner similar to Crossan (and N. T. Wright), Bock has Jesus act
with reference to a script that was not available to him, and Bock claims
to know why Jesus acted in the manner he did according to that script.
Second, by stating "Jesus saw his messianic activity as more complex"
Bock once more claims to have access to Jesus' own perception of reality. Again, this claim supposes that Jesus had an awareness of other
"varieties of messianic Jewish expectation" and was in a position to
choose among them. Third, Bock knows that Jesus "embraced the
view" that this key figure would suffer, again implying that there was
such a "view" concerning "this key figure" that Jesus could elect among
other competing views—and that the Gospel gives us direct access to
this choice by Jesus.

My complaint here is not nitpicking concerning Bock's prose. It cuts
to the heart of his enterprise. He is not expressing himself clumsily; he
is committing historiographical fallacy. The fact that other Jesus
questers (including Crossan, Meier and Wright) regularly commit the
same fallacy does not make it any more acceptable. As Chesterton once
remarked, "a fallacy does not become less of a fallacy merely because it
has become a fashion."

In the same discussion, Bock claims that it is unlikely that the early
church would have created the suffering dimension of Jesus' ministry.
He cites as evidence the fact that the Gospels have Jesus characterize
Peter as "Satan" when Jesus predicts his passion and resurrection. He
cites the criterion of embarrassment—the church would not create an
event in which the chief apostle is called Satan. He concludes that the
passage "points to a key feature of Jesus' depiction of himself." Bock

here follows the form of logic but not the substance. First, Mark has Jesus call Peter "Satan" because Peter rejects the prediction of *both* the suffering and resurrection. Second, the church certainly did not invent Jesus' suffering; it was, if anything was, part of the historical fact with which the church had to grapple. Third, it is false to suppose the only options are "the church made it up" and "Jesus saw himself this way." What intervenes is precisely the oral transmission of the memory of Jesus in assemblies after his resurrection, and, above all, the shaping of the image of Jesus by the Evangelist. It is above all because the suffering of Jesus has entered so completely into the memory of him as shaped by the Evangelists—and in every other major witness of the New Testament—that it becomes difficult to state without hesitation, "Jesus saw suffering as a dimension of his ministry."

But this is just what Bock claims, breaking down his insight into three distinct elements. First, "He was being careful not to be misunderstood and have his effort hijacked into a raw political movement." Second, "he sought to be clear in all that he did that he was more than one of the Jewish prophets." Third, "He was also undertaking an effort to reshape and recast the portrait of Messiah as Jewish people embraced it in its various forms at that time." And he states again, "This explains Jesus' call for silence and his increased instruction about suffering that immediately followed. Jesus saw himself as a messianic figure, but only when carefully defined in a way that incorporated his service into that role."

In all of these statements, Bock simply takes the compositional shaping by the Evangelists (above all Mark) as reporting the words, the intentions and even the inner thinking of Jesus. Bock has not yet really engaged the Gospels critically as sources. Despite the statements that open his essay, he has not yet grasped what historical analysis requires.

RESPONSE TO DARRELL L. BOCK

James D. G. Dunn

I welcome Darrell Bock's emphasis on Jesus remembered and on the impact made by Jesus—both points I have emphasized in my own essay. I accord with him on the value, though limited, of the non-Christian references to Jesus. I agree with him on the character of Jesus' ministry and on the various aspects of Jesus' proclamation of the kingdom of God (what Bock calls "the provision for the age"). And I argue a broadly similar case on the question of Jesus and messiahship and on the significance of the events leading up to Jesus' execution (the "atriumphal" entry into Jerusalem is a neatly made point). His resort to the criteria of multiple attestation is understandable, though I would prefer to work more from the "impact" made by Jesus and in terms of the "characteristic" Jesus, as I develop in my own essay. In fact this is in effect how Bock proceeds, with a summary of Jesus' mission that is close to my own.

The points where we diverge are less significant. I question some of the ways he develops his arguments; for example, given the extent of the territory administered from Caesarea Philippi ("the villages of Caesarea Philippi"), the event of Mark 8:27 need not have taken place in the immediate vicinity of Caesarea Philippi itself. On the miraculous dimension of Jesus' mission I would have wanted to push the "impact" line as I have done in *Jesus Remembered*, by arguing that the events were understood and even experienced as miracles from the first, rather than that a miraculous color was added to a nonmiracle event or story at some later date. On the trial narrative, much as I appreciate his explanation of the charge of blasphemy laid against Jesus, I am less confident that Psalm 110:1 was part of the original formulation of Mark 14:62.

And finally, the discussion of the resurrection of Jesus as "historical" I think needs to be more nuanced, particularly as the way the "resurrection appearances" were conceptualized is so unclear (from heaven? a tangible continuous presence on earth, though only occasionally visible?). In describing resurrection appearances as "historical," are we referring to the data that can be investigated and evaluated by historical method? That is, in saying that the "resurrection" is historical do we mean simply that the effect on those involved in these events (the effect being itself part of the events, of course) is in principle subject to historical investigation and analysis, including the fact that the events resulted in the conviction that Jesus had been raised from the dead, with all the improbabilities and theological complexities involved in that claim? Presumably, we do not also mean that the resurrected Christ as such is similarly in principle available for historical inquiry? Still less, of course, the event of resurrection itself, apart from the subject of the emptiness of the tomb where Jesus was laid.

The question of what we mean by *historical* is also raised by Bock's somewhat casual use of the term "the historical Jesus." It is important that the role of historical inquiry is made clear here. To do so includes acknowledging that, properly speaking, "the historical Jesus" denotes Jesus as discerned by historical study. Those engaged in the quest of the historical Jesus, those at least who have sought to clarify what the phrase "the historical Jesus" denotes, have usually made the point that the term properly denotes the life and mission of Jesus as they have been "reconstructed" by means of historical research—"historical" in that sense. Despite this, however, it is wholly understandable that "the historical Jesus" is regularly and popularly understood as a reference to the historical actuality of the first-century Jesus of Nazareth. Bock seems to slip into this way of thinking when he speaks of making "a case for the historical Jesus in detail." But here we have to recognize the dangers of historicism—that is, of assuming that Jesus is like an archaeological artifact that can be uncovered by digging down through history, like a physical object at the bottom of an archaeological tell, from which the accretions of dirt and later strata can be brushed away to reveal it (Jesus) in its (his) actual pristine antique actuality.

One of the things that needs to be made clear here is the distinction I made in *Jesus Remembered* between "data" and "facts." The data are the various reports we still have (particularly the Gospels, of course) and our knowledge of first-century Israel-Palestine, for example. From these data historical method attempts to derive facts. That is, "facts" properly speaking are always and never more than interpretations of the data. Here too we must avoid the oversimplification which speaks of "brute facts" or "hard facts," as though, once again, these were tangible entities that could be uncovered by archaeological/historical investigation. Such language, if it is to be used at all, applies only to the data—the Gospel accounts are themselves such data or, if you like, hard facts. But the events to which the Gospels refer are not themselves "hard facts"; they are facts only in the sense that we interpret the text, together with such other data as we have, to reach a conclusion regarding the events as best we are able. They are facts in the same way that the verdict of a jury establishes the facts of the case, the interpretation of the evidence that results in the verdict delivered. Here it is as well to remember that historical methodology can only produce probabilities, the probability that some event took place in such circumstances being greater or smaller, depending on the quality of the data and the perspective of the historical enquirer. The jury which decides what is beyond reasonable doubt is determining that the probability is sufficiently high for a clear–cut verdict to be delivered. Those who like "certainty" in matters of faith will always find this uncomfortable. But faith is not knowledge of "hard facts" ("we walk not by sight but by faith"); it is rather confidence, assurance, trust in the reliability of the data and in the integrity of the interpretations derived from that data. Probability, we now realize, is much more integral to daily living than was previously understood. So the acceptance of the fact that in historical investigation we are dealing with probabilities rather than certainties should not be so alarming to those of faith as it is sometimes thought to be.

It does seem important to me that those who speak for evangelical Christians grasp this nettle firmly, even if it stings!—it is important for the intellectual integrity of evangelicals. Of course any Christian (and particularly evangelical Christians) will want to get as close as possible to the Jesus who ministered in Galilee in the late 20s of the first century. If, as they believe, God spoke in and through that man, more definitively and finally than at any other time and by any other medium, then of course Christians will want to hear as clearly as possible what he said, and to see as clearly as possible what he did, to come as close as possible to being an eyewitness and earwitness for themselves. If God revealed himself most definitively in the historical particularity of a Galilean Jew in the earliest decades of the Common Era, then naturally those who believe this will want to inquire as closely into the historical particularity and actuality of that life and of Jesus' mission. The possibility that later faith has in some degree covered over that historical actuality cannot be dismissed as out of the question. So a genuinely critical historical inquiry is necessary if we are to get as close to the historical actuality as possible. *Critical* here, and this is the point, should not be taken to mean negatively critical, hermeneutical suspicion, dismissal of any material that has overtones of Easter faith. It means, more straightforwardly, a careful scrutiny of all the relevant data to gain as accurate or as historically responsible a picture as possible.

In a day when *evangelical,* and even *Christian,* is often identified with a strongly right-wing, conservative and even fundamentalist attitude to the Bible, it is important that responsible evangelical scholars defend and advocate such critical historical inquiry and that their work display its positive outcome and benefits. These include believers growing in maturity

- to recognize gray areas and questions to which no clear-cut answer can be given ("we see in a mirror dimly/a poor reflection"),

- to discern what really matters and distinguish them from issues that matter little,

- and be able to engage in genuine dialogue with those who share or respect a faith inquiring after truth and seeking deeper understanding.

In that way we may hope that *evangelical* (not to mention *Christian*) can again become a label that men and women of integrity and good will can respect and hope to learn from more than most seem to do today.

CONTRIBUTORS

Darrell L. Bock is research professor of New Testament studies at Dallas Theological Seminary, Dallas, Texas. He is the author of several books on Jesus and the Gospels, including *Jesus According to Scripture: Restoring the Portrait from the Gospels* (2007) and *Studying the Historical Jesus: A Guide to Sources and Methods* (2002).

James K. Beilby is professor of systematic and philosophical theology at Bethel University, St. Paul, Minnesota. He has edited several multiple-views books (with Paul Eddy) and is the author of a number of articles and books, including *Epistemology as Theology* (2006).

John Dominic Crossan is emeritus professor of religious studies, DePaul University, Chicago, Illinois. He was the cofounder of the Jesus Seminar and is the author of numerous works on or related to the historical Jesus, including *The Historical Jesus: The Life of a Mediterranean Jewish Peasant* (1991) and *Jesus: A Revolutionary Biography* (1994).

James D. G. Dunn is emeritus Lightfoot Professor of Divinity at Durham University, Durham, England. He has published widely on Jesus, Paul and early Christianity and is the author of *Jesus Remembered* (2003).

Paul Rhodes Eddy is professor of biblical and theological studies at Bethel University, St. Paul, Minnesota. He has edited several multiple-views books (with James Beilby) and has published a number of articles and books related to historical Jesus research including *The Jesus Legend* (2007).

Luke Timothy Johnson is R. W. Woodruff Professor of New Testament and Christian Origins at Candler School of Theology, Emory University, Atlanta, Georgia. Among his numerous books on the New Testament is his influential *The Real Jesus: The Misguided Quest for the Historical Jesus and the Truth of the Traditional Gospels* (1996).

Robert M. Price is professor of theology and scriptural studies at the Johnnie Colemon Theological Seminary, Miami Gardens, Florida, editor of *The Journal of Higher Criticism* and member of the Jesus Seminar. His books include *Deconstructing Jesus* (1999) and *The Incredible Shrinking Son of Man* (2004).

Name and Subject Index

Scripture Index

Finding the Textbook You Need

The IVP Academic Textbook Selector
is an online tool for instantly finding the IVP books
suitable for over 250 courses across 24 disciplines.

---

ivpacademic.com
